AF326969

Making New Time

M a k i n g N e w T i m e M a

k i n g N e w T i m e M a k i

n g N e w T i m e M a k i n g

N e w T i m e M a k i n g N e

w T i m e M a k i n g N e w T

i m e M a k i n g N e w T i m

e M a k i n g N e w T i m e M

a k i n g N e w T i m e M a k

i n g N e w T i m e M a k i n

g N e w T i m e M a k i n g N

e w T i m e M a k i n g N e w

T i m e M a k i n g N e w T i

m e M a k i n g N e w T i m e

MakingNewTimeMa
kingNewTimeMaki
ngNewTime**Making**
NewTimeMakingNe
wTimeMakingNewT
imeMakingNewTim
eMaking**New**TimeM
akingNewTimeMak
ingNewTimeMakin
gNewTimeMakingN
ewTimeMakingNew
TimeMakingNewTi
meMakingNew**Time**

Edited by Omar Kholeif

Making New Time

Sharjah Biennial 14: Leaving the Echo Chamber
Curated By Zoe Butt, Omar Kholeif and Claire Tancons

Published by:

Sharjah Art Foundation
PO Box 19989, Sharjah
United Arab Emirates
www.sharjahart.org

DelMonico Books, an imprint of Prestel, a member of Verlagsgruppe Random House GmbH

Prestel Verlag
Neumarkter Strasse 28
81673 Munich

Prestel Publishing Ltd.
14-17 Wells Street
London W1T 3PD

Prestel Publishing
900 Broadway, Suite 603
New York, NY 10003

www.prestel.com

ISBN 978-9948-38-743-5
(Sharjah Art Foundation)

ISBN 978-3-7913-5849-9
(Prestel)

Library of Congress Control Number: 2019931318

This book was published for
Sharjah Biennial 14: Leaving the Echo Chamber
March 7 – June 10, 2019

Sharjah Art Foundation, President and Director
Hoor Al Qasimi

Editor
Omar Kholeif

Publication Coordinators
Reem Shadid
Wasan Yousif

Copy editor
Eti Bonn-Muller

Designer
Kemistry Design

Printed in the United Arab Emirates

Sharjah Art Foundation Staff and Sharjah Biennial 14
. Sheikha Hoor Al Qasimi, Director and President
. Reem Shadid, Deputy Director

Curatorial and Programmes
. Momen Al Ajouz
. Mariam Al Askari
. Anahita Harding
. Carmen Hassan
. Ryan Inouye
. Zeina Al Kattan
. Amal Al Khaja
. Noora Al Mualla
. May Alqaydi
. Ambika Rajgopal
. Mahmoud El-Safadi
. Raneem Turjman
. Ayman Zedani
. Mohammad Asadullah (Intern)
. Amy-Clare McCarthy (Intern)

Exhibition Design and Production
. Eng. Hassan Ali Mahmood
. Mona El Mousfy
. Eng. Younus Suliman
. Aia Azad
. Mona Al Chaar
. Maria Kalaiji
. Tigran Kostandyan
. Hinjal Kumar
. Farah Al Qedra
. Lana El Samman
. Sirine El Samman (Intern)

Logistics
. Mohammed Fawwaz
. Mahmoud Al Jaddah
. Syed Kashif Syed Sibt
. Ali Tawfiq

Publications and Research
. Saira Ansari
. Dalia Chabarek
. Sheherbano Iqbal
. Areej Kaoud
. Wasan Yousif

Education
. Sana Haroon Abdulmajeed
. Madiha Adel
. Hessa Al Ajmani
. Tahani Y K AlAshqar
. Jinan Coulter
. Shefa Al Hammadi
. Maryam Ali AlHammadi
. Mouza Al Hamrani
. Heba Hosny
. Hussein Al Khayyat
. Sherine Mohammed
. Hamad Ghanim Mughawer
. Manal Al Muttawa
. Nasir Ahmed Nasrallah
. Arwa Nasreldin
. Mahmood Bin Shamsan

Marketing and Communication
. Yusra Abdelhakam
. Ragaa Amin
. Huda Amini
. Lojain Ismail

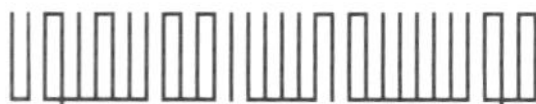

SHARJAH ART FOUNDATION

. Nawale Lacroix
. Naveed Majeed
. Ali Mrad
. Alyazeyah Al Reyaysa
. Carine Rizk
. Tracy Jad Sawan
. Tuba Tortob

Design, Image and Archives
. Hind Al Ali
. Alia Al Amri
. Dima Bittard
. Mohammed Al Hmadi
. Shanavas Jamaluddin
. Ghaya Bin Mesmar
. Unnikrishnan Suresh
. Louie Aloc De la Torre
. Magdi Emad (Intern)
. Rahaf Jumran (Intern)

Editing and Translation
. Ismail AlRifaie
. Ziad Abdullah
. Kathleen Butti
. Abdullah Hussein
. Sezar Ibrahem

International Programmes and Development
. Judith Greer
. Nawar Al Qassimi
. Alaeldin Ahmed
. Ali Al Hadidi
. Eshtar Hussain
. Ruqaia Ibrahim
. Sara Imad Eldin
. Maryam AlQassimi
. Suraya El Amin (Intern)

IT
. Mahesh Kumar
. Nitin Alden Mathias
. Noaf Yousif

Finance and Administration
. Fatma Al Jasmi
. Dalia Al Shehhi
. Abdulhamed Abdulghfor
. Humam Ahmad
. Mansour Ahmed
. Amina Al Ali
. Amjeth Khan Muhamed Ali
. Huda Al Ali
. Khaula Al Ameri
. Sara AlBloushi
. Maitha Buti Bin Ashoor
. Babylyn Tacos Deliva
. Mark Gillbert
. Aisha Al Hammadi
. Amal Al Hammadi
. Nouria Al Hammadi
. Aisha Al Hashmi
. Alyaa Al Hosani
. Sufiyan Iqbal
. Saifuddin Klzhakkedath
. Ann Tharwat Milad
. Alyazyah Ahmed Al Raeesi
. Nafeesa Umma
. Abdul Rahman Al Yafeai

Hospitality
. Najeeba Aslam
. Abdelhamid Ayesh Abo Ebeiid
. Shaima Hussain (Intern)

Visitor Services
. Ali Ahmad
. Ibrahim Ahmed
. Ahmed Ali
. Saeed Ali
. Ayoub Arbaoui
. Hajer Boulahbel
. Zahra Al Hassan
. Mahmoud Hatem
. Ahmed Hussain
. Hassan Madhlom
. Khalid Mohammed
. Abdul Haseeb Moidunni
. Abdullah Al Shamsi
. Saleh Al Soufi
. Khalifa Sultan
. Omar Al Obaidly
. Faisal Ali (Intern)
. Fatima Amjath (Intern)
. Abderrahmane Ammar (Intern)
. Yousif Hussein (Intern)
. Mahmoud Kandeel (Intern)
. Mustafa Kandeel (Intern)

Installation Technicians
. Salil AbdulSalam
. Suhaib Ali Abdul Shakoor
. Masroof Ahmed
. Habib Akhtar
. Javed Ali
. Hamed Allah
. Mark Anthony
. Mohamed Atif
. Minhad Azeem
. Hussain Baloch
. Sameer Chalil
. Sameer Cuto
. Ali Suliman Darweesh
. Hassan Darwish
. Sunil Devasia
. Mahesh Dharmmarjan
. Muhammad Farooq
. Muhammed Fazal
. Abdul Ghaffar
. Mohamed Ghalib
. Ameen Ul Haq
. Irfan Iqbal
. Syed Jalaluddin
. Arshad Khalil
. Abid Amir Khan
. Asad Ullah Khan
. Atlas Amir Dawar Khan
. Ayoub Khan
. Ibrahim Khan
. Mohamed Khan Mira Khan
. Muslim Khan
. Nadeem Khan
. Savdar Khan
. Wasseem Khan
. Sudheersha Mohamed Khani
. Mustafa Kinagat
. Shabeer Kizhakkedath
. Noufal Koya
. Shrinidhi Madival
. Sunil Mathew
. AbdulRahman Mavella
. Satheesh Mundeerath
. Aswani Kummar Raveendran Nair
. Andre Perez
. Tahir Pervez
. Shihabudheen Poonthala
. Shuaib Poonthala
. Joy Pulikkottil
. Fazel Rahman
. Raqib Said
. Moidu Koroth Saidalu
. Alaa Sami
. Khalid Sami
. Manu Scaria
. Abdul Khaliq Shan
. Aboobacker Siddeque
. Sreerenj Sudhakaran
. Shajahan Kannokaran Sulaiman
. Zathbit Ullah Welayat Ullah

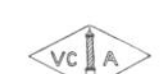

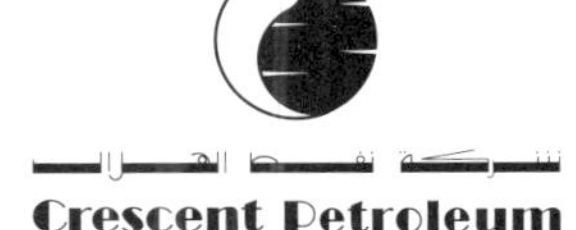

Contents

011 Foreword by Hoor Al Qasimi
015 Acknowledgements by Omar Kholeif
019 ***Making New Time: An Itinerary*** by Omar Kholeif
027 Artist Pages
183 ***The Unknowing X*** by Sophia Al-Maria
189 ***Intimate Clocks: A Provocation*** by Khalid Abdalla
197 ***Too Stupid to Fail*** by Douglas Coupland
203 ***Earlye in the Morning*** by Heather Phillipson
211 ***The Order of Time*** by Yasmine El Rashidi
219 ***Ouroboros*** by Sean Gullette
233 ***What we talk about when we talk about time*** by Hannah Feldman
241 ***I'm Ready Now*** by Aram Moshayedi
247 ***Pretty Green City*** by Todd Reisz
253 ***To Hold My Breath*** by Sofia Victorino
259 ***Endings and Other Things*** by Oraib Toukan
265 ***The Whispering Gallery*** by Koyo Kuoh
271 ***Cordoba House*** by Koray Duman
279 ***Encroachments*** by Shezad Dawood
289 ***Making New Time: An Afterword*** by Omar Kholeif
293 List of works
303 Contributors

N e w T i m e M a k i n g N e
w T i m e M a k i n g N e w T
i m e M a k i n g N e w T i m
e M a k i n g N e w T i m e M
a k i n g N e w T i m e M a k
i n g N e w T i m e M a k i n
g N e w T i m e M a k i n g N
e w T i m e M a k i n g N e w
T i m e M a k i n g N e w T i
m e M a k i n g N e w T i m e
M a k i n g N e w T i m e M a
k i n g N e w T i m e M a k i
n g N e w T i m e M a k i n g
N e w T i m e M a k i n g N e
w T i m e M a k i n g N e w T

imeMakingNewTim
eMakingNewTimeM
akingNewTimeMak
ingNewTimeMakin
gNewTimeMakingN
ewTimeMakingNew

Time **Foreword** Mak

ingNewTimeMakin
gNewTimeMakingN
ewTimeMakingNew
TimeMakingNewTi
meMakingNewTime
MakingNewTimeMa
kingNewTimeMaki
ngNewTimeMaking

Extending Sharjah Biennial's engagement with artists from different countries and generations, Sharjah Biennial 14: *Leaving the Echo Chamber* continues its history of support for art and culture in the region and beyond. The fourteenth edition of the biennial, established in 1993, provides an international platform for artists to present work that engages with their local environments but also resonates more broadly with a global audience.

Invited for their substantial work and research, curators Zoe Butt, Omar Kholeif and Claire Tancons collectively conceived of 'leaving the echo chamber' as the framework for Sharjah Biennial 14. In the context of the biennial, the 'echo chamber' encompasses the noise of mainstream media coverage, conspiracy theories, sensationalised storytelling and social media feeds that reverberates within closed systems and networks that prevent people from engaging with each other in complex ways. Although the biennial does not propose answers or solutions, it does offer opportunities to closely examine how stories are told and from what perspectives they are communicated and historicised. In distinct and interrelated platforms, each curator endeavours to amplify the development of new and ongoing ideas through artistic and cultural production that moves beyond existing models of thought and relationships.

Together, the three platforms encourage thinking about interconnectedness across time, culture and geography as new horizons of thought and experience emerge. In *Journey Beyond the Arrow*, Butt takes a long look at the movement of humanity and the tools that have enabled its survival. Artists grapple with practices that have facilitated the transference of knowledge across land and sea as well as the profound intergenerational impact of colonialism, economic exploitation and ideology, which requires nuanced insight and response. Kholeif's *Making New Time* examines today's experience of accelerating time in the midst of seismic technological, social and political change. Artists in this platform encourage consideration of how both new technology and histories of material culture augment the limits of perception and belief that inevitably shape an understanding of reality. Tancons' *Look for Me All Around You* underscores displacement as a foundational experience of modernity, drawing on pan-African thinker and activist Marcus Mosiah Garvey Jr's (1887–1940) call to 'Look for me in the whirlwind or a storm, look for me all around you...' (1925). She has assembled a group of artists who predominantly work in performance to acknowledge the presence of people and histories that often only register in fleeting or immaterial forms.

At March Meeting 2019, during the opening week of the biennial, three days of talks, readings and performances by local, regional and international speakers expand on the dynamic presentations of the more than 80 artists in the biennial. The invited speakers broaden the dialogue beyond the biennial by mobilising related discussions in art, architecture, education, philosophy and more. In so doing, Butt, Kholeif and Tancons prompt a reassessment of our moment and contribute to the development of Sharjah as an important meeting place for artists and the public.

M a k i n g N e w T i m e M a
k i n g N e w T i m e M a k i
n g N e w T i m e M a k i n g
N e w T i m e M a k i n g N e
w T i m e M a k i n g N e w T
i m e M a k i n g N e w T i m
e M a k i n g N e w T i m e M
a k i n g N e w T i m e M a k
i n g N e w T i m e M a k i n
g N e w T i m e M a k i n g N
e w T i m e M a k i n g N e w
T i m e M a k i n g N e w T i
m e M a k i n g N e w T i m e
M a k i n g N e w T i m e M a
k i n g N e w T i m e M a k i

ngNewTimeMaking
NewTimeMakingNe
wTimeMakingNewT
imeMakingNewTim
eMakingNewTimeM
aking**Acknowledg**
ementsNewTimeMa
kingNewTimeMaki
ngNewTimeMaking
NewTimeMakingNe
wTimeMakingNewT
imeMakingNewTim
eMakingNewTimeM
akingNewTimeMak
ingNewTimeMakin

Omar Kholeif would like to personally thank all the artists, lenders, catalogue contributors and advisors to Sharjah Biennial 14. Special thanks to:

. Frank Gallacher
. Laurie Simmons
. Susan Chun
. Sultan Sooud Al Qassemi
. Todd Reisz
. Chris McCormack
. Terence McCormack
. Sofia Victorino
. Eline van der Vlist
. Hannah Feldman
. Joana Hadjithomas and Khalil Joreige
. Sarah Perks
. Andreas Gegner
. Simon Sakhai
. Maureen Paley
. Andrée Sfeir Semler
. Sunny Rahbar
. Amanda Schmidt
. Galerist, Istanbul
. Brigitte Caland
. Malado Baldwin
. Richard Flaata
. Veronica So
. Amrita Jhaveri
. Justine Durrett
. Angela Choon
. Lisa Panting
. Malin Stahl
. Guillaume Bleret
. Femke Cools
. Laure Poupard
. Masahito Ono
. Stefania Bortolomi
. Claire Bergeal
. Marie Krauss
. Angelika von Schwedes
. Fabienne Leclerc
. Rhona Hoffman
. Tobias Steinle
. Factum arte
. Simon Preston
. Sree Goswami
. Courtney Plummer
. Andrew Leslie Heyward
. Zipho Dayile
. Alexander Richards
. Yasmine Atassi
. Tasveer Shemza
. The Sharjah Art Foundation team, who made this all possible
. And mama, baba (Manar Farahat and Yasser Kholeif), Nahoula, and my brothers, Yousef, Ali, and Shereif.

T i m e M a k i n g N e w T i

m e M a k i n g N e w T i m e

M a k i n g N e w T i m e M a

k i n g N e w T i m e M a k i

n g N e w T i m e M a k i n g

N e w T i m e M a k i n g N e

w T i m e M a k i n g N e w T

i m e M a k i n g N e w T i m

e M a k i n g N e w T i m e M

a k i n g N e w T i m e M a k

i n g N e w T i m e M a k i n

g N e w T i m e M a k i n g N

e w T i m e M a k i n g N e w

T i m e M a k i n g N e w T i

m e M a k i n g N e w T i m e

MakingNewTimeMa
kingNewTimeMaki
ng**New**TimeMaking
NewTimeMakingNe
wTimeMakingNewT
imeMakingNewTim
eMakingNew**Time:**
MakingNewTimeMa
king**An**NewTimeMa
king**Itinerary**Ne
wTimeMakingNewT
imeMakingNewTim
eMakingNewTimeM
akingNewTimeMak
ingNewTimeMakin

In *Água Viva*, Brazilian writer Clarice Lispector opens her 1973 autobiographical book by describing a 'fourth dimension' that she dubs 'the instant-now': a transitory space where we experience a moment in time. The instant-now is the space for breath, a cosmos where one can 'possess the atoms of time'. With her book, Lispector had hoped to capture the present as it so rapidly slipped through her fingers. In the text, she speaks of producing electronic drawings devoid of a past or a future, and she proclaims to write 'with her whole body' that she would dance into an end, an 'intangible' realm, in order to make sense of herself.

The journey to *Making New Time* was as much about the instant-now as it was about taking inventory of the urgencies of the now. In turn, the exhibition became both a call and a response to artists. Artists who became friends. Artists who spoke different languages, whose work created ruptures, fissures, holes through an echo chamber – a space with multiple surfaces, contortions and resonances.

Who was I searching for? Or rather, what was I searching for?

There was never a clear answer. That was not the point. The question was this: In an era of accelerated and mediated tumult, why bother with art? What can art do? What can art demand of the viewer, the person, of us as humans?

Art has, for me, been a barometer of radical social change since I was a child confronted with Salvador Dalí's *Christ of St. John of the Cross* (1951) at Kelvingrove Art Gallery and Museum in Glasgow. Perhaps it was a phenomenological effect: I am not entirely certain why, but this painting changed something within me. It gave me room to think of possibilities that existed outside of the bounds of a confined reality. It was anything and everything, all at the same time. That, indeed, is the power of art – to be of many things at once. Art has the potential to open up the wounds of the past, so that they may be unfurled and sutured. It holds the possibility to help us create new alphabets, dreamscapes and maps for the imagination.

The contoured forms of identification that art produces enable us to envisage new forms of understanding and experiencing time. Time is as much a marker of lived experience as it is a thing, an entity, a container. *Making New Time* is an exhibition as anti-museum. It is a museum torn apart; not a mausoleum, but a space for the living!

A Meditation

Ours is an age of constant speed; we barely have a moment to breathe. Time is the irreversible, indefinite and continued process of existing in the world. Yet technological, social and political changes have altered the means by which we relate to images, objects and the concept of history, itself. Spatial and temporal orders have shifted with the advent of a reality that moves like mercury, in and out of our hands (our bloodstream) and into an abyss, a space of chaos – but also towards a new portal, a space of possibility: reality and history have been augmented by the realm of the virtual. This process encourages us to cast a critical eye on the history of material cultures as we think we know them. With all this in mind, how do we slow down and 'experience' the experience? How do we make 'new time'?

Making New Time is a provocation: How can material culture be reimagined through the lens of a group of artists whose political agency, activism and astute observations encourage us to extend beyond the limits of belief? We consider how economies have formed around technological culture, how narrative is created and deconstructed, and how these forces enable a reconstitution or, indeed, a restitution of a history lost, or even unknown. Drifting in and out of hegemonies and entrenched structures of power, here the sensorial and the bodily intertwine, becoming archaeological sediments in the landscape of Sharjah, asking viewers to consider their complicity in a world that is forever fleeting.

Tactile Time

The body moves and shifts to the contours of history. Artists rupture, fragment and distil the body into a sensorial experience. The body, here, undergoes a process that seeps through our skin, that forms scripts, new languages. Its scale morphs and contorts until we are formless, bound by nothing else but earth. Semiha Berksoy was one of the leading cultural figures in Turkey. She was, at any one time, an opera singer, a poet, a performance artist and a painter, whose amorous limbs flowed freely into each other, forming palpable embraces. Huguette Caland, the daughter of the first Lebanese president, used abstraction to carve out a new form of sensorial sensuality – an erotic configuration of ebullient colour, contoured out of sumptuous textures ranging from canvas to fabric.

Stan Douglas uses computerised technology to create constructions that reflect on the nature of photographic representation. In his *DCT* series

(2016), he manipulates a sequence of data points referred to as a 'DCT' (discrete cosine transform), manually inputting data to create photographs divorced from any reference to the real world. The DCTs play with light, as does Ann Veronica Janssens's *Volute* (2006–19), an environment in which the viewer is disoriented and flooded into a spectral universe, where the body is upturned from the confines of its own physicality.

The materiality of the body is examined in Barbara Kasten's photography from the 1970s, which seeks to interrogate material culture with its amplified and staged settings of saturated colour. Here, stage sets resemble bodies, but the body is absent; all we are left with is a palpable feeling of its absence. Bodies morph into landscapes in the paintings of Marwan and Bruno Pacheco, a historic figure and a contemporary one, respectively, whose investigations into canvas seek to push the formal limits of figuration.

Otobong Nkanga collaborates with Emeka Ogboh to create a sonic garden, a space that is public, but made to foster private experiences. Pamela Rosenkranz also deploys techniques that blur the public and the private, offering a courtyard as a resting place for a controlled ancient species. Anwar Jalal Shemza's calligraphic forms are a carefully choreographed antecedent to the bodily, to the cityscape and to the all-encompassing universe that shrouds us in its tactile material.

Playing Time

Technologies have fragmented us, but they have also reconstituted us. They create possibilities, openings and fissures. These spaces, however, are open to tampering, suspension, surveillance and corruption. So how, then, have our spatial and temporal senses shifted in light of the digital realities that have started to consume us? A quest for liberation ensues.

Cory Arcangel contorts forms of identification often synonymous with branding in order to create habitats that surprise and enthral. Ian Cheng proposes a form of acting out with his simulations, which are entirely algorithmically generated. Shezad Dawood's virtual world, in his project *Encroachments* (2019), takes us through a history of Lahore and Karachi. Heather Phillipson's multiverse is one of perpetual free fall. Jon Rafman's modular installation *The Ride Never Ends* (2019) questions technologies from the Jurassic period to contemporary times, and considers how we engage in an algorithmically predetermined universe.

Trialing Time

History is that most elusive of things. It proclaims to account for our time, but it is marred or, at the very least, contorted by the subjectivity of others as well as notions of what might constitute tradition. Can we invent new modes of time in the face of competing narratives? How do we negotiate the trauma wrought by perpetual conflict and the echo chamber that circulates around it? Embers turn to dust.

Lawrence Abu Hamdan presents the time traveling life of a 30 year old writer and historian whose trans-migrated soul leads him to a rare political archive. Marwa Arsanios's investigation into communal labour practices puts women first in a narrative of constant decay. Lubaina Himid's sculptural paintings unbuckle colonial histories, blood on their hands. Alfredo Jaar shines a light on the women of our time, whilst Astrid Klein asks, 'What are we fighting for?' Michael Rakowitz tells the tale of Special Ops Cody in a meditation on war and its artefactual traces. Hrair Sarkissian questions the movement of a fleet of birds that have re-emerged after extinction in one of the most violently contested parts of the world.

Candice Breitz presents a video installation without an image, presenting a morgue that traces the end of subjectivity associated with the analogue era. Munem Wasif documents the degeneration of an urban landscape that keeps eating itself. Kemang Wa Lehulere creates a meditation on memory – sewing back together the wounds of his past through palimpsestlike renderings. Alessandro Balteo-Yazbeck interrogates Sharjah's port economy, the rise and fall of colonialism, and Akram Zaatari digs beneath the sands of time to reveal a little-known piece of mythology.

Collective Weaving

This brief, cursory glance speaks to an act of curatorial practice; that is, one of collective weaving. How does one tell a macro tale of our times when looking at a single object abstracted from the context of its making and transplanted to the temporal juncture of Sharjah's heritage houses, museums and new spaces? These are works of art that are stitched into the fabric of a city – its smells, its tastes – leaving remnants for the minds of its citizens. These are materials that eschew the practice of museology and its display mechanisms, sometimes sedimenting into the gravel; at other times, fleeing like cigarette ash, leaving but small traces.

The works included in *Making New Time* represent a different kind of ordering – of things, of time. It is hot time, deep time, a past that is not fixed as well as a future that may or may not be open. This is, as Italian theoretical physicist Carlo Rovelli, invoking Aristotle, articulates, a time that 'crumbles', that is digestible, that is beautiful and that is troubled. One thing is transformed into another – rendered simultaneously meaningful, yet meaningless. These are networks of events that affect each other, dreams that delude and sully each other. Eternal currents that flow in and out of sync, creating moments of entropy. These are birds that caw and cats that shriek and sleep at the entrances of buildings; they rest, they sleep, in two temporal zones, awake at times, fast asleep at others. Collectively, they weave a map of a condition of time that demands re-examination, a reimagining of the instant-now.

Self, Other, West/Non-West

The echo chamber, as articulated in the theme of the 14th Sharjah Biennial, can be interpreted as the voice box of the West. In this case, the West is the hegemonic organ that flattens everything in its wake – or does it? In *A Cyborg Manifesto* (1985), Donna Haraway discusses the dualisms that the West produces. For instance, mind/body, culture/nature and active/passive are terms that are often aligned. Whether or not these terms are opposed to each other, they create dialogical meaning because of the way that Western culture structures its society.

Within this framework is the discussion of the Self and the Other, as well as how we see each other. The Self dominates, whilst the Other is dominated. Likewise, the Self is active, whilst the Other is passive; the Self is concerned with the mind, whilst the Other is concerned with the body – this is one version of the echo chamber. *Making New Time* does not propose to explain how we leave the echo chamber; rather, it posits a world, a position in which agency is not given to the Western Self to dominate a narrative or a subject. Instead, it is bestowed upon a multiplicity of actors, whose practices fundamentally interrogate the roles that we play within society.

The Beginning of the Script

A biennial is an event that is a constant work in progress. This itinerary is but a preamble; what you read here will shift and contort through time. This is but a fragment that maps a route, a course that is subject to constant change.

N e w T i m e M a k i n g N e
w T i m e M a k i n g N e w T
i m e M a k i n g N e w T i m
e M a k i n g N e w T i m e M
a k i n g N e w T i m e M a k
i n g N e w T i m e M a k i n
g N e w T i m e M a k i n g N
e w T i m e M a k i n g N e w
T i m e M a k i n g N e w T i
m e M a k i n g N e w T i m e
M a k i n g N e w T i m e M a
k i n g N e w T i m e M a k i
n g N e w T i m e M a k i n g
N e w T i m e M a k i n g N e
w T i m e M a k i n g N e w T

imeMakingNewTim
eMakingNewTimeM
akingNew**Artist**T
imeMakingNewTim
eMakingNewTimeM
akingNewTimeMak
ingNewTimeMakin
gNew**Pages**TimeMa
kingNewTimeMaki
ngNewTimeMaking
NewTimeMakingNe
wTimeMakingNewT
imeMakingNewTim
eMakingNewTimeM
akingNewTimeMak

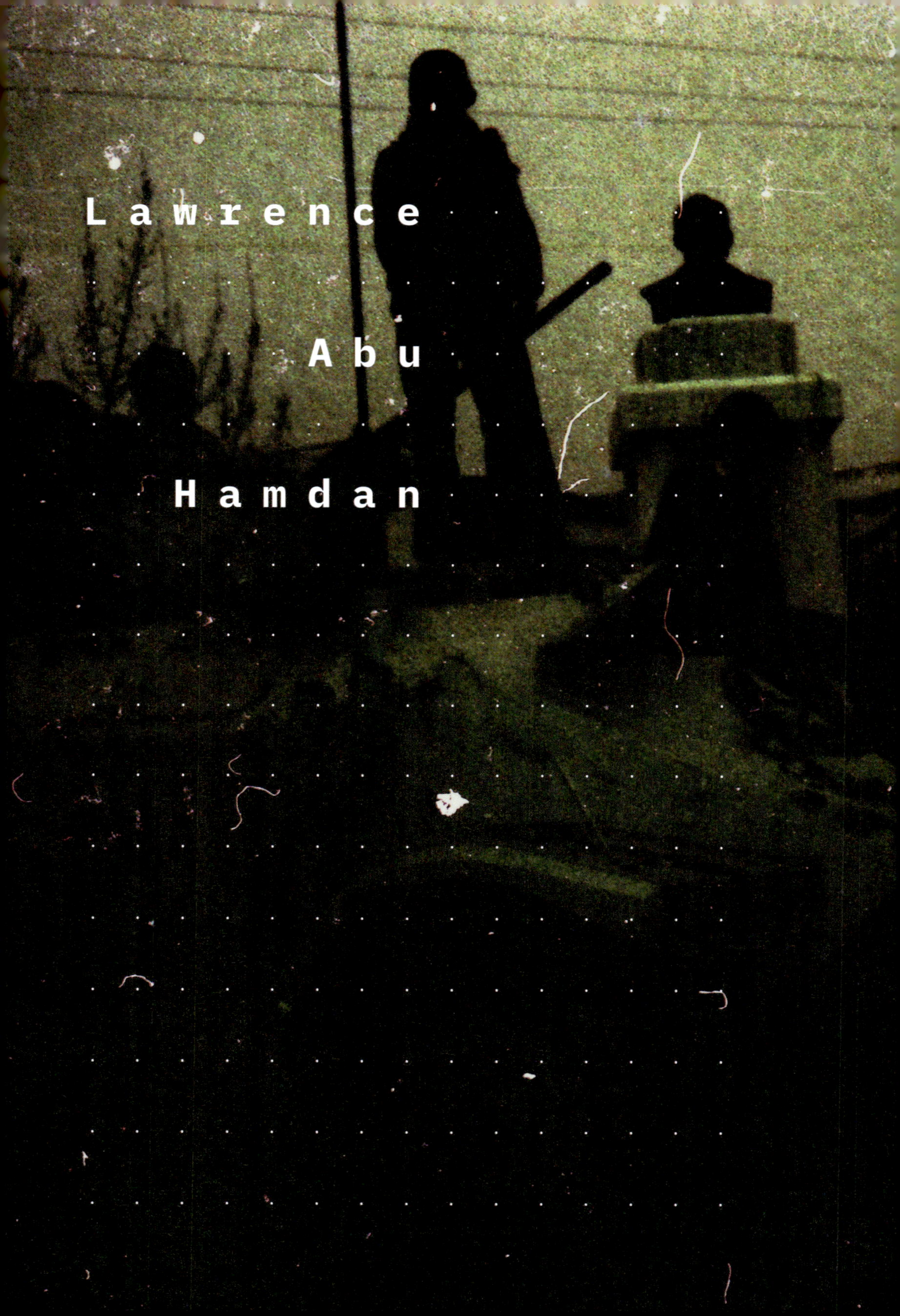

Lawrence

Abu

Hamdan

b. 1985, Amman, Jordan; lives in Beirut, Lebanon
Commissioned by Sharjah Art Foundation

In his new commission, *Once Removed* (2019), Abu Hamdan presents an audiovisual installation that acts as a portrait of the time-travelling life and work of Bassel Abi Chahine, a thirty-one-year-old writer and historian who managed to obtain an unparalleled, comprehensive inventory of extremely rare objects, photographs and interviews of the PLA and PSP socialist militia led by Walid Jumblatt during the Lebanese Civil War. As Abi Chahine amassed this archive, he taught himself how to read and identify all manner of military equipment – including every pattern of camouflage and the origin of every AK-47, whether Bulgarian, Polish, Soviet or Chinese – in each of the images. Through his obsessive analysis and unprecedented research, the writer also pursued materials that could reconstitute what he describes as 'flashbacks' and unexplainable memories from a previous life. Abi Chahine belongs to the Druze, an Islamic sect whose members believe in the transmigration of the soul after death. Through his research, he came to realise that his lucid and personal memories of the war, with which he had lived his whole life, were due to the fact that he was the reincarnation of a soldier named Yousef Fouad Al Jawhary, who had died on 26 February 1984, when he was sixteen years old, in the town of Aley, Lebanon. Since the end of the war, specific details pertaining to sectarian conflicts had been suppressed in the interest of national security, so as not to incite further tensions between the formerly warring parties. This has meant that, for Abi Chahine's generation, very little is known (or can be verified) about what happened during the war. His generation grew up with rumours and tales, as well as suggestions not to ask too many questions. Yet former soldiers and commanders of the PSP felt at ease to confide in him, thus imparting to Abi Chahine information that had been deemed unspeakable – only because they believed him to be the reincarnation of one of their former comrades. Abi Chahine's reincarnation and his research are inseparable. Yet the writer does not intend to expose the silenced events that he has uncovered regarding what happened during the war. Instead, he seeks material and tangible traces that it happened at all; and most of all, despite not having been alive at the time, that it happened to him.

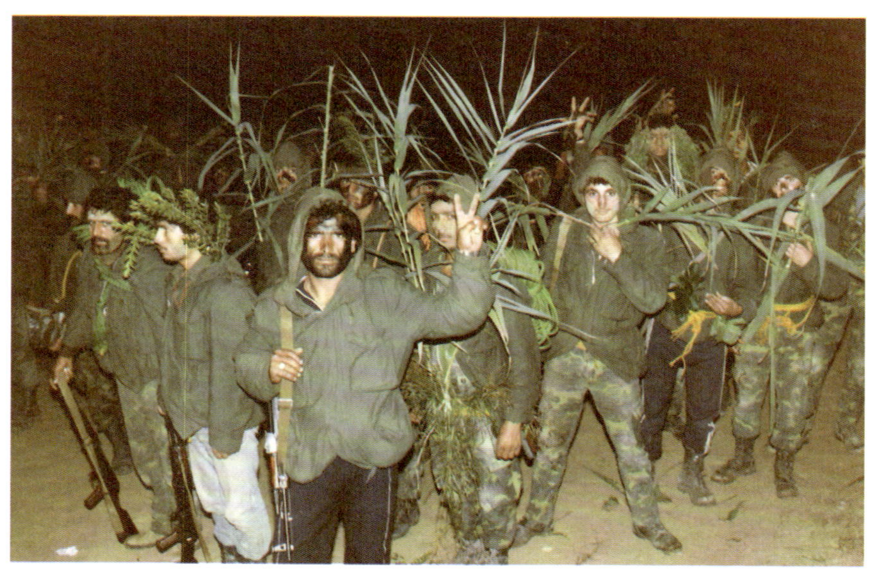

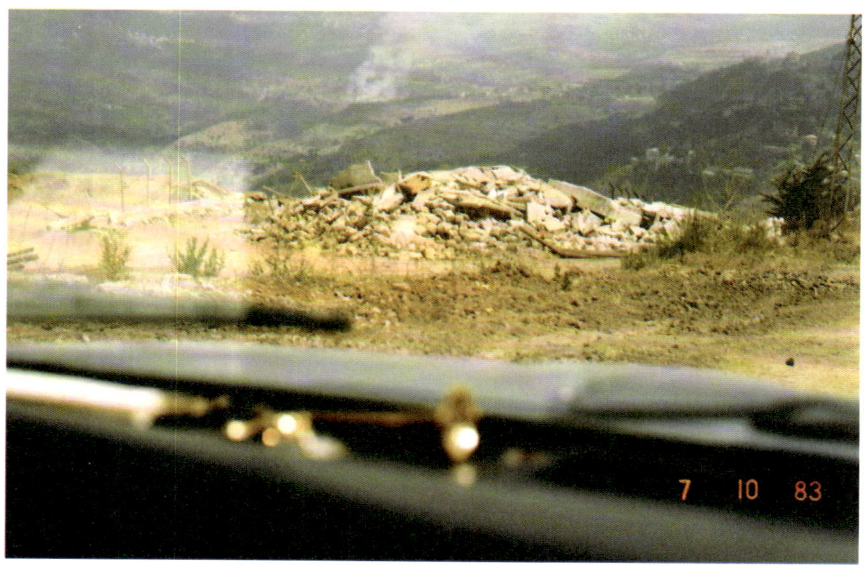
7 10 83

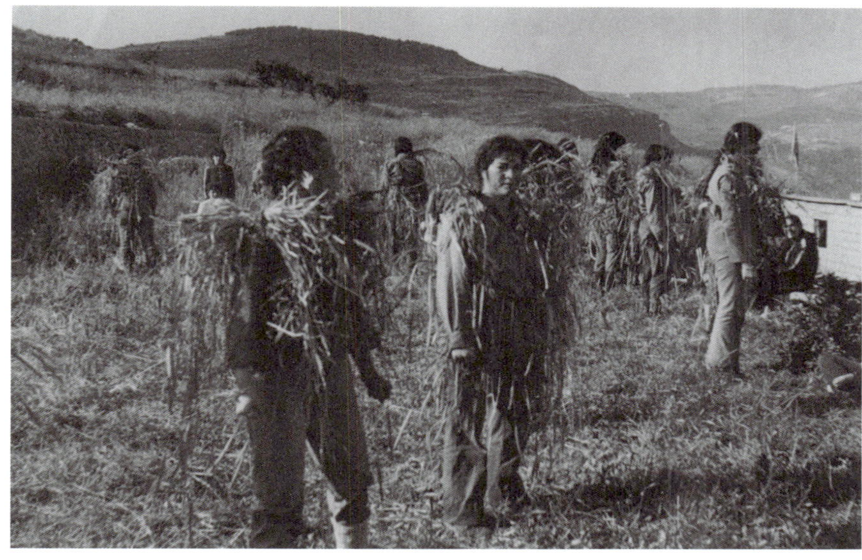

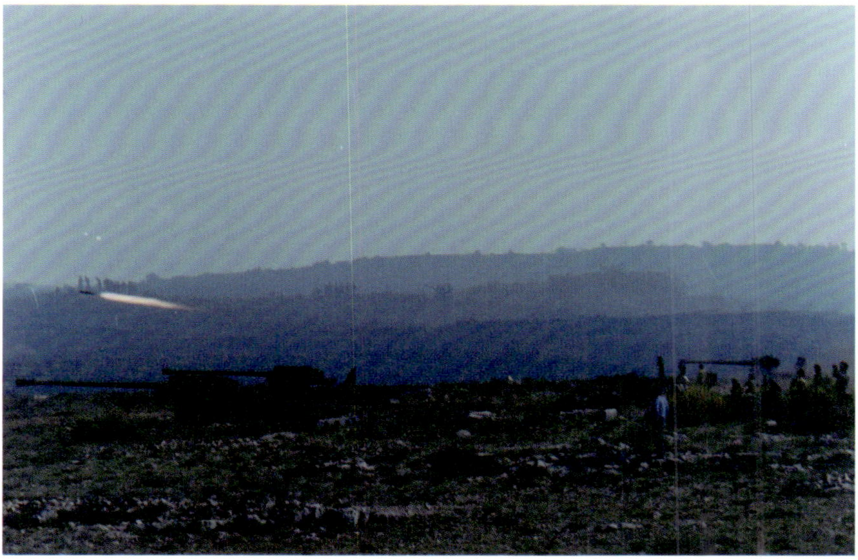

Production stills
Courtesy of the artist and Bassel Abi Chahine

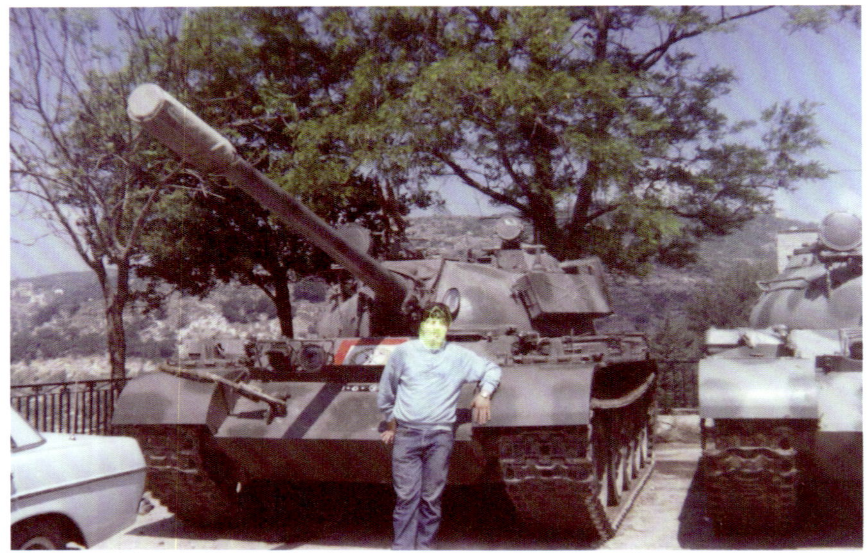

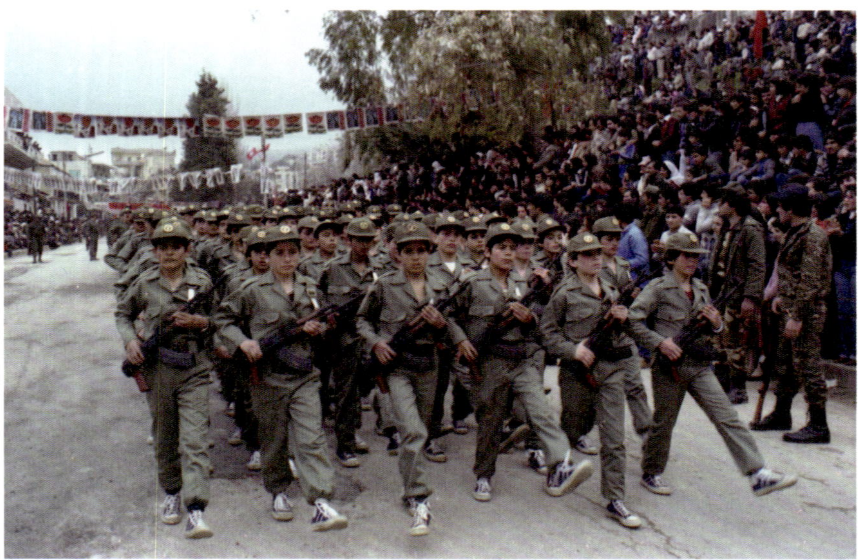

Production stills
Courtesy of the artist and Bassel Abi Chahine

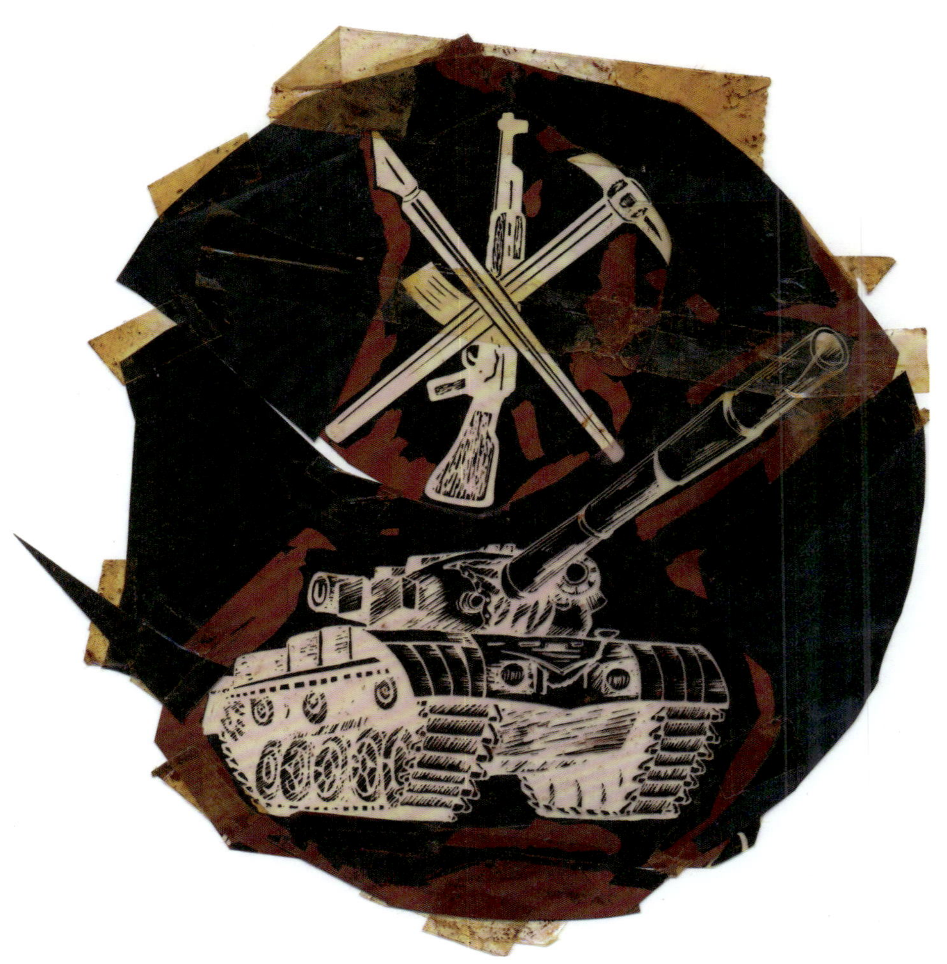

Cory Arcangel

b. 1978, New York, USA; lives in New York and Stavanger, Norway
Commissioned by Sharjah Art Foundation

Cory Arcangel is one of the leading artists working with emerging technology. He often explores the potential of software to create community, aesthetics and a shared visual language. Arcangel contorts and manipulates everyday technologies, from video games to YouTube clips, to produce works that reflect technology's uncomfortable role in our everyday lives. For the Sharjah Biennial, he has developed a suite of new works, including wall banners, a set of lasers and a soundtrack intervention. In a nod to global circulation, an abstracted audio-organ piece plays in the gym at the Radisson Blu Hotel amidst the ongoing soundtrack. Outdoor lasers project an animation of a basketball player dunking a ball into a hoop – perhaps a metaphor for the desire for success in the post-capitalist era. Meanwhile, appropriated and manipulated images of faded jeans give life to a street parade on the facade of the Sharjah Art Museum, a comment on the commoditisation of global culture.

Nanos
2018
Blueberry, Raspberry on Somerset Paper
19.05 x 27.94 cm
Courtesy of Cory Arcangel, Galerie Thaddaeus Ropac and Lisson Gallery

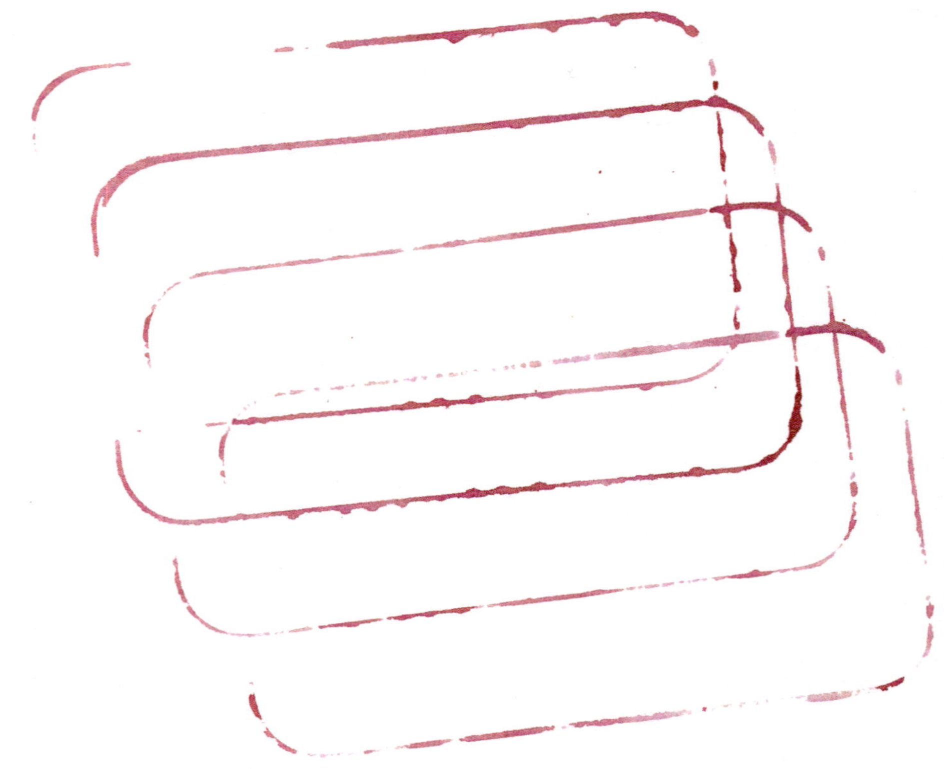

Nanos
2018
Blueberry, Raspberry on
Somerset Paper
19.05 x 27.94 cm
Courtesy of Cory Arcangel,
Galerie Thaddaeus Ropac and
Lisson Gallery

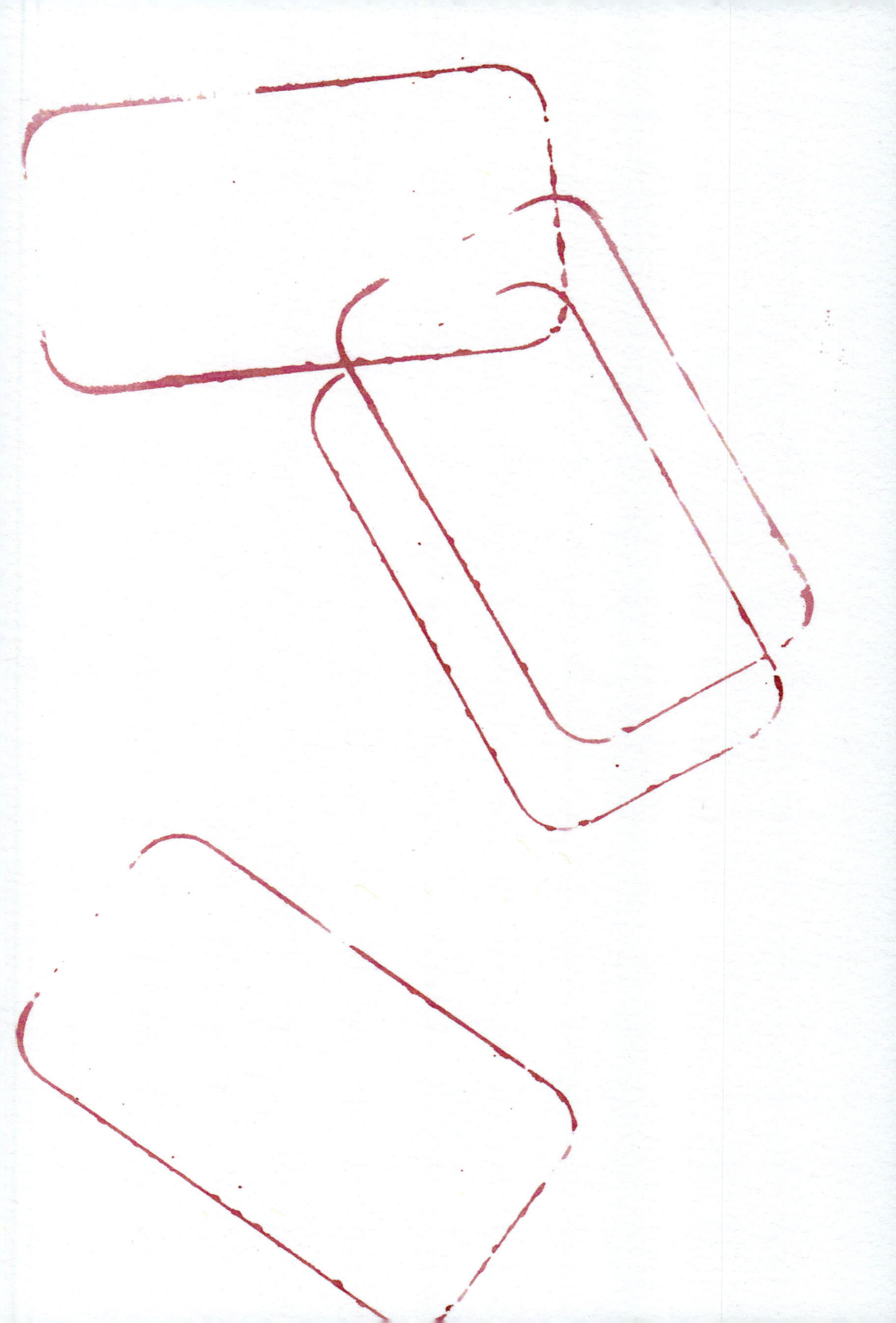

Marwa Arsanios

b. 1978, Washington, D.C., USA; lives in Beirut, Lebanon, and Berlin, Germany.

Commissioned by Sharjah Art Foundation and co-produced with San Francisco Museum of Modern Art, Fast Forward Festival Athens and Vooruit Belgium

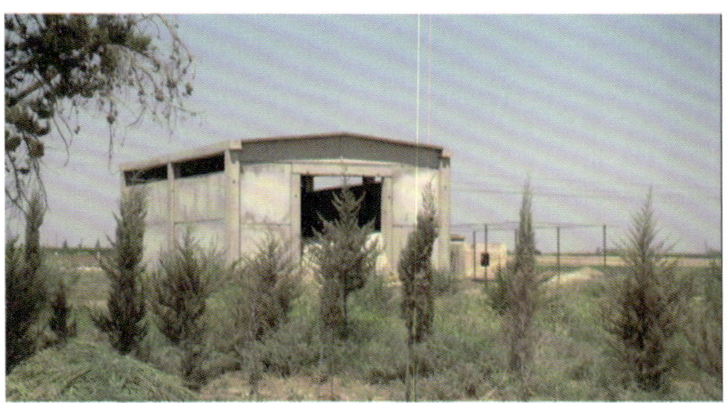

Marwa Arsanios is an artist, filmmaker and researcher who reconsiders Middle Eastern politics of the mid-twentieth century from a contemporary perspective, with a particular focus on gender relations, urbanism and industrialisation. For her new commission, *Who's Afraid of Ideology* II, Arsanios studies the ecofeminist community of Jinwar, a village in Rojava, in northern Syria, which was built by an autonomous women's movement. Here, the artist considers what it means to organise a communal life melding nature and non-human species. She also explores a farming cooperative in Bekaa Valley in Lebanon on the border with Syria – an informal NGO-like structure that has become a safe space for female Syrian refugees. Her new film, reveals how land has been re-appropriated by different groups under the agricultural policy of the political Ba'ath regime. Critiquing how ideology is constructed, Arsanios's work explores the possibilities of creating a countercultural movement under the oppressive force of a dictatorial political regime.

Who is Afraid of Ideology? part 2
2019
From 'Who is Afraid of Ideology?'
Video still
Video and installation;
27 minutes
Courtesy of the artist and Mor-Charpentier Gallery, Paris

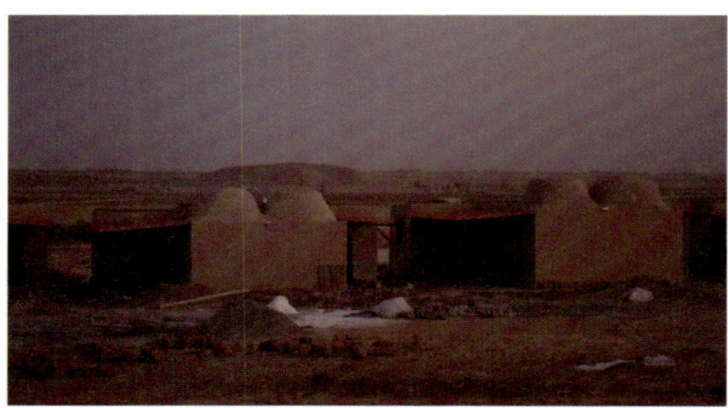

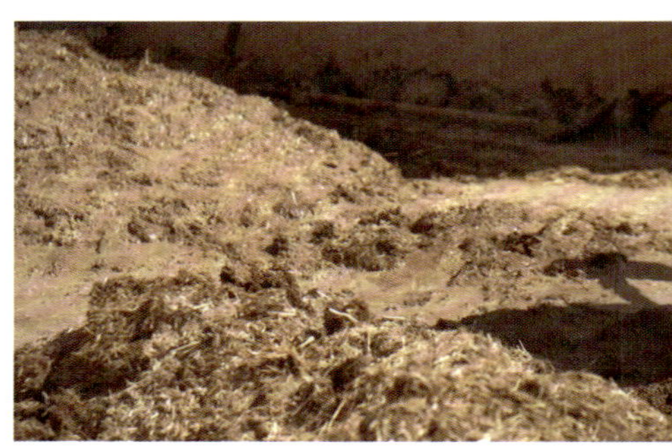

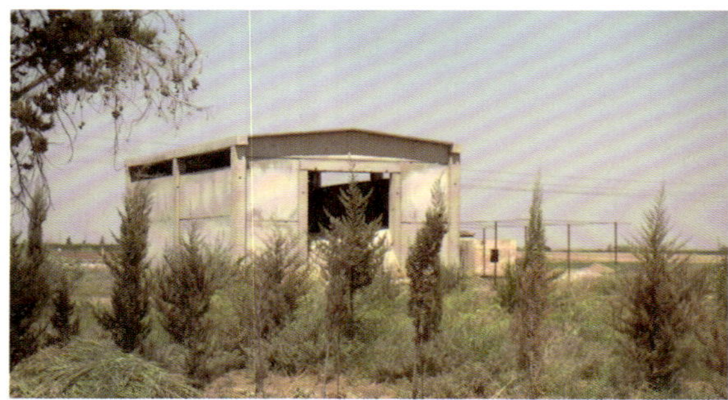

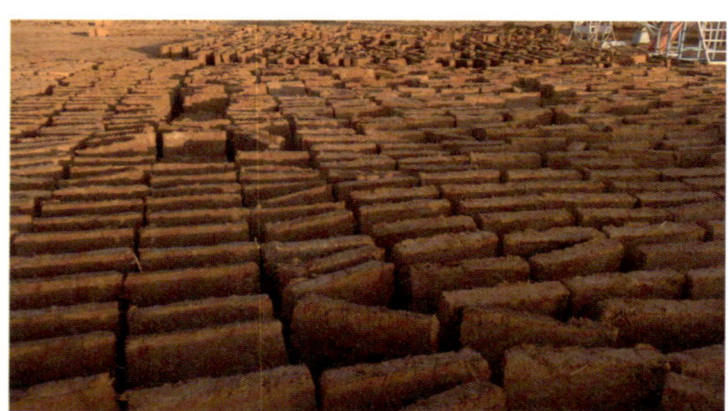

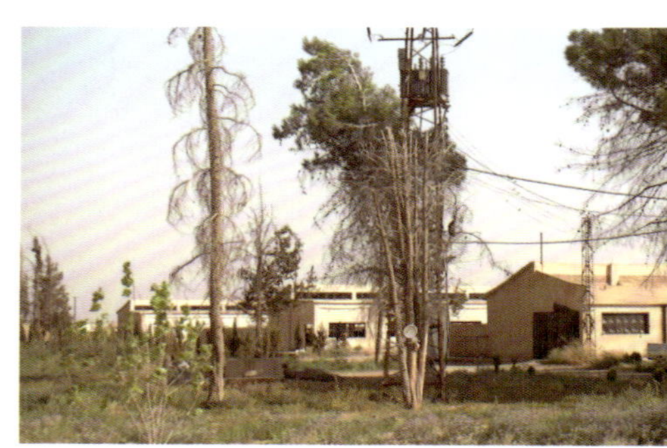

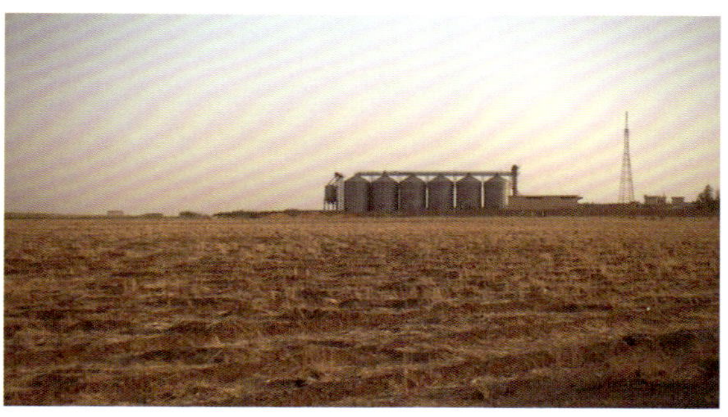

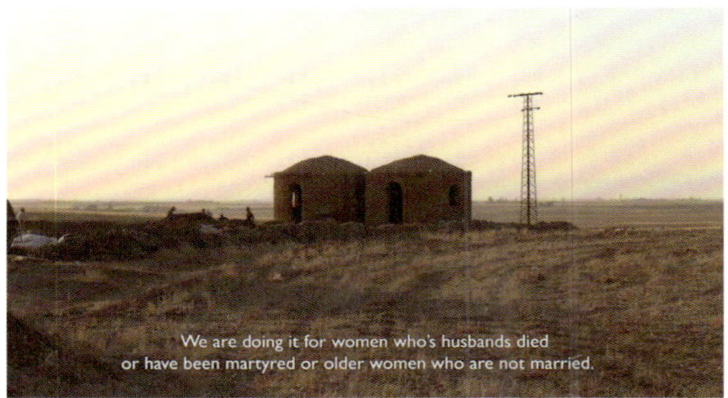
We are doing it for women who's husbands died
or have been martyred or older women who are not married.

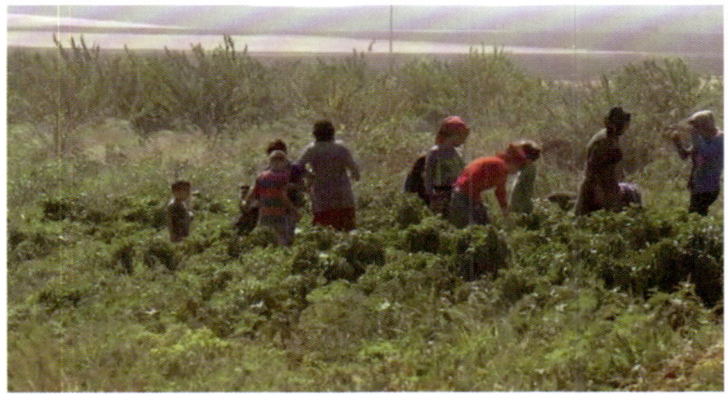

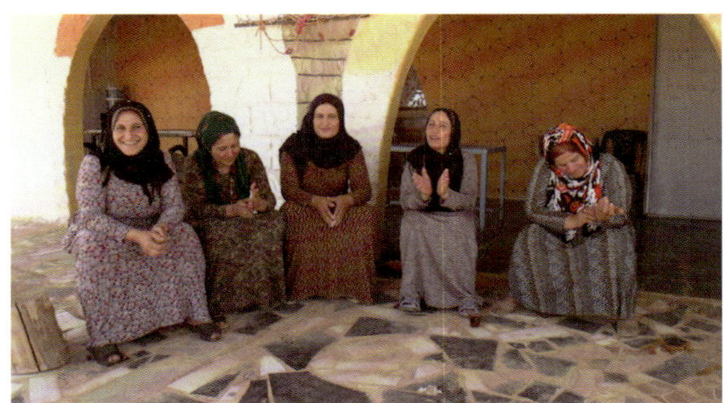

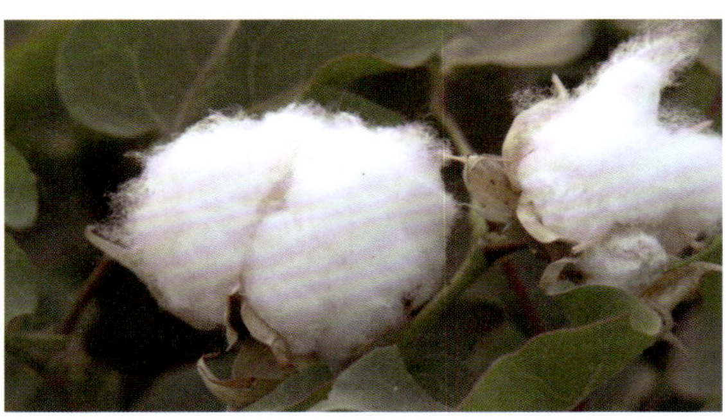

Alessandro Balteo-Yazbeck

b. 1972 Caracas, Venezuela. Lives in Berlin, Germany. In collaboration with Atilio Napolitano, b. 1936 Modica, Italy. Lives in Modica, Italy
Commissioned by Sharjah Art Foundation

With the exhibition format as his medium, Balteo-Yazbeck's hybrid practice incorporates the activities of a researcher, archivist, historian and curator. Attempting to reveal the political strategies and motives at work in the world, his oeuvre focuses on power and propaganda in modern history. For his installation, *All the lands from sunrise to sunset,* (2019) in the historical house of the British Political Agent, Issa Bin Abdul Latif Al Serkal, the artist conceived of a temporary wall acting as a warping white cube, formally and metaphorically intersecting the vernacular architecture. Focusing on the decorative remains of the original utilitarian wall niches as openings for indirect sunlight and ventilation, Balteo-Yazbeck highlights architecture as an expressive construct of local identities and as a strategy to simultaneously adopt and confront global trends. The selection of sunlight as an architectural leitmotif echoes the historical British political agency of the venue, as the title of the site-specific intervention refers to the phrase: "The empire on which the sun never sets". This is the context for the presentation of a heterogeneous grouping of objects and materials that refer to the port economy and its present historicisation. Ranging from centenary olive tree wood carvings depicting hand gestures (made by Atilio Napolitano) to vintage regional maps and other publications found during the artist's *dérive,* these objects alude to multiple and entagled narratives.

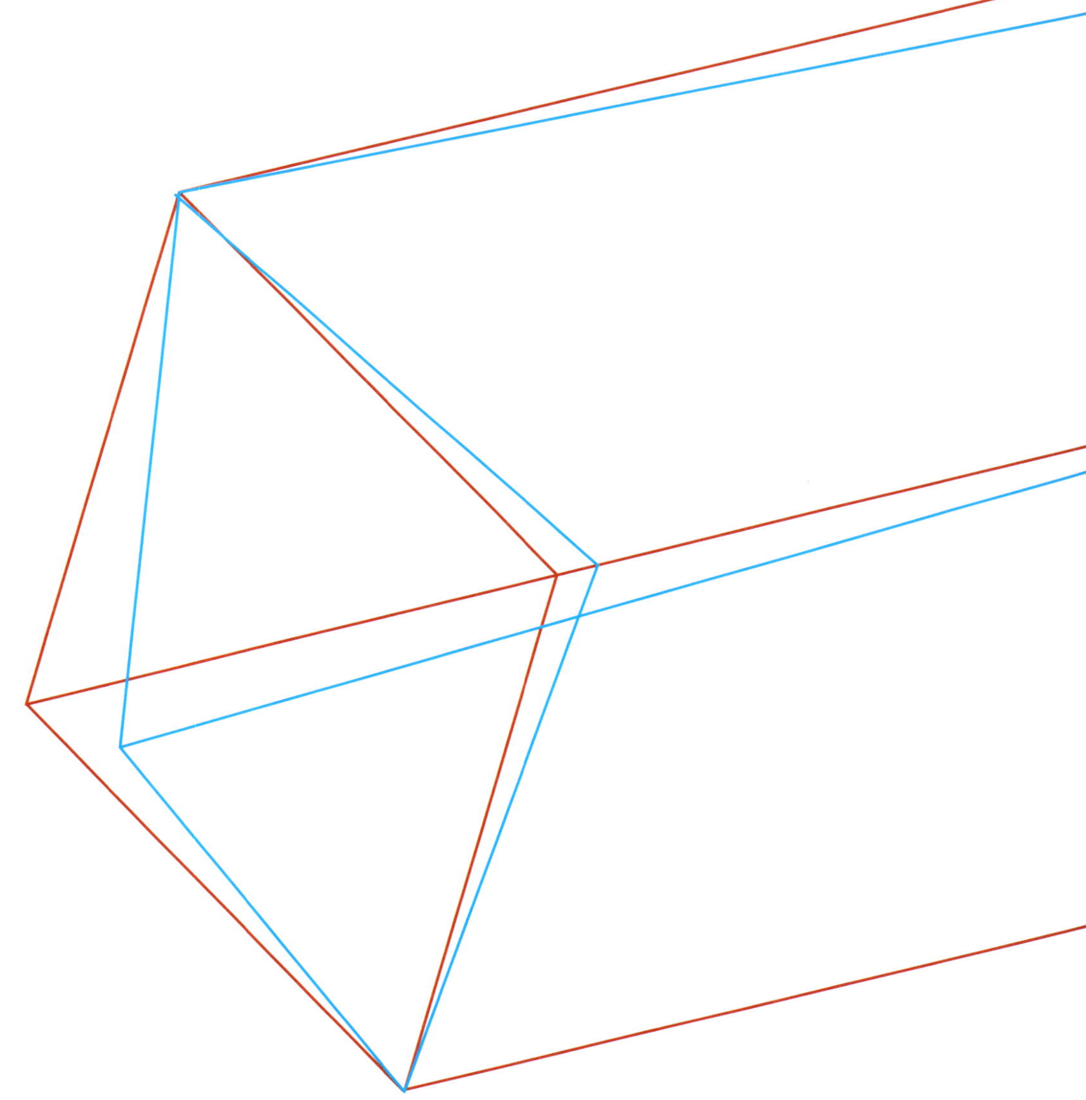

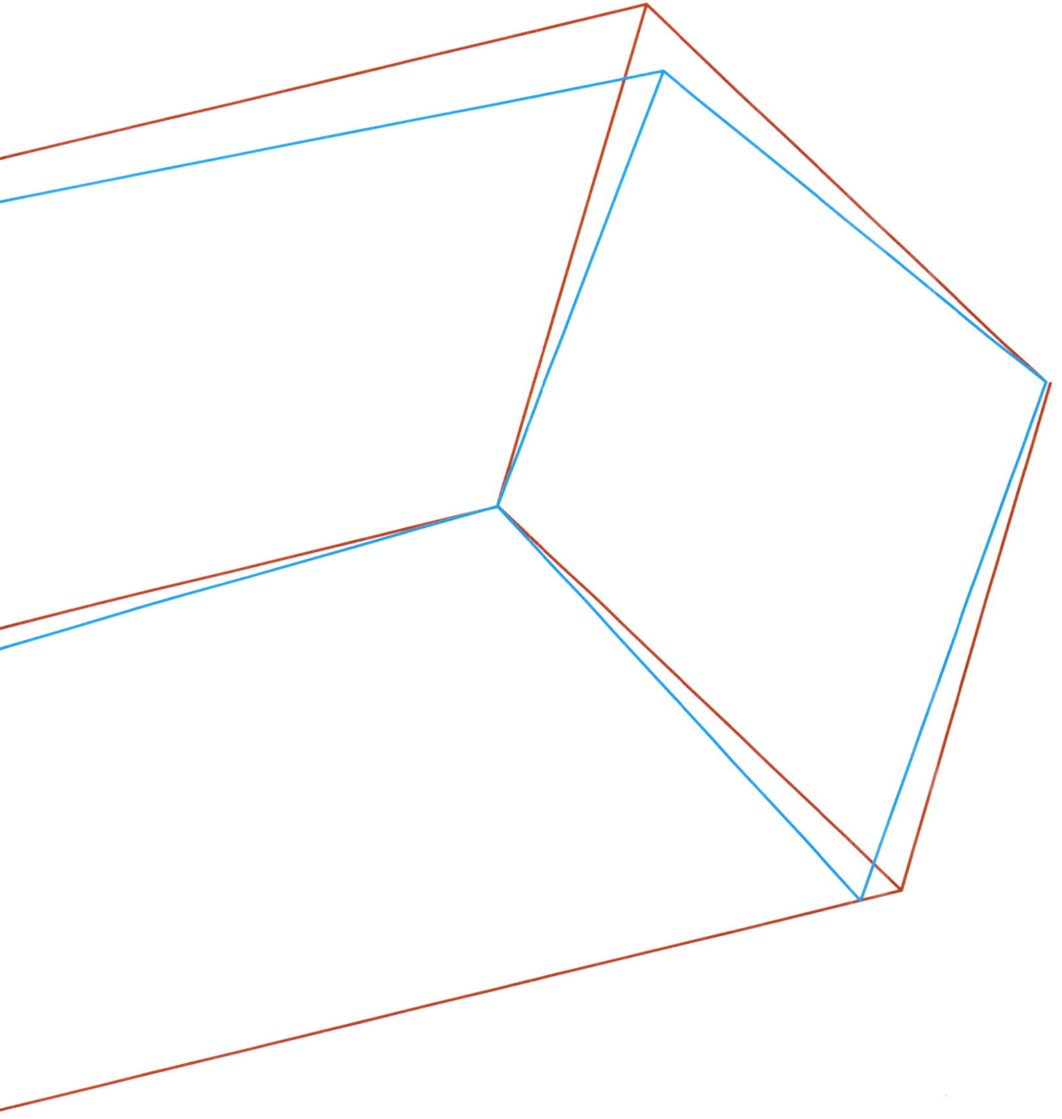

Warping the White Cube
2018
Concept drawing for an architectural intervention
Courtesy of the artist

dominion@PlanetEndure.com

neocon1997@NewAmericanCentury.org

usa1940s@americancentury.com

britain1821@SunNeverSets.co.uk

columbus1492@SunNeverSets.es

cesar@marenostrum.AD

sea-to-sea-from-river-to-end-of-earth@oldtestament.net

pharoh@all.that.sun.encircles.eg

all.lands.sunrise.to.sunset@mesopotamia.com

#EncodingWorldDominationGenealogy /

#warpingTheWhiteCube #ShowOff

#architectureAsBranding #archeologyAsAdvertisement

#DwellingExhibitionAsMedium /

#benevolentglobalhegemony

#miningTheArchive #skeptodelutional #utopicHope #homeopaticPolitics

#opposablethumb #ancientblingbling

#DiminishingReturn, fosil@fuel.org,

propaganda@geography.gulf, free@doom.bye

merchandise@biomass.com

free@doom.bye

Semiha Berksoy

My Mother The Painter Fatma Saime
1972
Oil on hardboard
100 x 70 cm
Courtesy of the artist and Gallerist

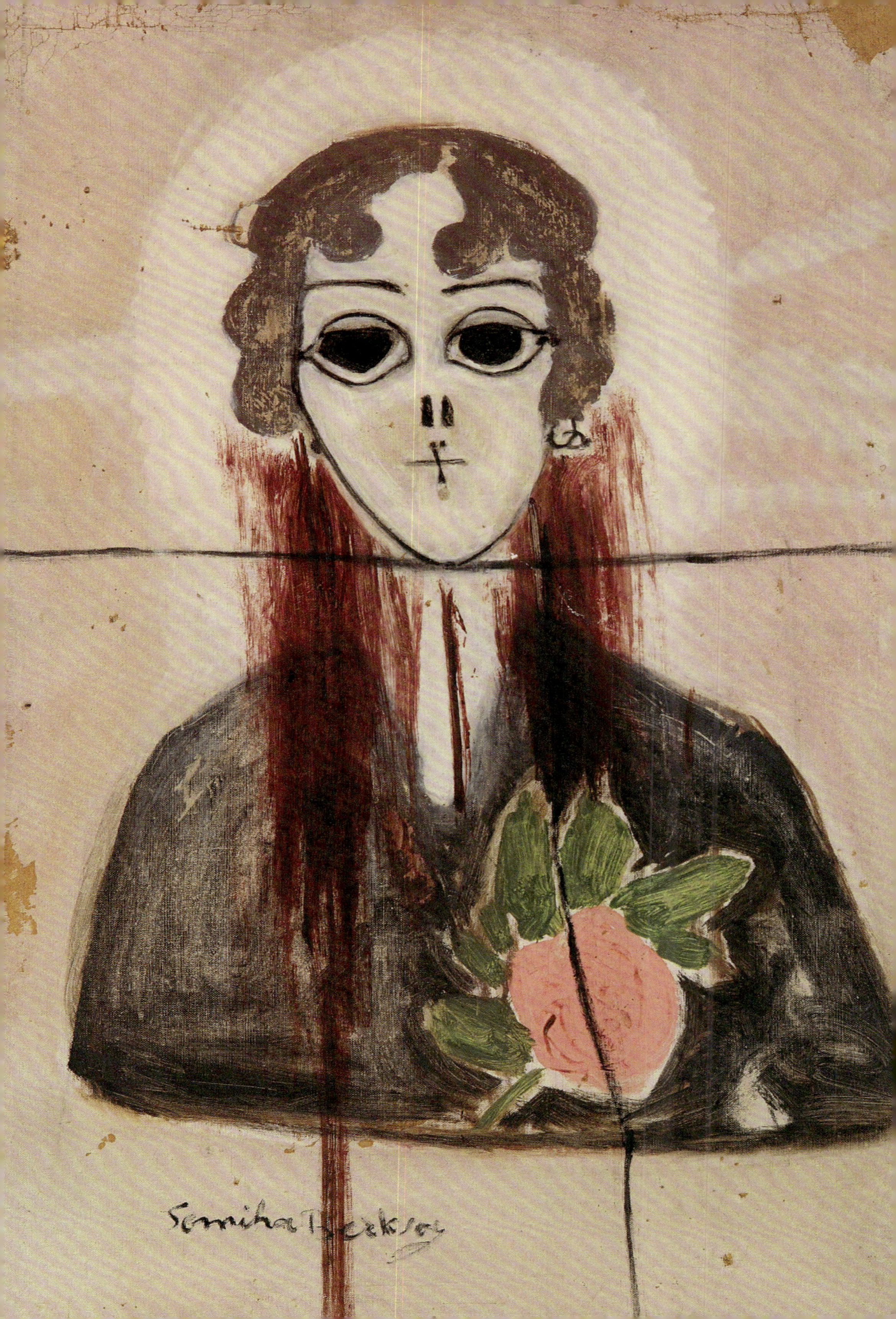
Semiha Berksoy

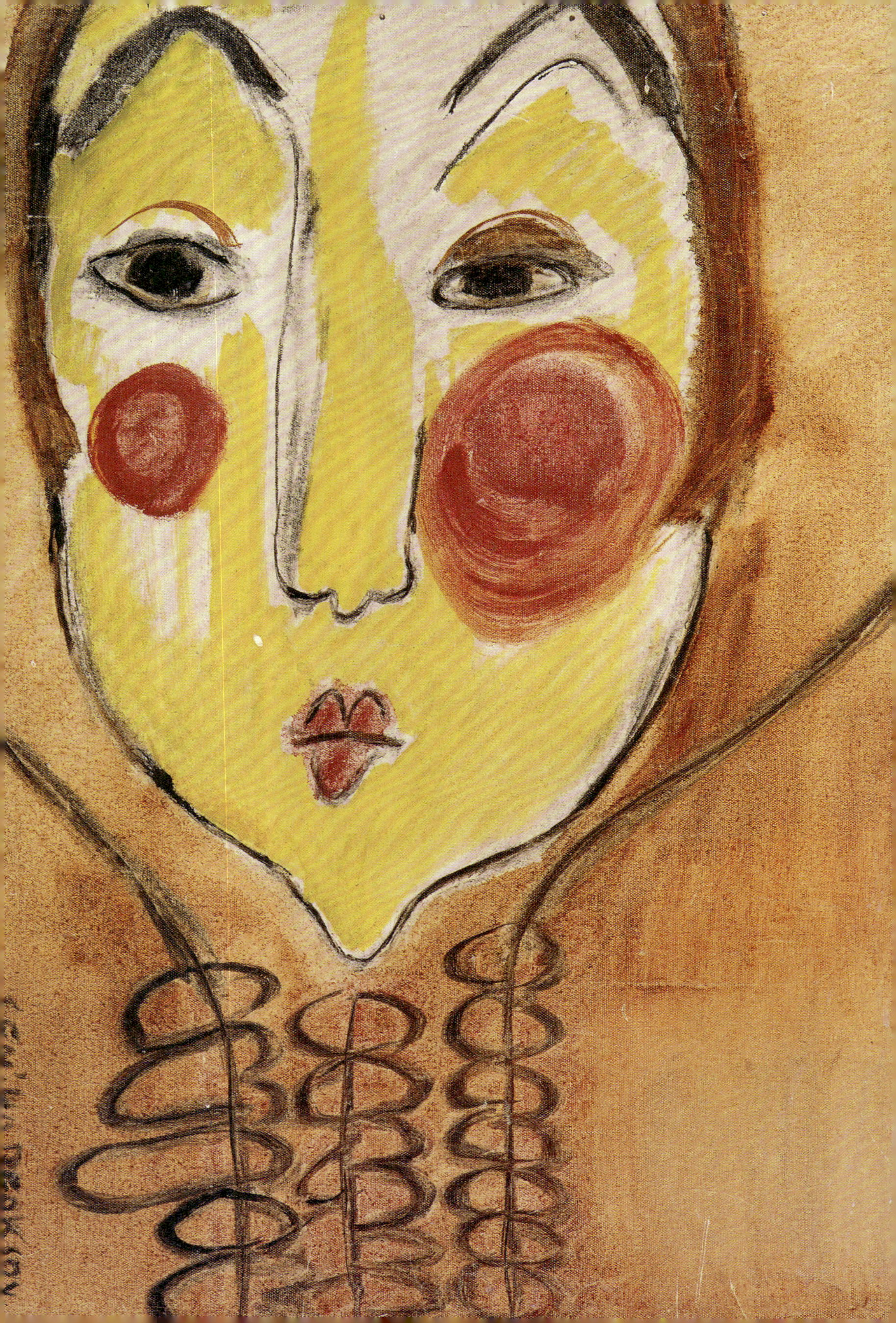

b. 1910, Istanbul, Turkey; d. 2004, Istanbul

Semiha Berksoy was a leading figure in the history of Turkey's cultural scene. A descendant of an artistic family (her mother was a painter and her father a poet), she was a pioneering painter, actress and opera singer. Berksoy started her career as a performer in the early 1930s and played numerous leading roles in Turkish and international opera houses and theatres. She starred in *Tosca* (1941), Turkey's first professional opera production, and *In the Streets of Istanbul* (1931), its first sound film. Berksoy studied at both the Music Academy of Berlin, graduating in 1939, and the Academy of Fine Arts, Istanbul (1929), where she developed a practice in painting. She also pursued her interests in performance and music at the Darülbedayi Drama School and Istanbul Music Conservatory. Her paintings have a distinctly free and sensual style that reflects her fluid movement across art disciplines. Berksoy continued her career as a painter and writer until she passed away in 2004.

In SB14, a selection of Berksoy's paintings from the 1950s to 1970s explores a playful interrelation between life and performance and an existential take on time, framed by the limits of birth and death. Revealing the artist's simple but spirited approach to the medium, the oil paintings include *My Mother Playing Oud* (1958) and *My Mother the Painter Fatima Saime* (1972), which present straightforward, uncomplicated representations of her mother, and *Love Story* (1968), a sinister self-portrait that conveys an ebullient and abject interiority. In another self-portrait, *Chain Breaker* (1968), Berksoy depicts herself surrounded by talisman, her shackled figure emerging and receding from a dark background, or according to the artist, between animal and human. In direct conversation with the self-portraits, a number of more sombre portraits of her mother watching over her introduce a spiritual dimension to this presentation of works.

Daime Koray
1959
Oil on hardboard
34 x 24 cm
Courtesy of the artist and Gallerist, Istanbul

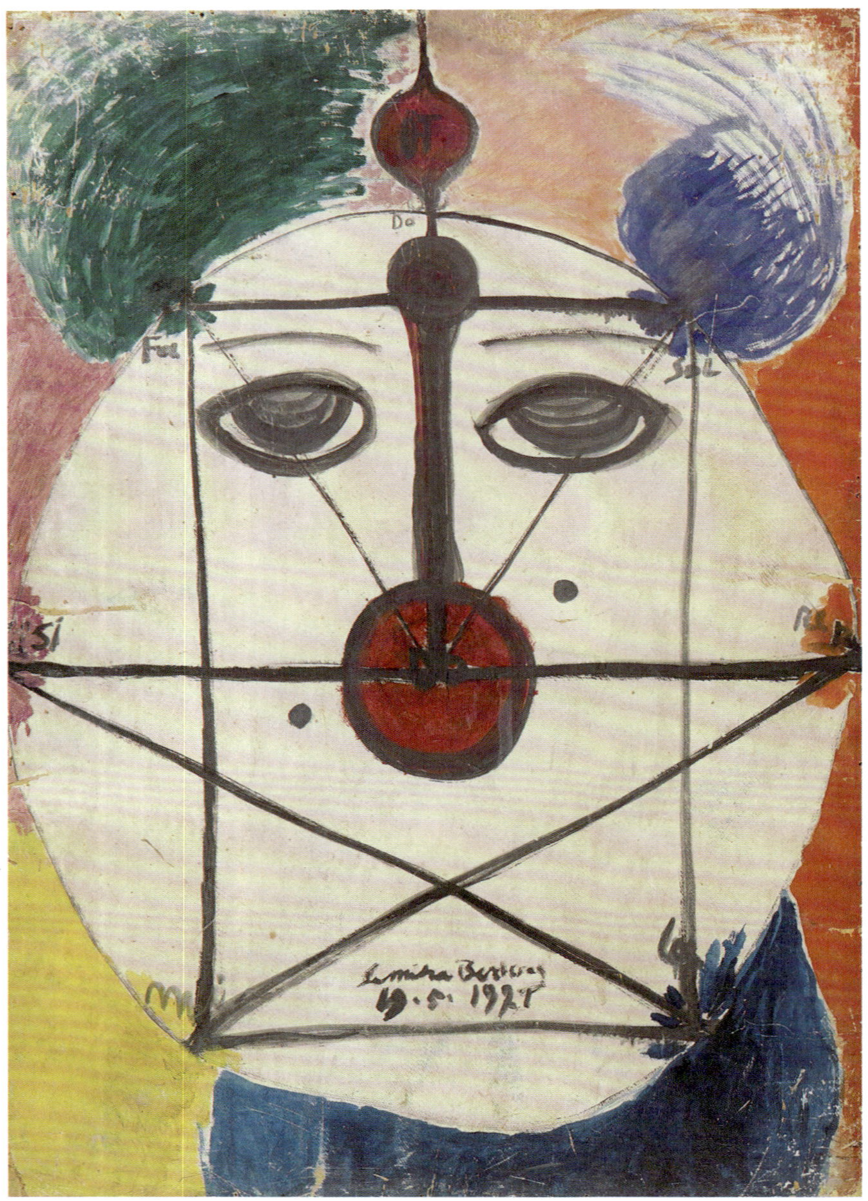

C Zeliha Berksoy
1971
Oil on hardboard
100 x 70 cm
Courtesy of the artist and Gallerist, Istanbul

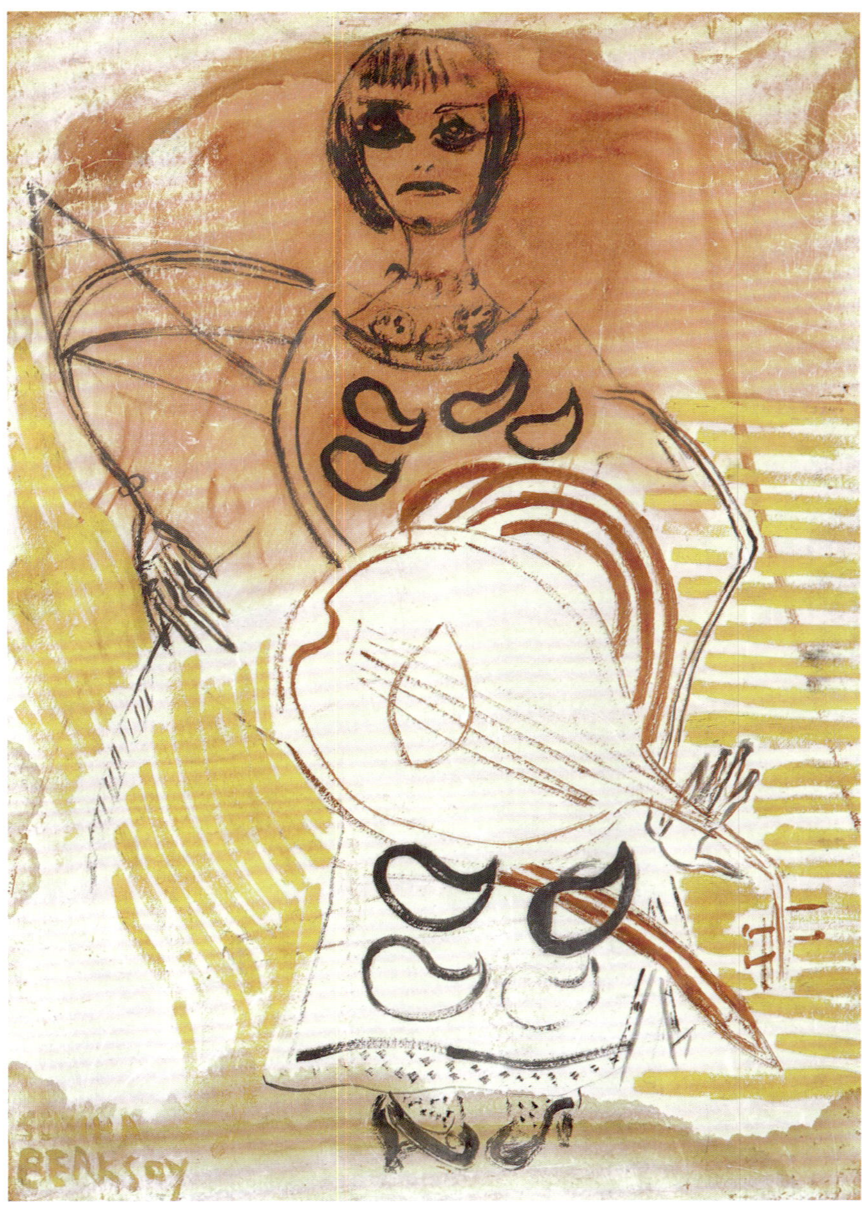

My Mother Playing the Oud
1958
Oil on hardboard
99 x 69 cm
Courtesy of the artist and Gallerist, Istanbul

Candice Breitz

Digest, 2019
A multichannel video installation
300 units: 20.3 x 12 x 2.7 cm each
70 shelves, 300 videotapes in polypropylene boxes, paper and acrylic paint
Courtesy Goodman Gallery (Johannesburg), Kaufmann Repetto (Milan) and KOW (Berlin)

b. 1972, Johannesburg; lives and works in Berlin
Commissioned by Sharjah Art Foundation

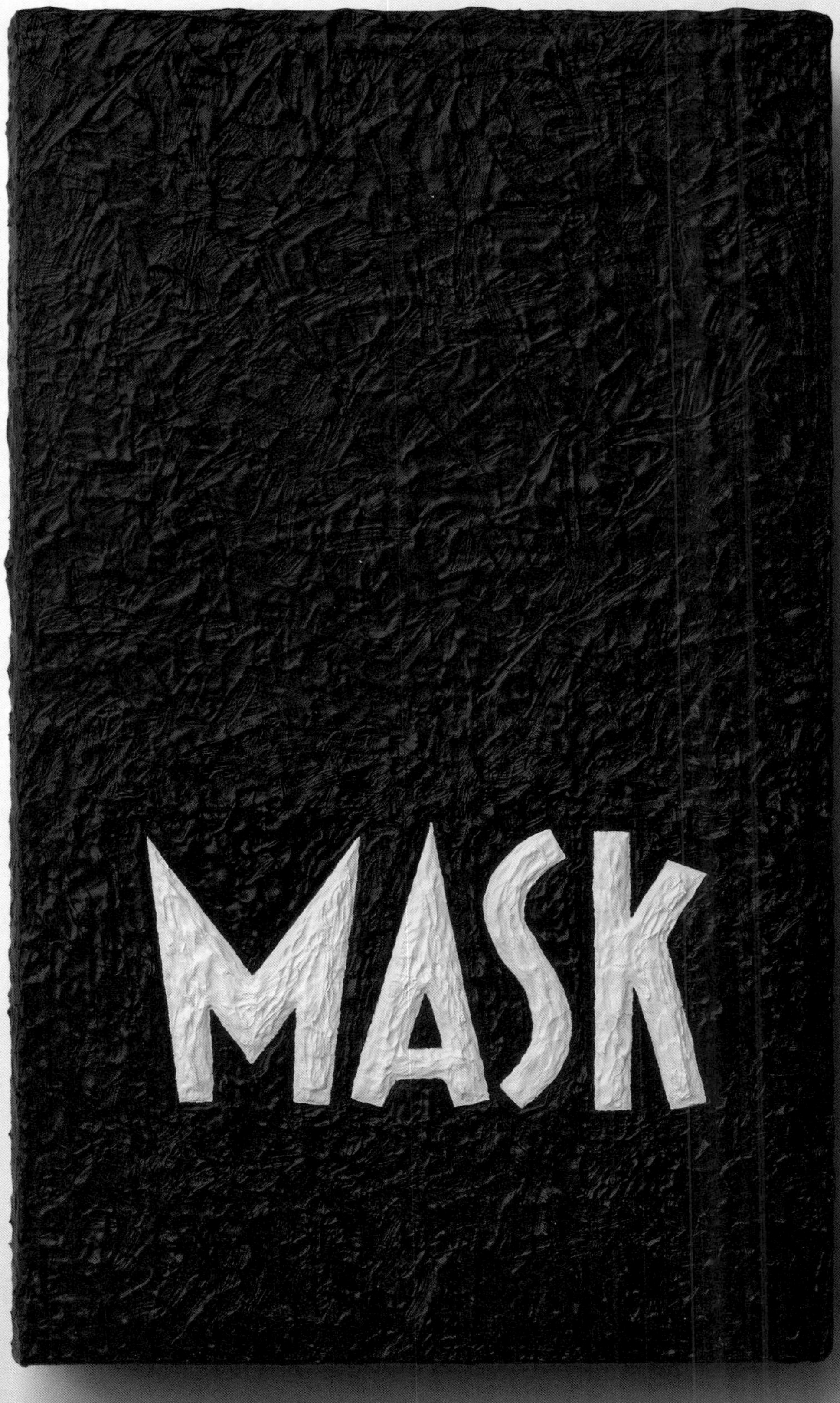

MASK

Touch

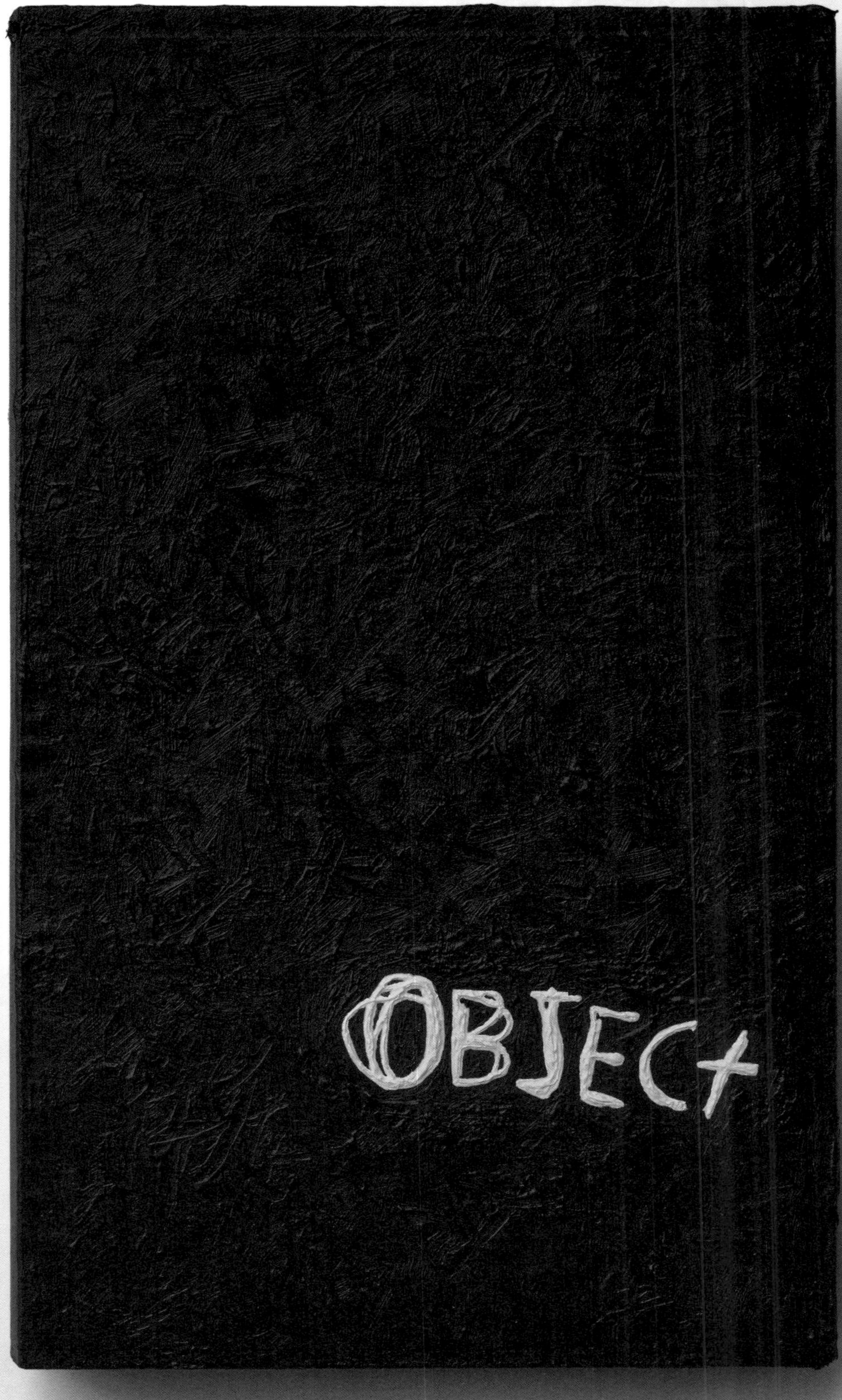

OBJECT

PROJECT

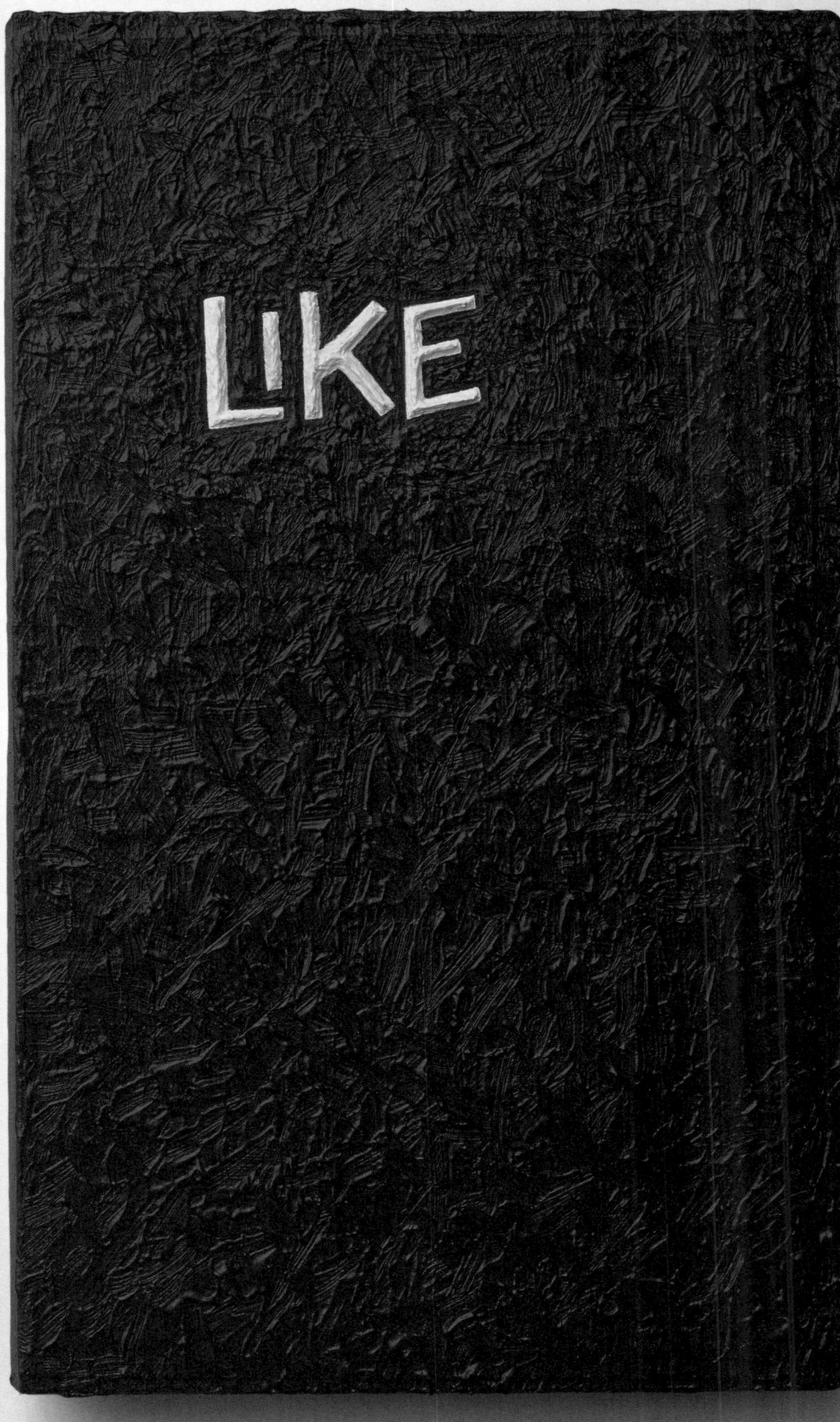

LIKE

To abduct, to accuse, to act, to adapt, to age, to air, to alter, to analyze, to anger, to answer, to assault, to attack, to babysit, to bear, to become, to believe, to blackmail, to blackout, to bleed, to bless, to blind, to block, to blow, to bomb, to boogie, to boomerang, to borrow, to boss, to boycott, to brainwash, to breed, to brood, to burn, to bust, to buy, to catch, to challenge, to champion, to cheat, to chill, to choose, to chuck, to click, to climax, to clone, to collect, to command, to confess, to confuse, to control, to corrupt, to cover, to crack, to crash, to cry, to curse, to cut, to dance, to decline, to desire, to die, to disappear, to dive, to doubt, to dream, to drive, to eat, to elect, to enter, to envy, to erase, to escape, to exist, to express, to face, to fall, to farm, to fast, to fear, to feast, to fiddle, to fight, to finger, to fire, to fist, to flash, to flirt, to fly, to follow, to forget, to frame, to friend, to gaslight, to get, to groom, to hate, to have, to hit, to honor, to hope, to hustle, to influence, to intern, to intrude, to jump, to kid, to kidnap, to kiss, to last, to like, to live, to love, to mask, to massacre, to master, to matter, to mind, to mob, to mother, to mute, to name, to network, to obey, to object, to other, to out, to panic, to park, to party, to perfect, to play, to possess, to potter, to pray, to present, to project, to promise, to rage, to raid, to react, to rebel, to recall, to record, to reek, to remember, to return, to ride, to riot, to rob, to rock, to rule, to scare, to school, to scroll, to sell out, to sense, to shame, to shampoo, to shiver, to shop, to shrink, to sight, to silence, to slay, to sleep, to smile [...].

Disclaimer:
This incomplete survey of the analogue intestines of home video is not titled *Merda d'artista* or *Boîte-en-valise*. Despite its investment in strategies of *Reversal* and *Retrospection*, this mute depository comes both too early and too late to serve as a convincing *Pense-Bête*. These are neither the tales of Scheherazade nor the boxes of Pandora. These miniscule coffins are not *Date Paintings* or *Time Capsules*, nor are they adequate *Surrogates* for the moving images that they obscure. This *Verb List* is not a definitive *Atlas*. Nor is it an encyclopedia or compendium or index or library or collection or dictionary or inventory or archive or catalogue. *Digest* could not accurately be described as a monograph or a biopic or a catalogue raisonné. This is not art about art or about artists or about the art market. This is not a love song or a selfie.

Illustrated on the previous pages:
'mask', 'touch', 'object', 'project' and 'like'

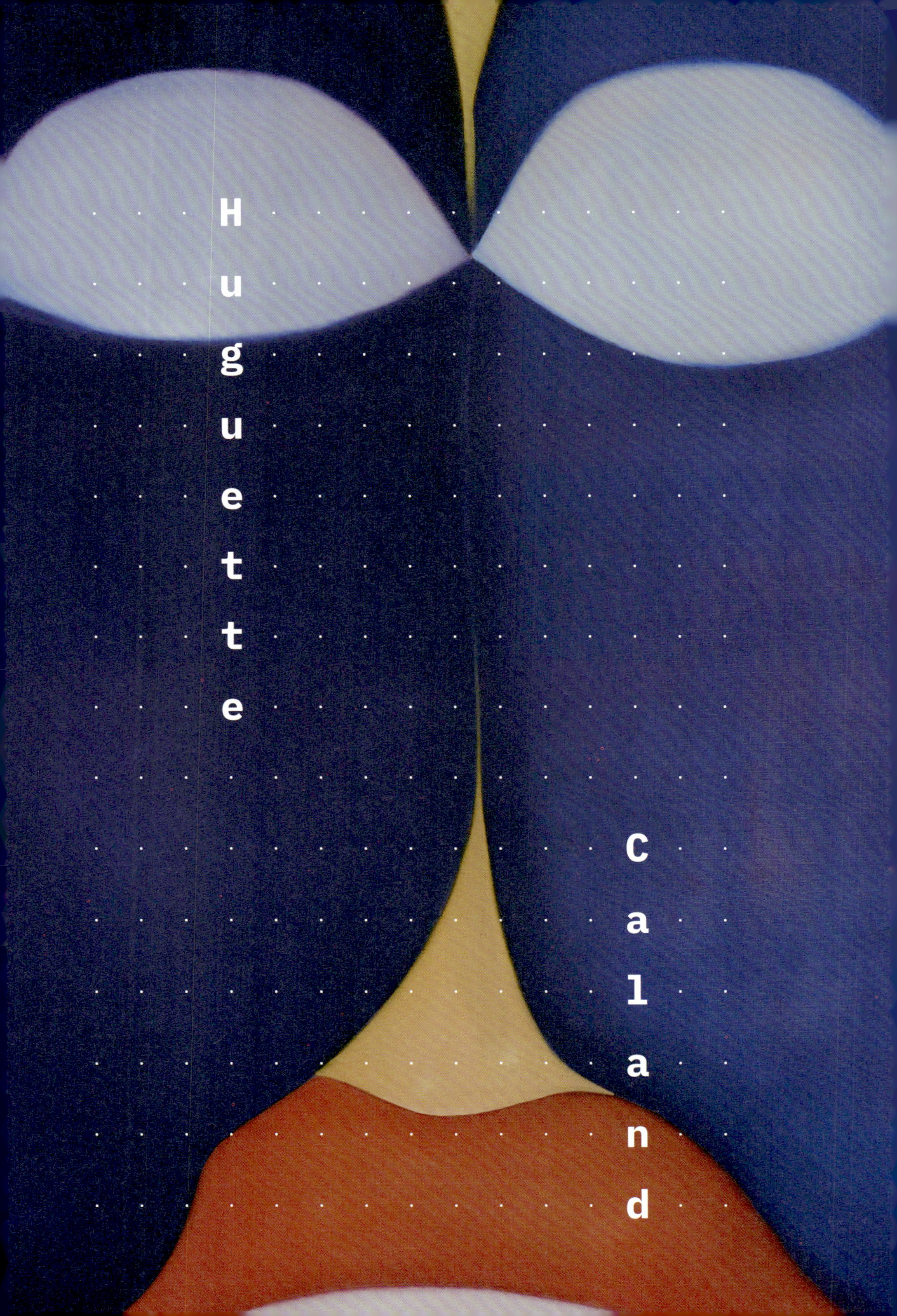
Huguette
Caland

b. 1931, Beirut, Lebanon; lives in Beirut

Huguette Caland is a pioneering figure of abstract modernism. Her carefully crafted lines create contortions that look, at once, like bodily forms and cityscapes. Often erotic in subject matter, her alluring paintings are preoccupied with feminine representations and subjects, creating a conversation between the male and the female gaze. The works presented at the Sharjah Biennial focus largely on her formative period in the 1970s, when the artist lived in Paris. On view is a series of kaftans that the artist created for French designer Pierre Cardin, as well as smocks, which are intricately detailed with Caland's signature lines and bodily shapes. The daughter of the first post-independence Lebanese president, Caland later lived and worked in Venice, California, where she was reported to have been a doyenne of the Los Angeles art world, hosting guests whilst she sat and worked. Now, having worked for more than five decades, she is finally receiving overdue recognition. Caland's sensual, curved contours leave space for viewers to imagine what they will.

Self Portrait (B.d.c.) (58) / Category 1
1973
Oil on linen / Category 1
128.27 x 88.9 cm
Courtesy of the artist

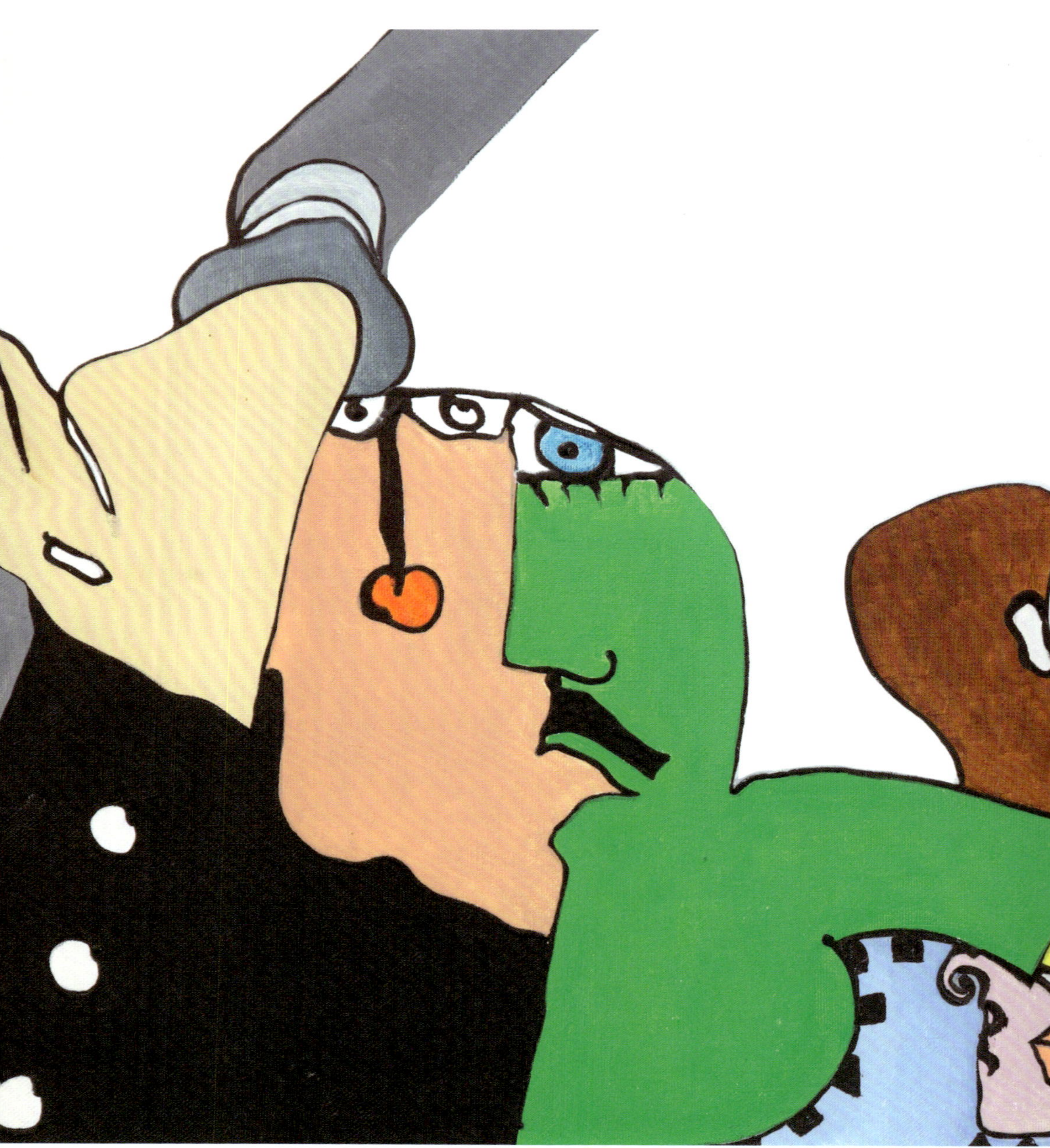

Enlève ton doigt (109) / Category 2, 1971. Oil on canvas / Category 2
38.1 x 76.2 cm, Courtesy of the artist

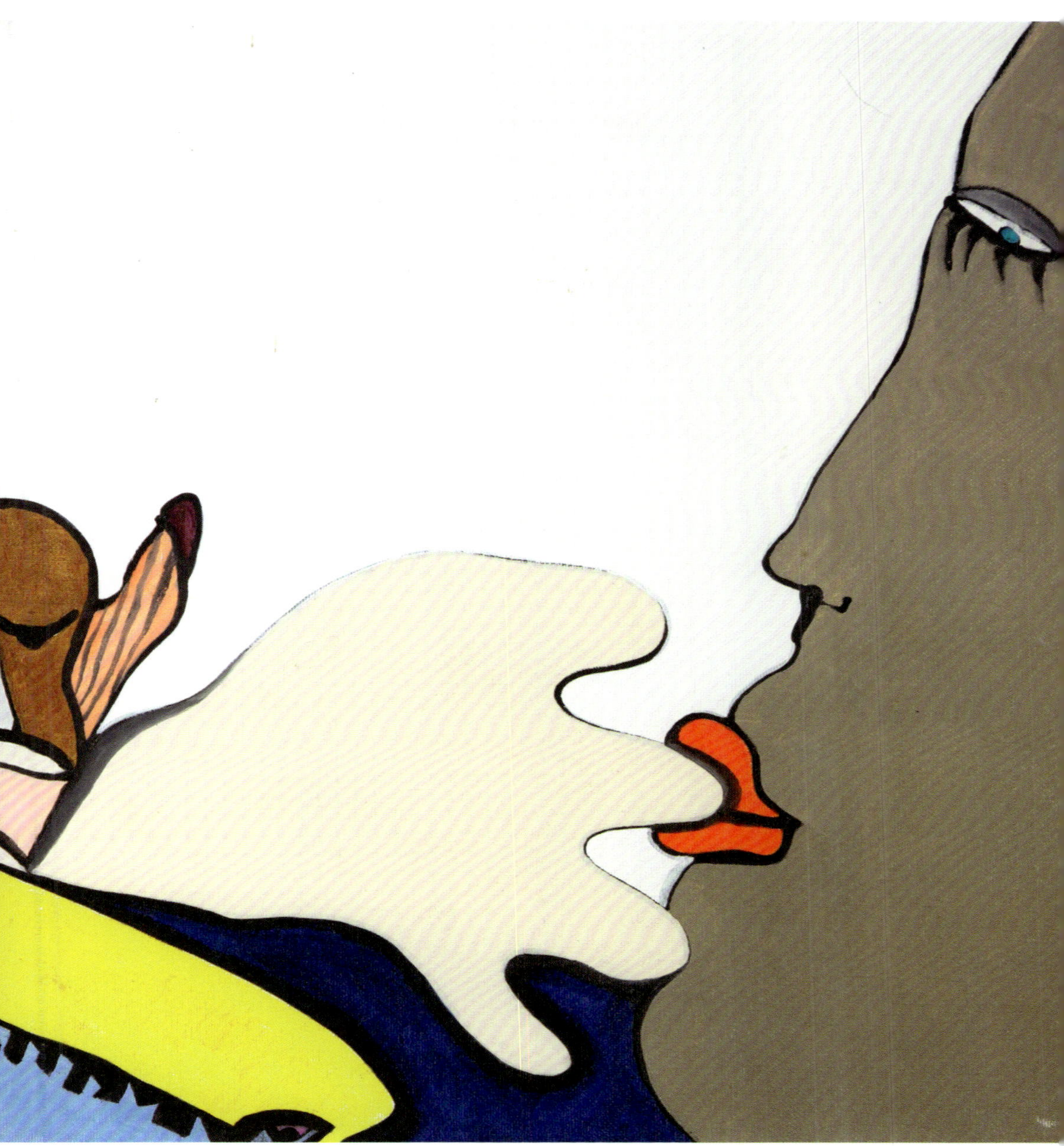

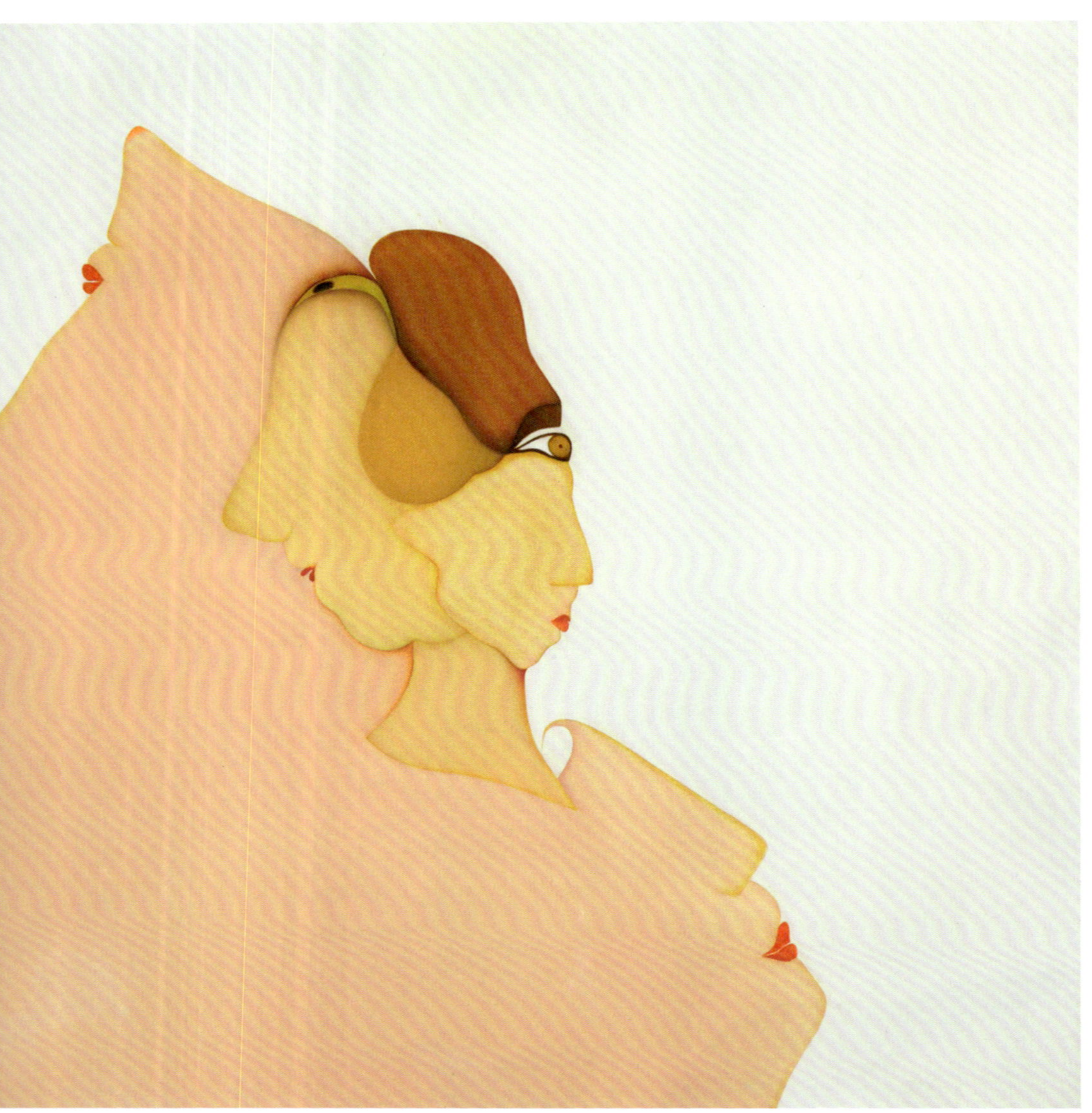

Eux (55) / Category 4
1975 circa
Oil on linen / Category 4
100.33 x 100.33 cm
Courtesy of the artist

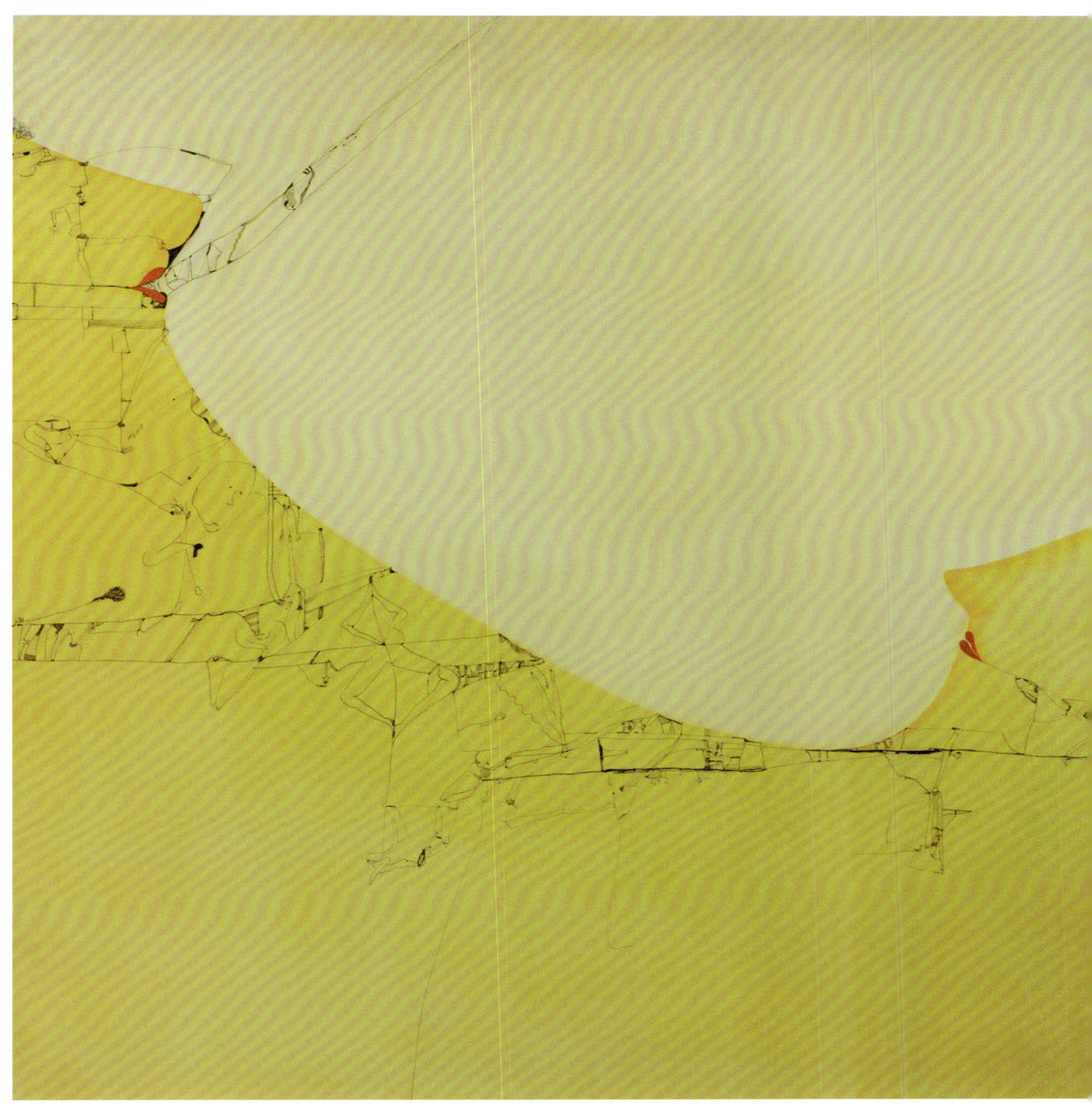

Bribes de corps (293) / Category 4
1973
Oil on linen / Category 4
130.8 x 130.8 cm
(Main Studio, Conserv)
Courtesy of the artist

Ian Cheng

b. 1984, Los Angeles, USA; lives and works in New York

Ian Cheng is renowned for his simulations – a series of live, open-ended works created using a computerised engine similar to those in video games. Described by the artist as 'video games that play themselves', these works are made up of computer-generated simulations akin to those used in predictive technologies – software that helps large, often consumer-facing businesses to reduce risks or foretell certain trends or experiences, such as election results. In this presentation, Cheng takes over Sharjah Art Foundation's Arts Square with his complete *Emissary* trilogy (2015–17). Occupied by a cast of characters and different forms of wildlife that create interrelated, open-ended narratives, the artist's simulations evolve endlessly. They are self-contained ecosystems: no two experiences of the works are ever the same. The series contemplates questions of time, including progress, consciousness and existence.

Emissary Forks At Perfection
2015-2016
Live simulation and story, infinite duration, sound
Dimensions variable
Courtesy of the artist, Pilar Corrias London, Gladstone Gallery, Standard (Oslo)

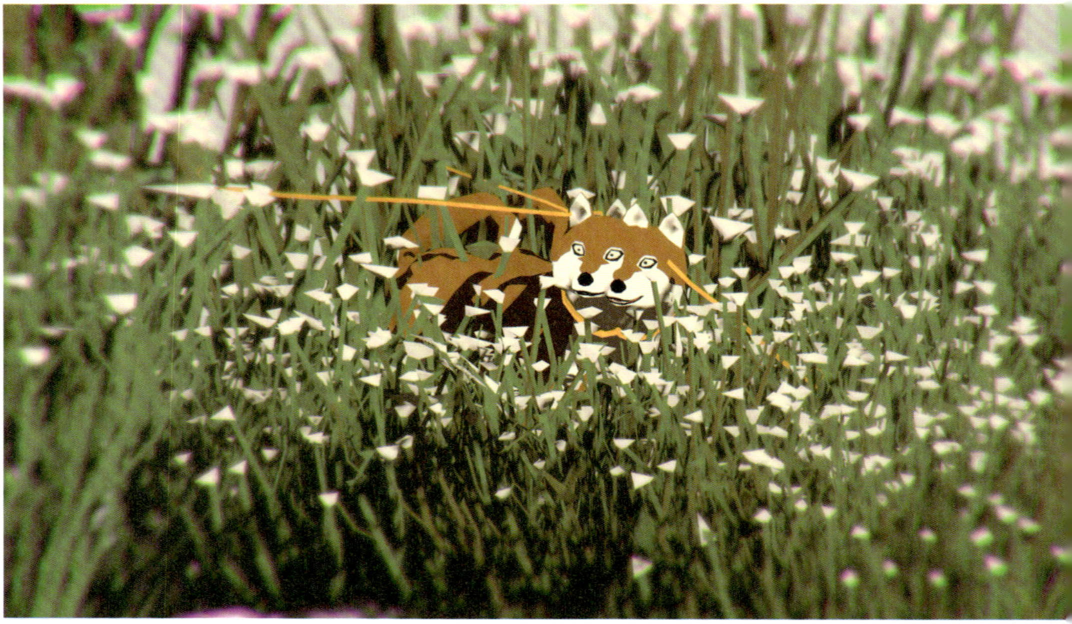

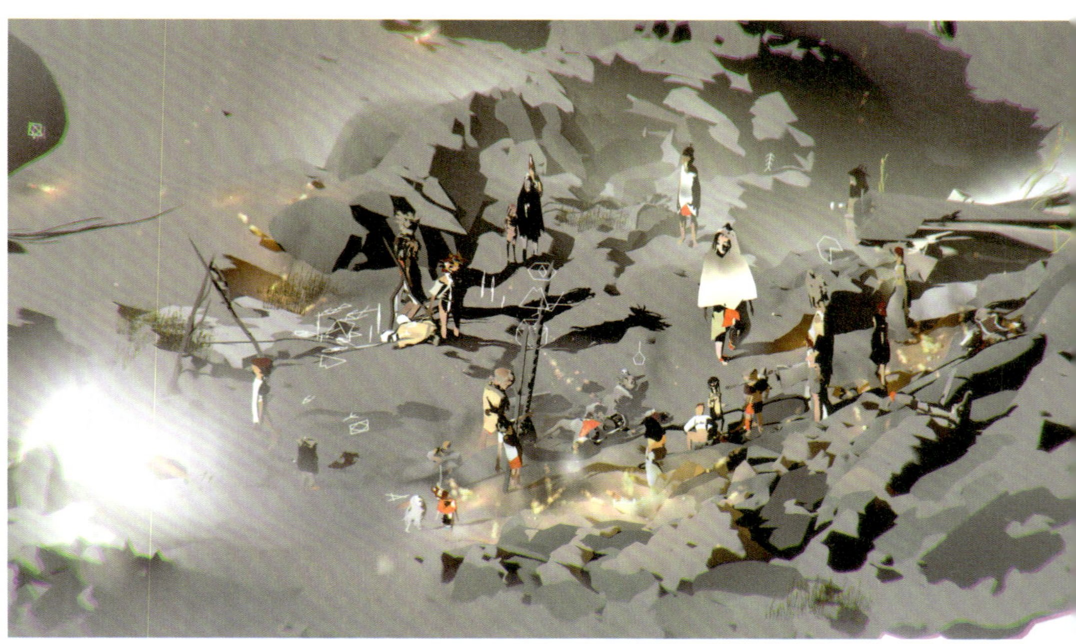

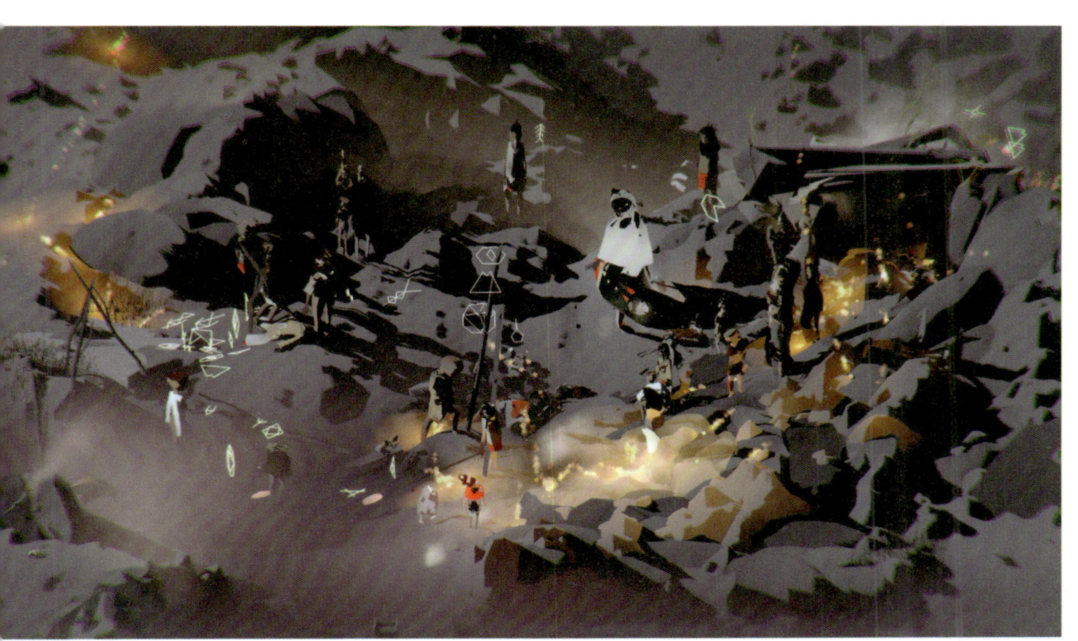

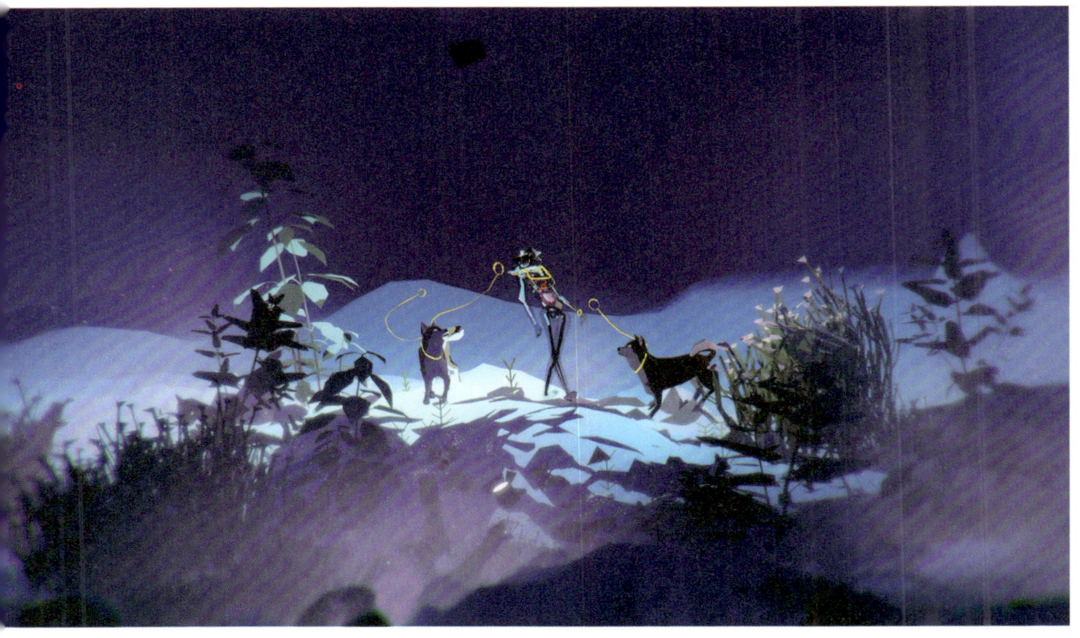

Shezad Dawood

b. 1974, London, UK; lives and works in London

Co-commissioned by Sharjah Art Foundation and New Art Exchange, Nottingham. Generously supported by the Bagri Foundation. Produced by Sharjah Art Foundation and UBIK Productions. Special Thanks to the Hashoo Group, Gul Ahmed, EMI Pakistan, Jhaveri Contemporary, Mumbai and Timothy Taylor, London.

Shezad Dawood works across various media, often in collaboration with others and frequently with unique networks around a given project or site. These networks map various geographic locations and communities, and are particularly concerned with acts of translation and restaging. His new commission, *Encroachments* (2019), is anchored in an immersive virtual reality (VR) experience that explores the concepts of sovereignty, private property and the politics of space in Pakistan's two largest cities, Lahore and Karachi. The term 'encroachments' refers to the backlash in politics against the so-called 'illegal structures' built into and onto existing private and state infrastructure. These zones have become social spaces for the lower classes, reflecting what the artist has dubbed 'grassroots entrepreneurialism'. They represent a grey area of ownership: Who has the right to communal space? Dawood uses specific sites to play on this question, including the grounds of the intended United States Embassy in Karachi in the 1950s, local pop-up video arcades in the 1980s and a colonial-era bookshop. Presented in an immersive installation, the VR experience is shown alongside Dawood's signature textiles, neon and custom-designed wallpaper.

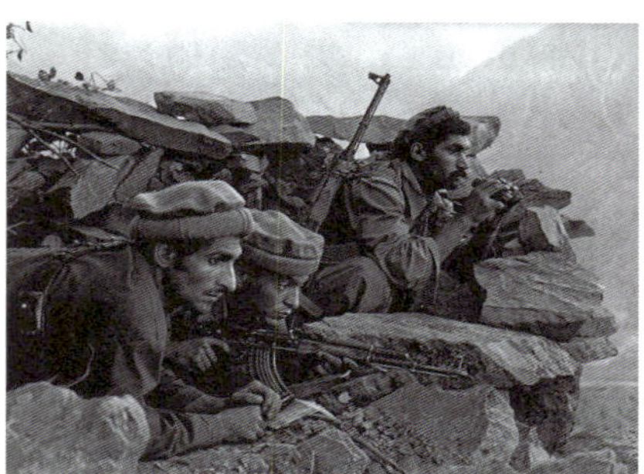

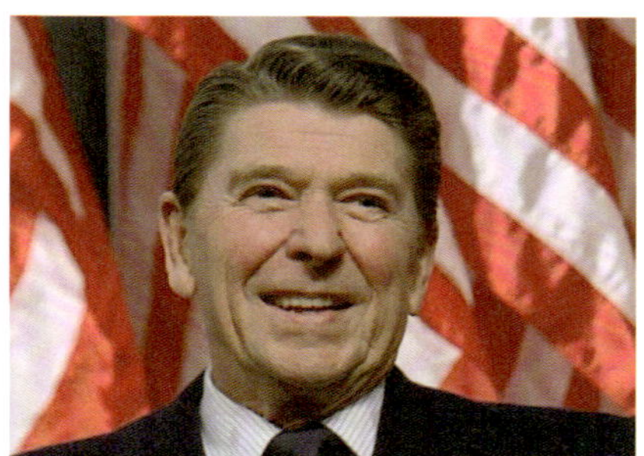

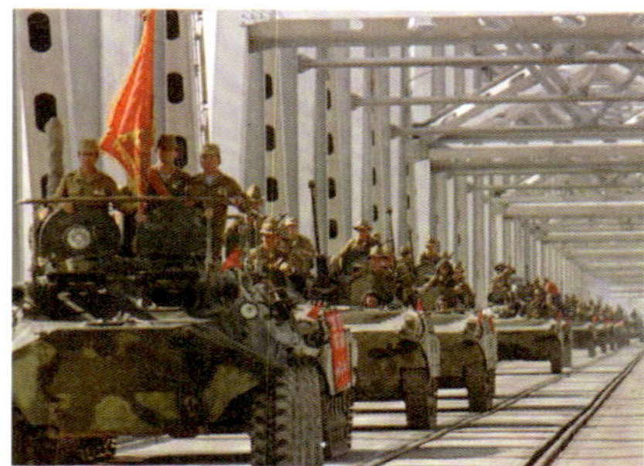

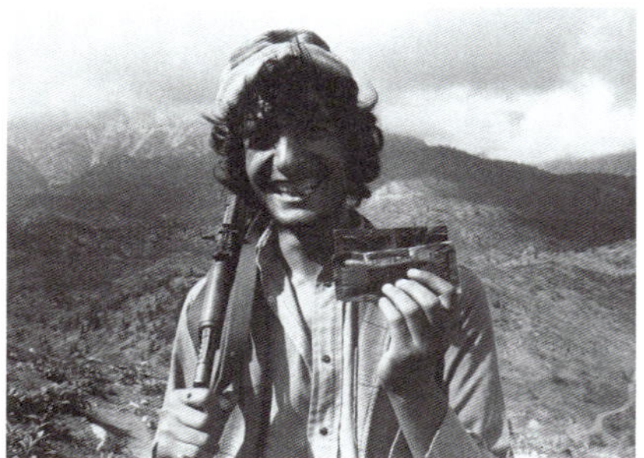

Afghan Mujahideen; The Reagan years; Soviet tanks leave Afghanistan in February 1989

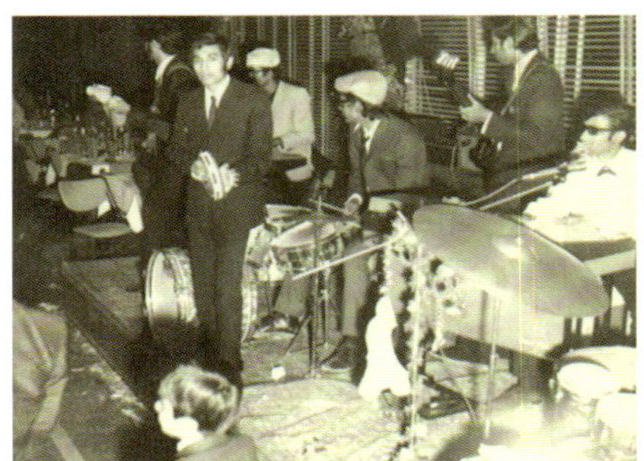

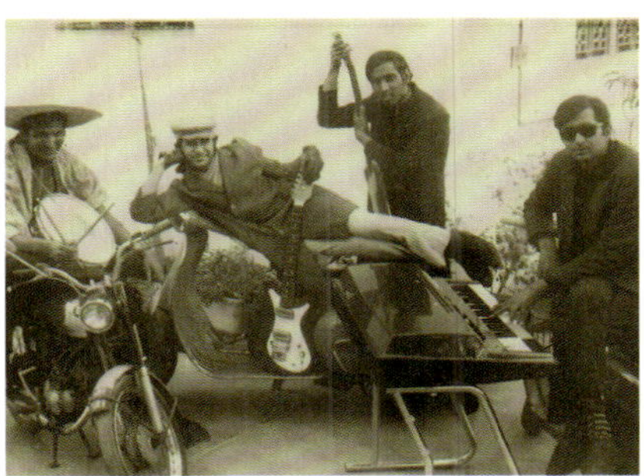

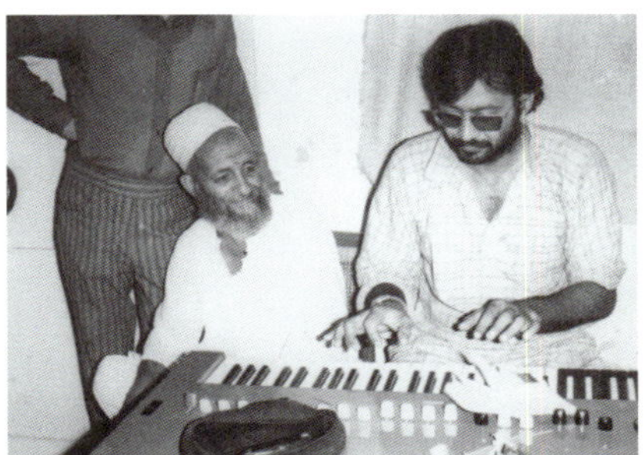

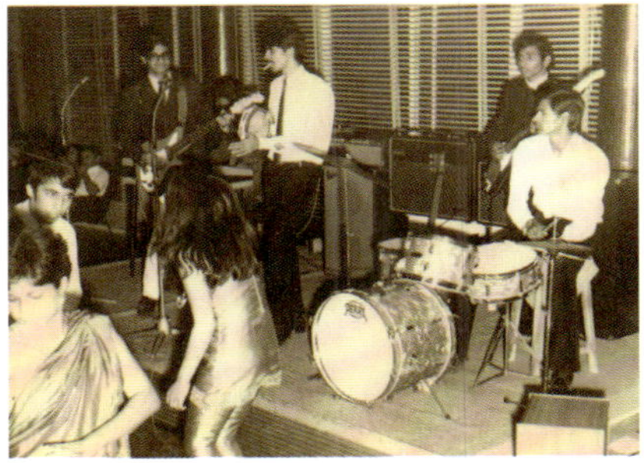

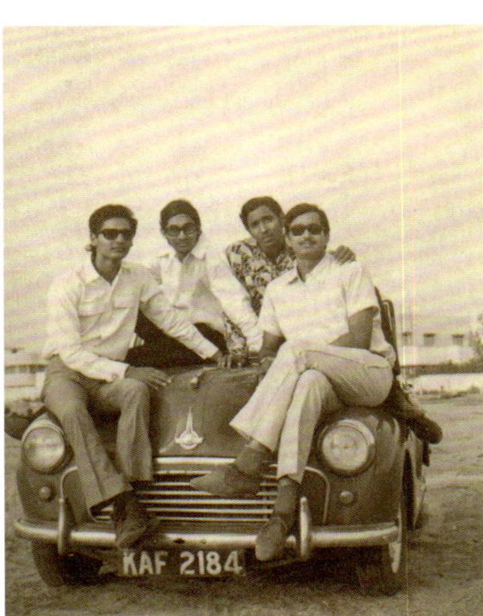

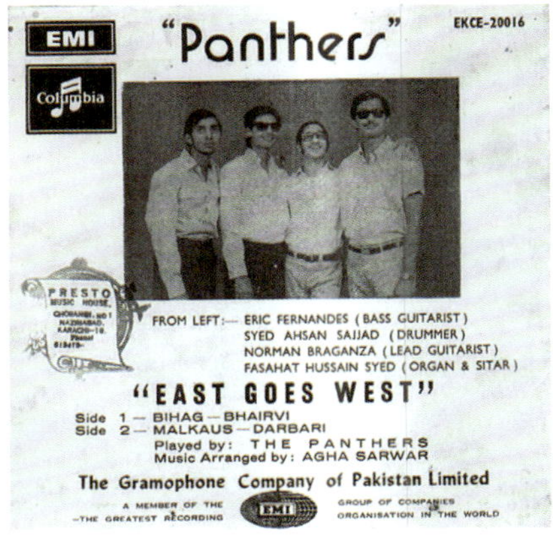

The club scene at the Metropole Hotel, Karachi and promotional photos of The Panthers and their EP release 'East Goes West'. Courtesy of Fasahat Hussain Syed and Ahsan Sajjad

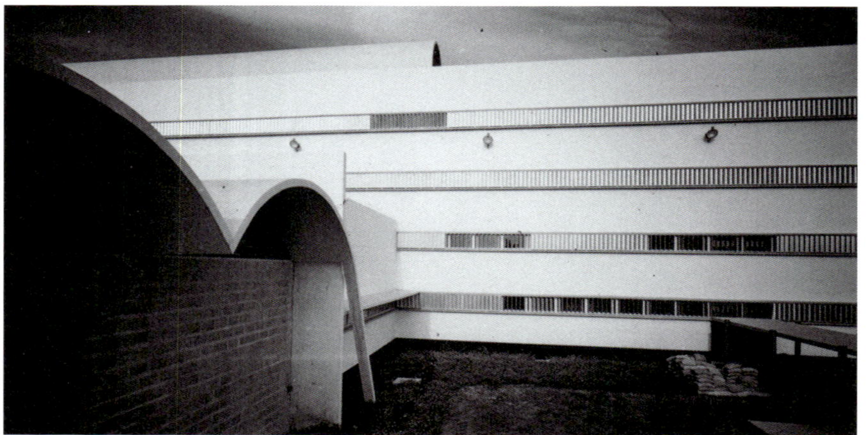

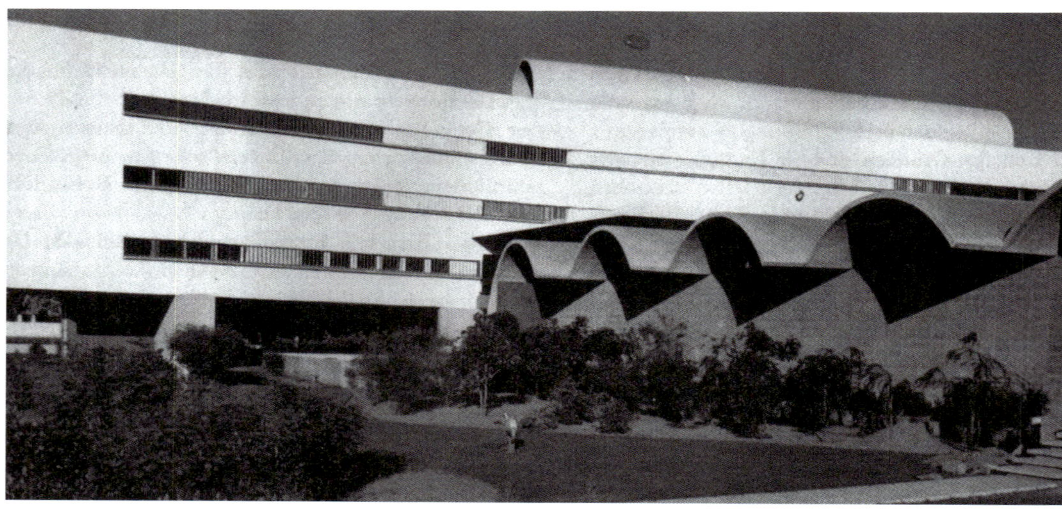

The administrative and ambassadorial wing; warehouses; and reflecting pool of Richard Neutra and Robert Alexander's US Embassy in Karachi (which was downgraded to a consulate in 1966, after the capital was moved to the newly-constructed city of Islamabad in 1961). Photos: Rondal Partridge

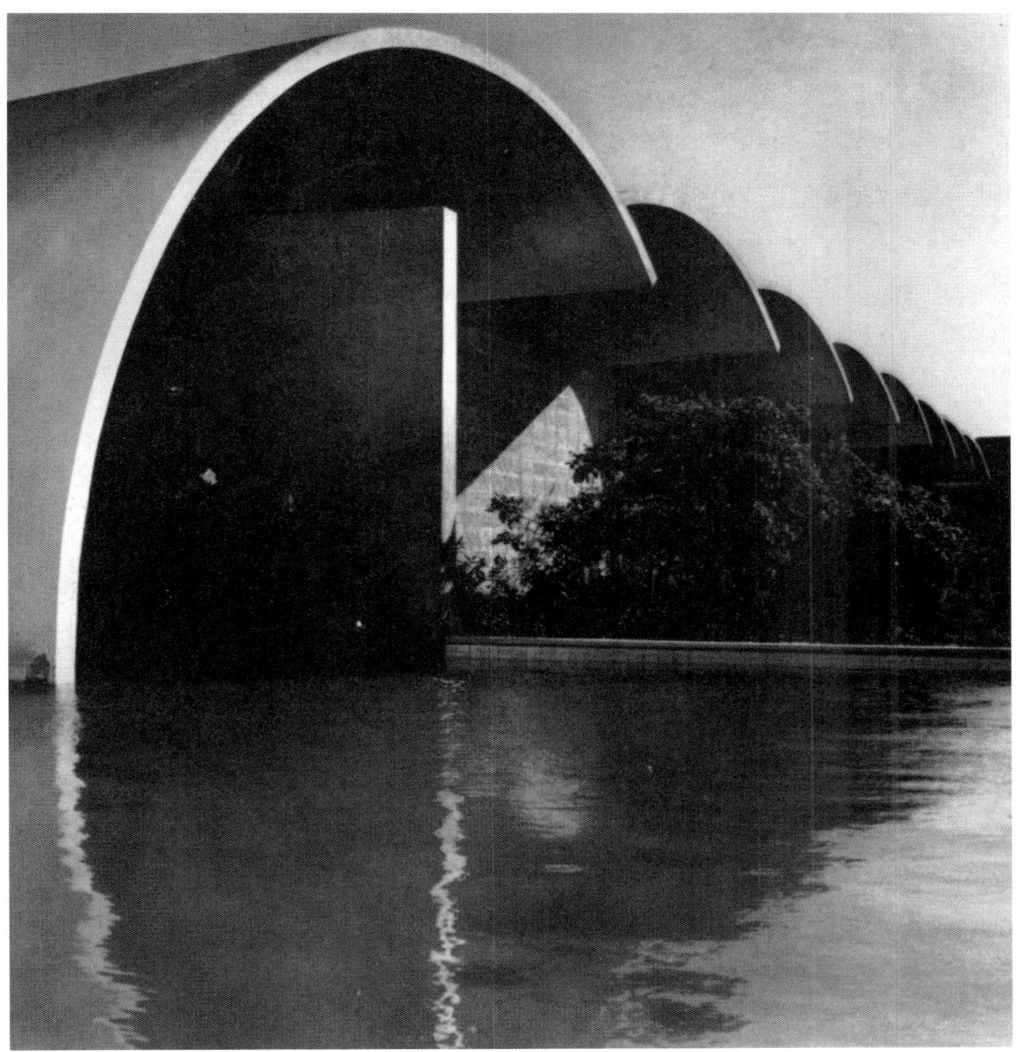

Stan Douglas

b. 1960, Vancouver, Canada; lives and works in Vancouver

This project has kindly been supported by Canada Council for the Arts

Through photography, film and installation, Stan Douglas has, since the late 1980s, examined complex intersections of narrative, fact and fiction, whilst simultaneously scrutinising the media he employs and how it shapes our understanding of reality. In his *DCT* series (2017), the artist presents what he has dubbed 'synthetic pictures' that consider the optical qualities of photography. To create these works, Douglas manipulated a sequence of data known as DCT (discrete cosine transform) that stipulate how JPEG images are compressed. In this case, he altered their frequencies, amplitudes and colour values by entering numbers in a custom-made programme. The photos, in turn, are separate from any image that could be produced in the real world. Printed on large, square panels and primed with gesso, these light abstractions, which dialogue with Sharjah's light-filled landscape, contort the notion of the photographic and blur the formal boundaries between photography and painting.

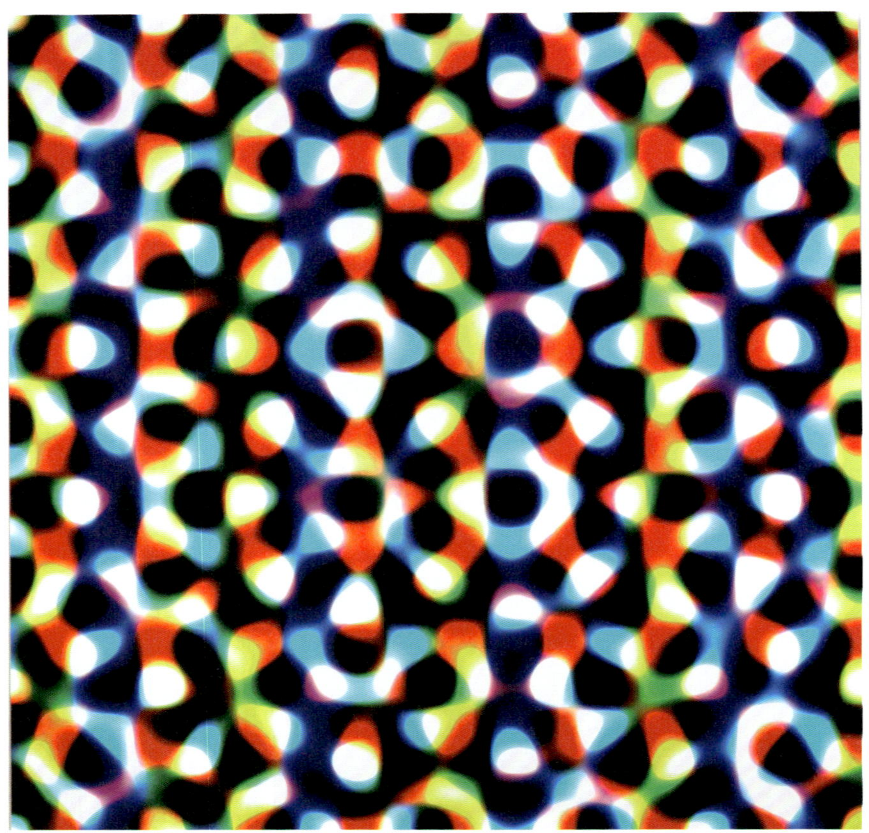

AMMA
2017
Lacquered UV ink on gessoed panel
150 x 150 x 5.1 cm
Edition 1 of 1, 1 AP
Signed verso
Courtesy of the artist and David Zwirner

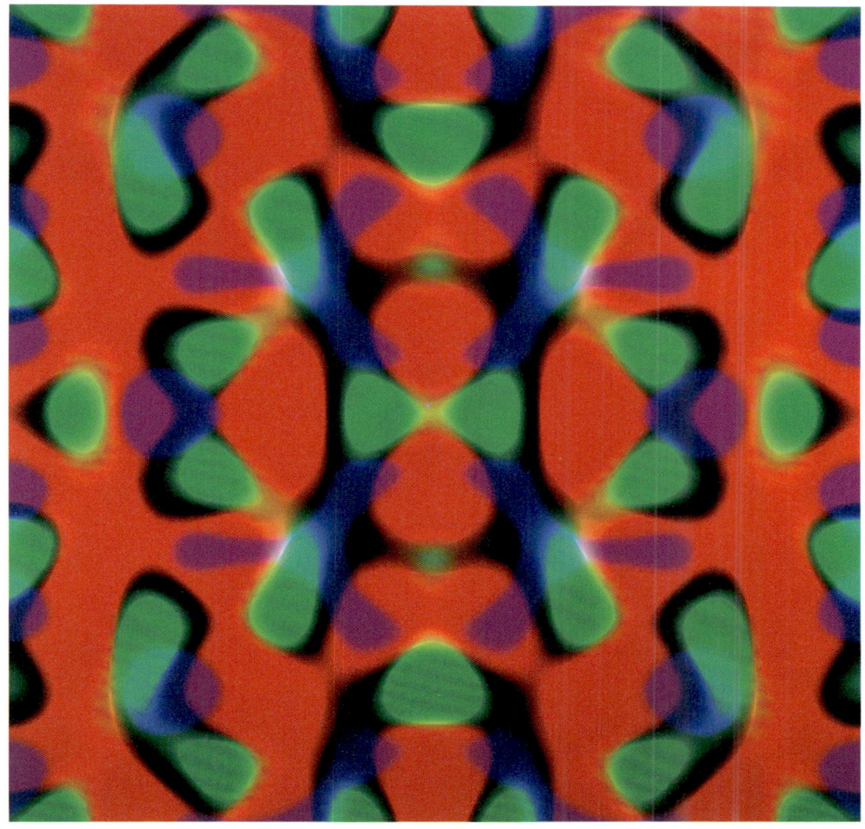

4CC4
2017
Lacquered UV ink on gessoed panel
150 x 150 x 5.1 cm
Edition 1 of 1, 1 AP
Signed verso
Courtesy of the artist and David Zwirner

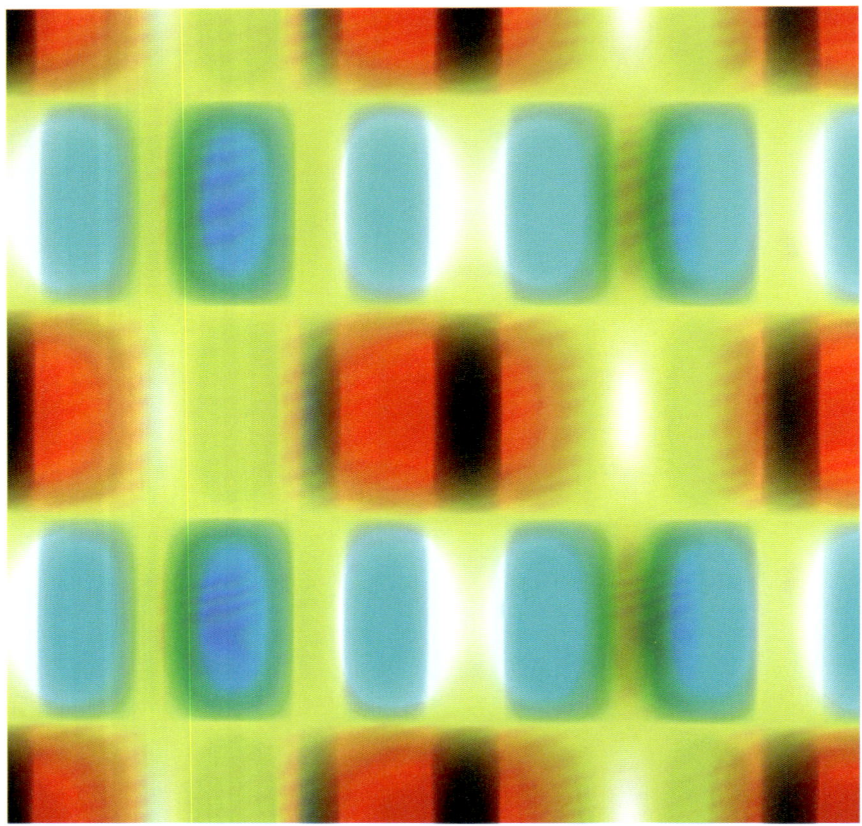

4400
2017
Lacquered UV ink on gessoed panel
150 x 150 x 5.1 cm
Edition 1 of 1, 1 AP
Signed verso
Courtesy of the artist and David Zwirner

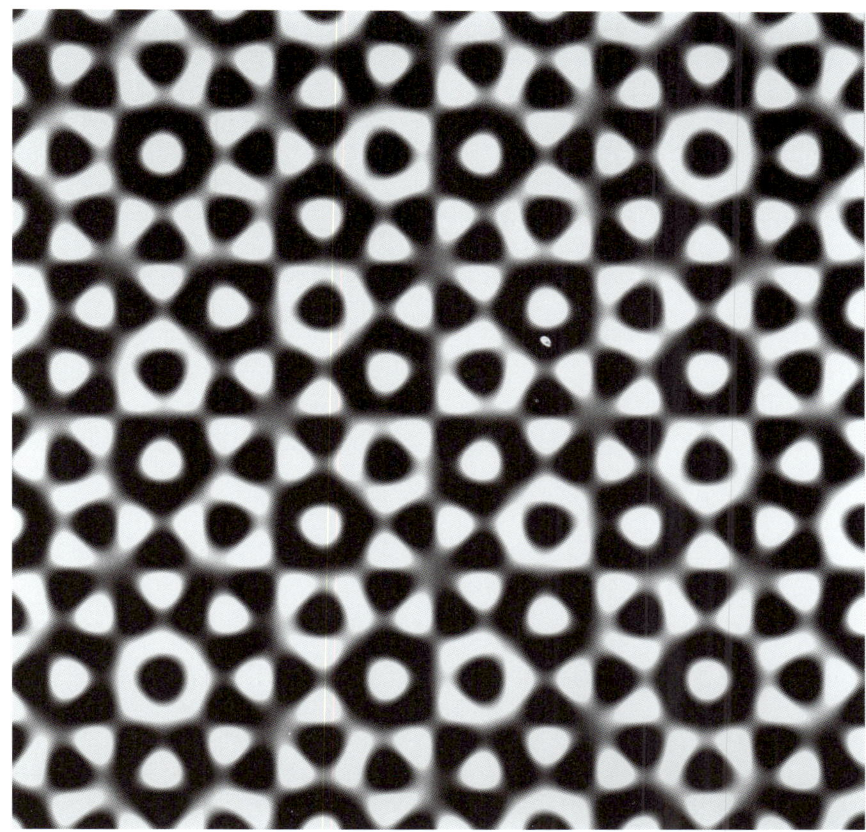

RCCR
2017
Lacquered UV ink on gessoed panel
150 x 150 x 5.1 cm
Edition 1 of 1, 1 AP
Signed verso
Courtesy of the artist and David Zwirner

Lubaina

Himid

b. 1954, Zanzibar, Tanzania; lives and works in Preston, UK

In her paintings, colourful prints, patterned drawings, figurative cut-outs and installations, Lubaina Himid approaches questions of identity through the celebration of Black creativity and political agency. Her overarching practice as an artist, curator and professor challenges institutional narratives that have systematically overlooked and erased the enduring legacy of slavery as well as the foundational contributions to society that have been made by people of the African diaspora. Himid's practice services as a reimagining, a memorialising and reconfiguring of the world she wishes to see.

For SB14, the artist presents six of her works in a range of mediums, including painting and installation, which provide insight into the artist's wry, spirited and serious sensibility. In *Man in a Stationary Drawer* (2017–2018) and *Man in a Jumper Drawer* (2018) the artist has painted the portrait of a man inside a drawer. The 'men in drawer' series comments on Himid's investigation into the invisible representations of Black men in art and society. The use of the drawer as *object trouvé* extends Himid's interest in painting on all kinds of surfaces that have included wood, ceramic and fabric.

The painting *The Captain and the Mate* (2017–2018) explores Himid's long-term interest in the work of James Tissot (1832- 1902). Since the early 90s Himid has been recasting paintings from his period of painting fashionable women, replacing white figures with black figures, suggesting alternative stories that could have been concurrent, but that also operate in their own time space continuum. Whilst far removed from the original, the pulleys on the ship have been faithfully painted - the mechanisms in the painting asking for as much attention as the drama unfolding in front of us; oblivious of their audience, the figures are caught up with each other. *Bone in the China: Success to the Africa Trade* (1985) was made in response to a ceramic punch bowl celebrating the slave trade in a museum in Stoke. Some of Himid's significant early work has been born from responding to site and objects that form the backbone of British cultural heritage that still remain in museum collections unchallenged, forgotten and undiscussed.

The Carrot Piece
1985
Acrylic on wood, card, string
243 x 335 cm
Courtesy of the artist and Hollybush Gardens
Photo: Andy Keate

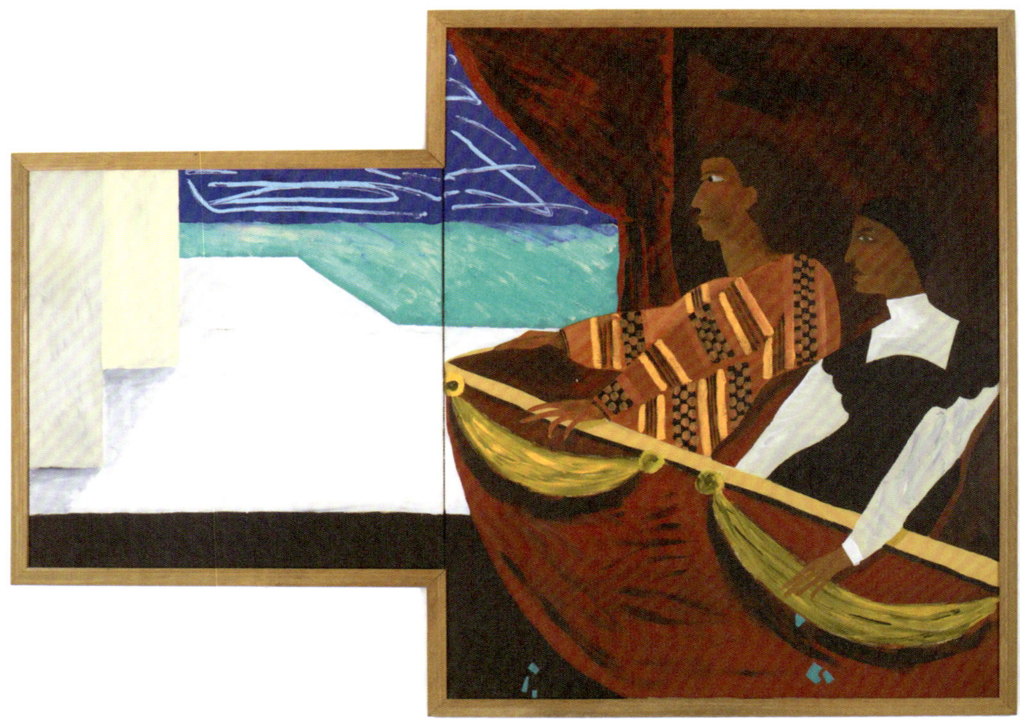

Act One No Maps
1992
Acrylic on canvas
150 x 210 cm
Courtesy of the artist and
Hollybush Gardens
Photo: Andy Keate

The Captain and the Mate
2017-2018
Acrylic on canvas
183 x 244 cm
Courtesy of the artist and
Hollybush Gardens
Photo: Andy Keate

This work brings to the fore a discussion between British industrialisation and slavery and the role of slavery in the building of wealth in Britain.

Act One, No Maps (1992) and *Memorial to Zong* (1992) come from a painting cycle entitled *Revenge. Act One, No Maps* references the work of Tissot, where *Memorial to Zong* commemorates the people held on a slave ship and thrown overboard in the Zong massacre, to allow the ship's captain to make an insurance claim for their bodies.

This presentation, spanning work made over a 30- year period continues to question the representation and place of the Black body within art history, imagined futures and current day realities.

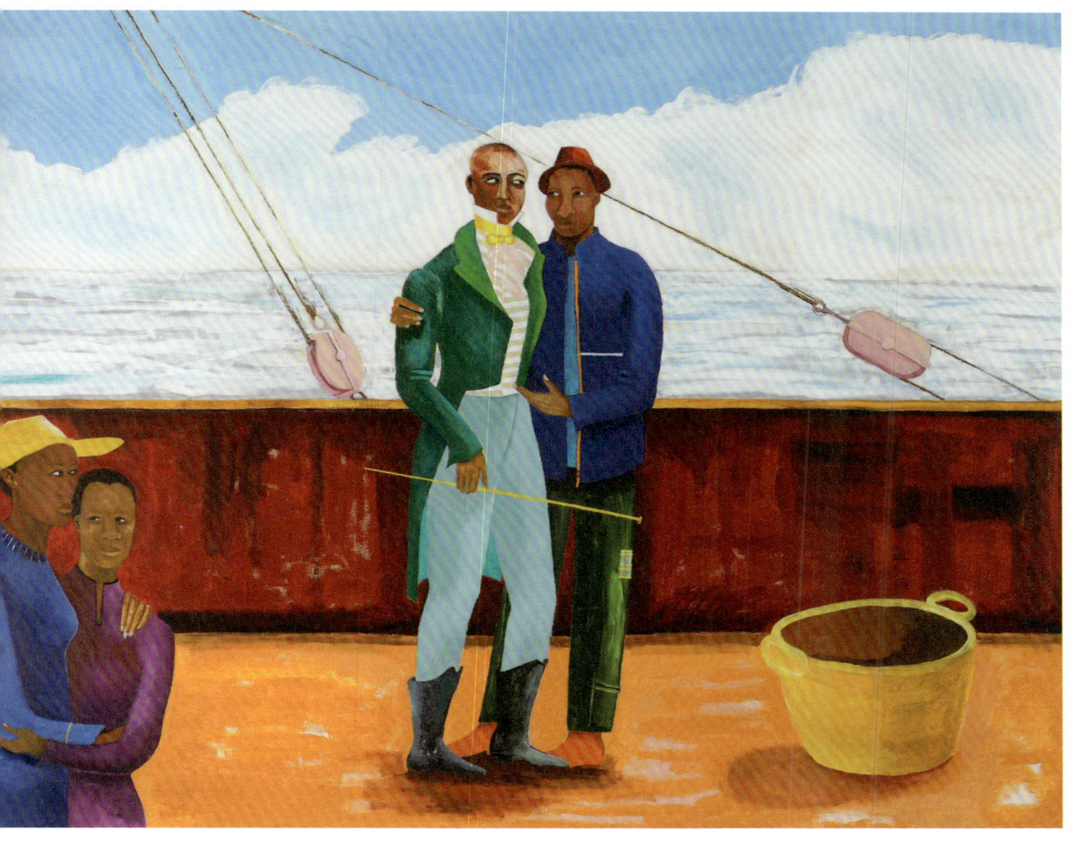

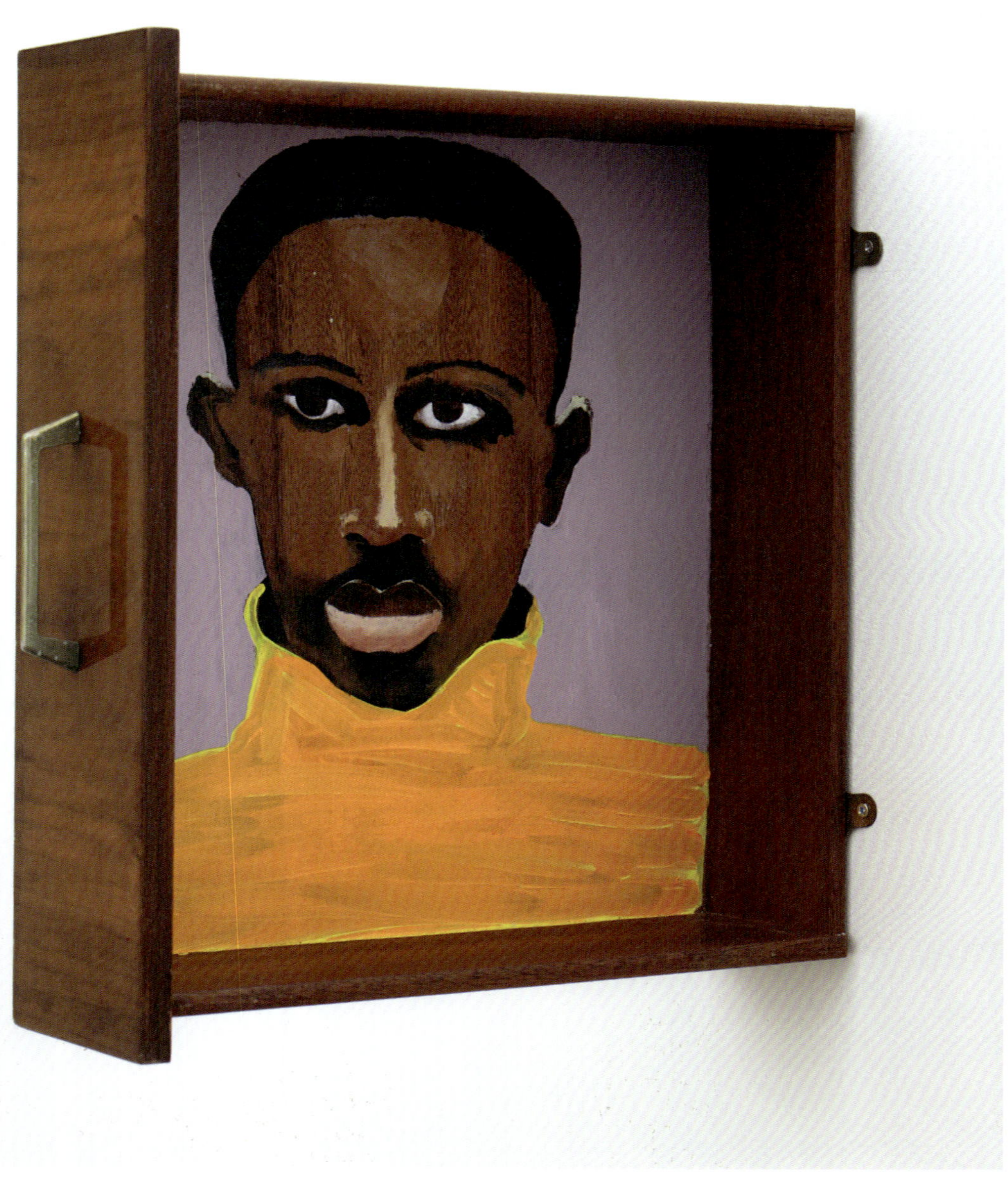

Man in a Jumper Drawer
2018
Acrylic on wood
44 x 37 x 12 cm
Courtesy of the artist and
Hollybush Gardens

Man in A Stationery Drawer
2017-2018
Acrylic on wood
45 x 36.50 x 8 cm
Courtesy of the artist and
Hollybush Gardens
Photo: Andy Keate

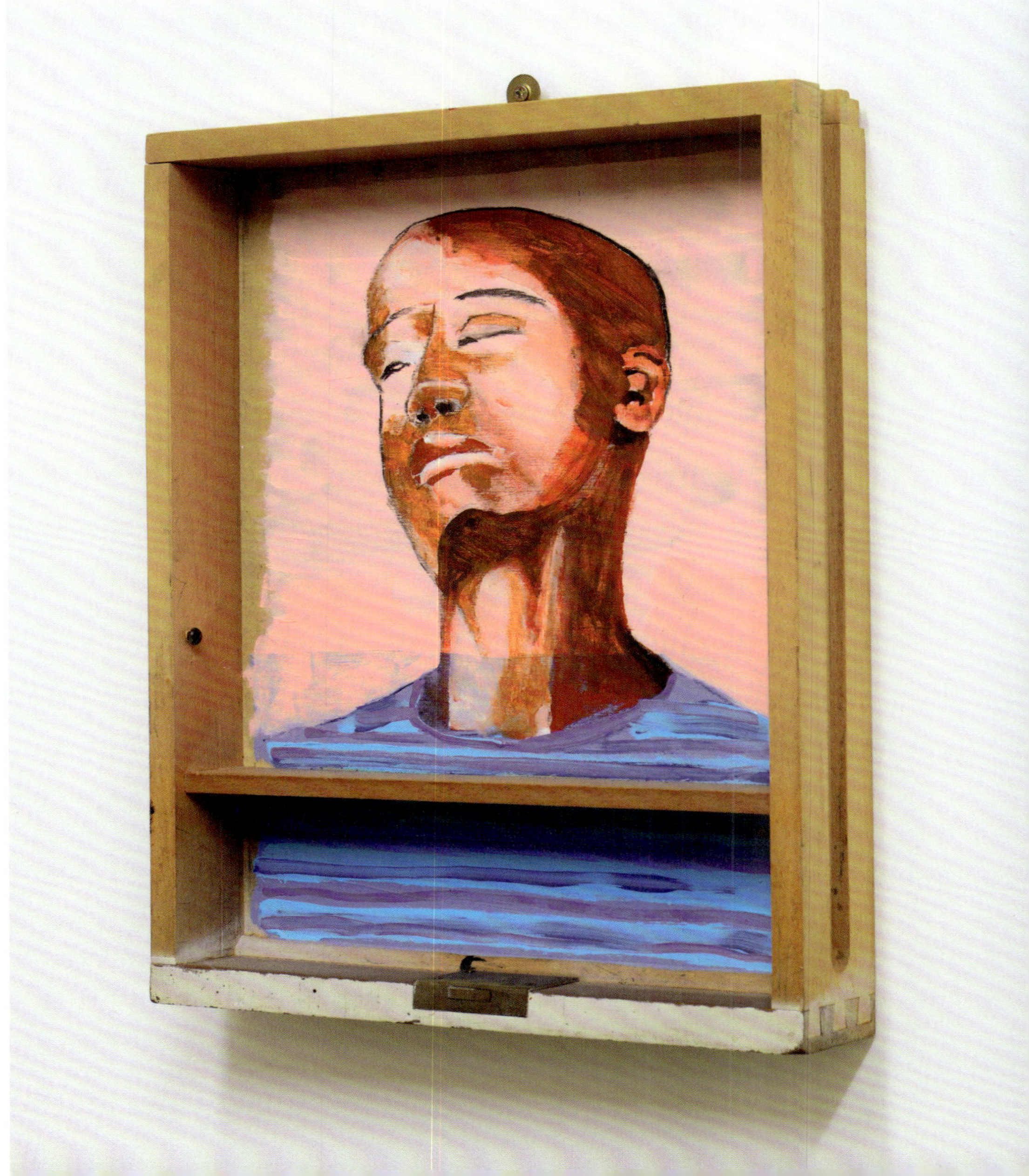

Alfredo

Jaar

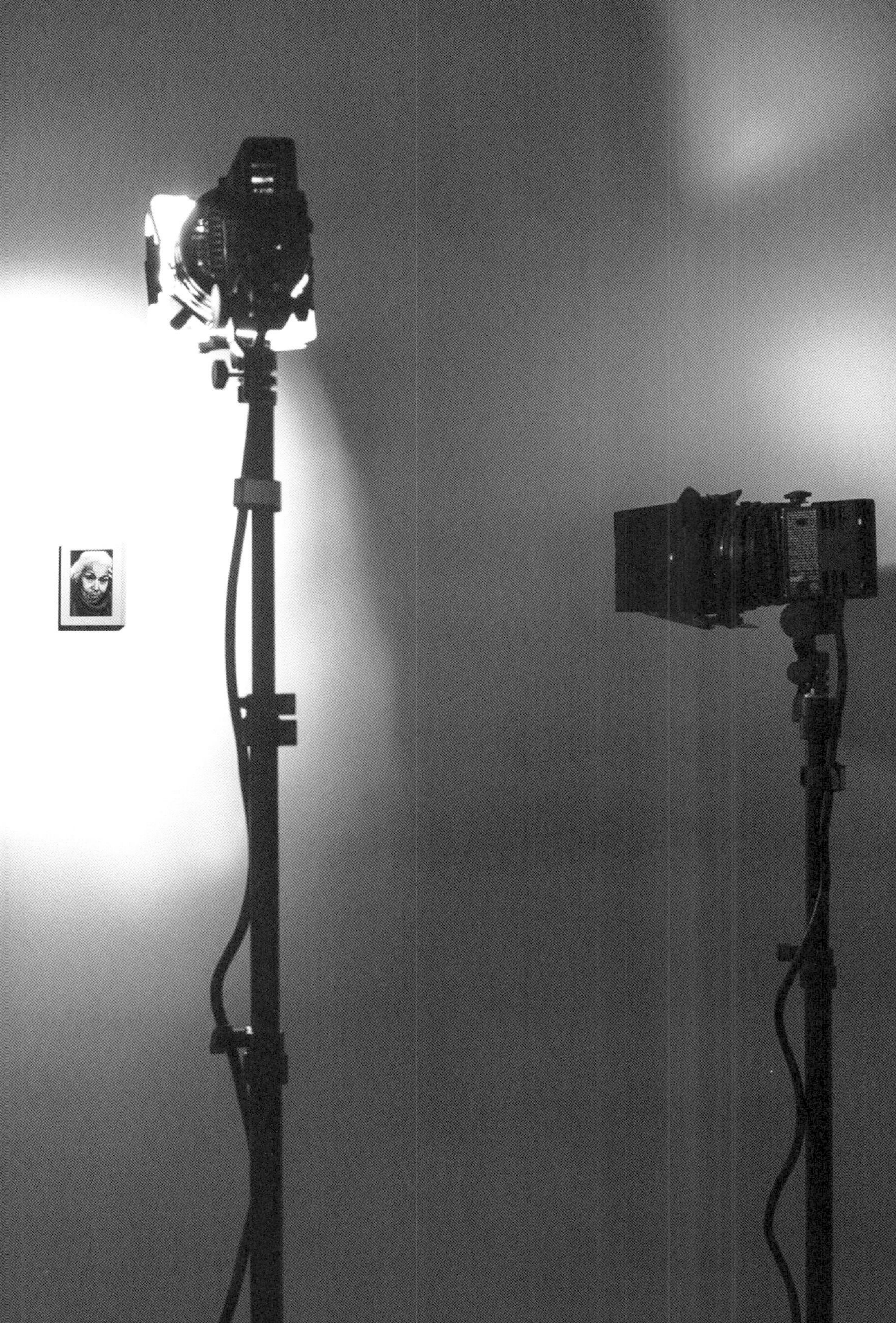

b. 1956, Santiago, Chile; lives and works in New York, USA
Commissioned by Sharjah Art Foundation

Alfredo Jaar is an artist, architect and filmmaker. In his new commission, *33 Women* (2019), he extends his ongoing project that sheds light on the work of extraordinary women. By physically spotlighting their images, he begs the question: Have these figures remained invisible from public view? Jaar presented the first iteration of this project, which illuminated three women, in 2010. As he continues to expand it, he ultimately endeavours to reveal the lives of at least 100 significant women. The women featured in this project are all fearless protesters and advocates who, despite their outstanding achievements, remain generally unknown to the wider public; their work is often under-recognised, inhibited or snubbed. The artist's work provides a means to pay homage to the efforts of these individuals to overcome prejudice. It both acknowledges and counters the lack of acknowledgement that they have received to date. All of them exemplify resistance in their given fields – fighting human rights violations, sexual violence, censorship and ethnic persecution, amongst other causes.

22 Women
2014
From '100 Women'
22 framed pigment prints, 132 light fixtures
Overall dimensions variable
Courtesy of the artist and SKMU, Norway

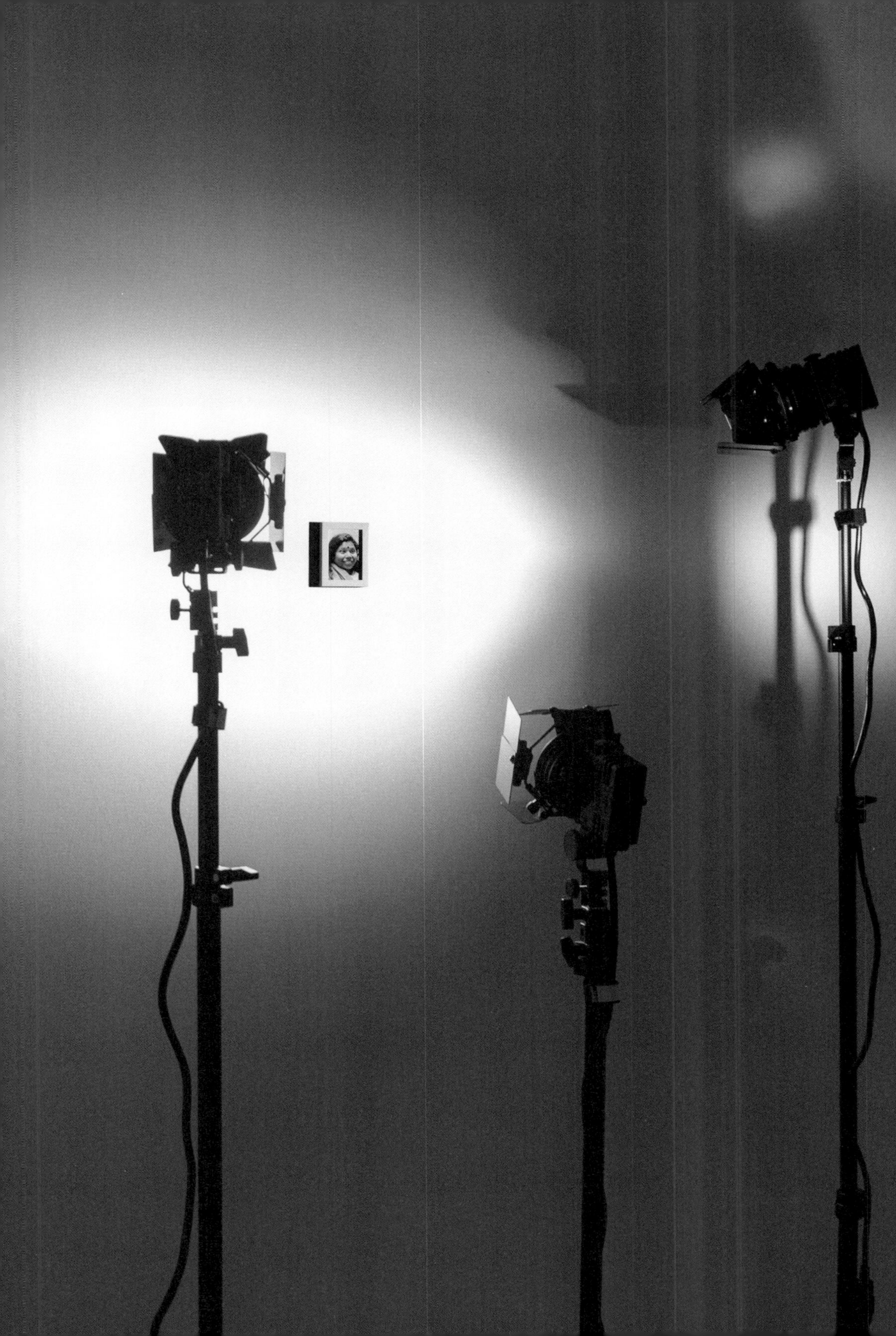

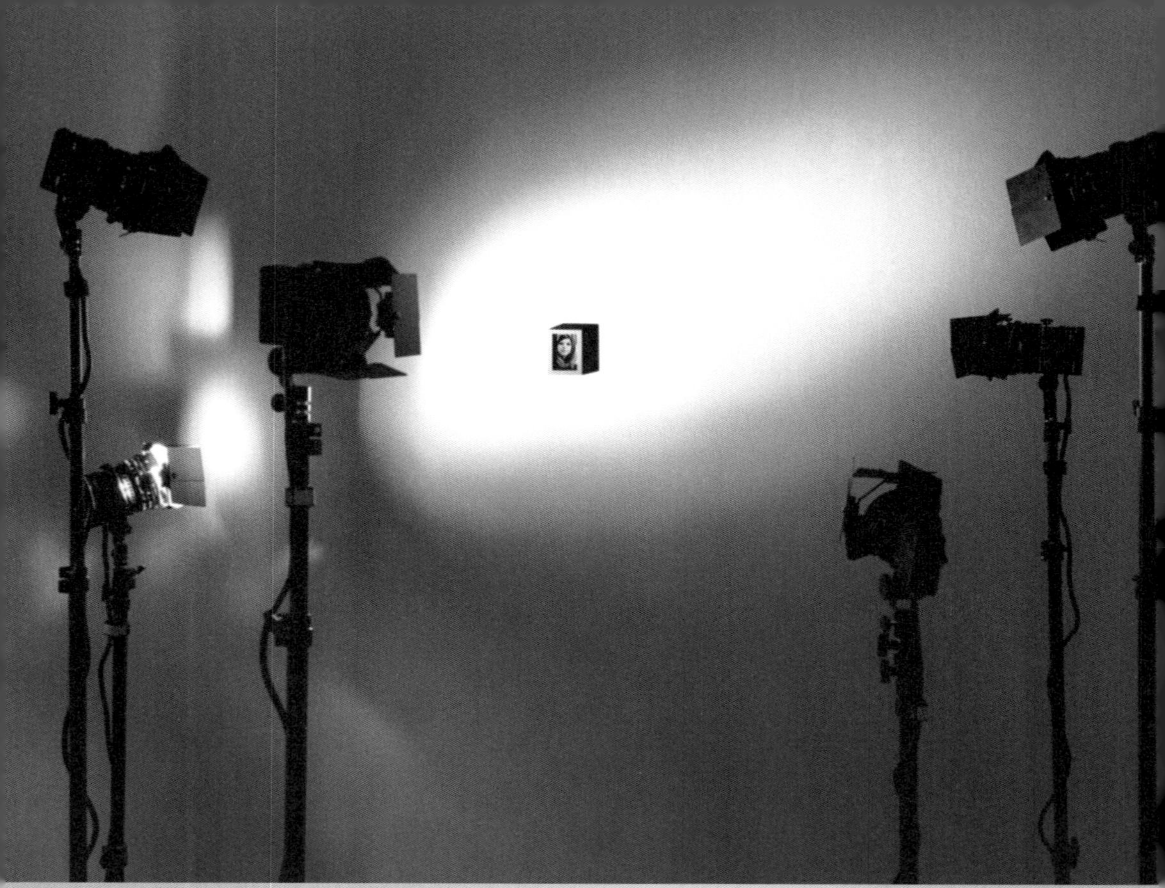

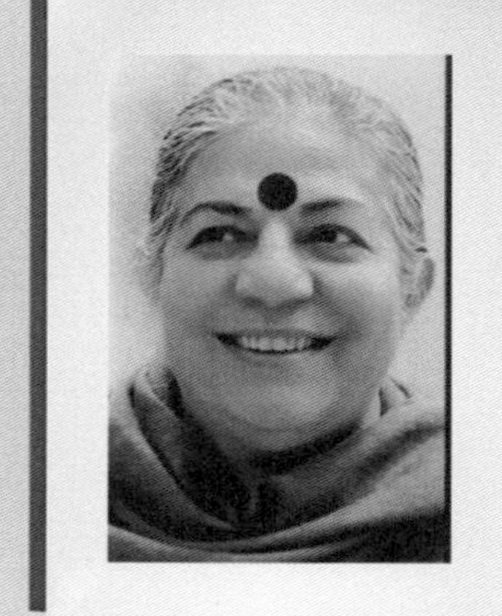

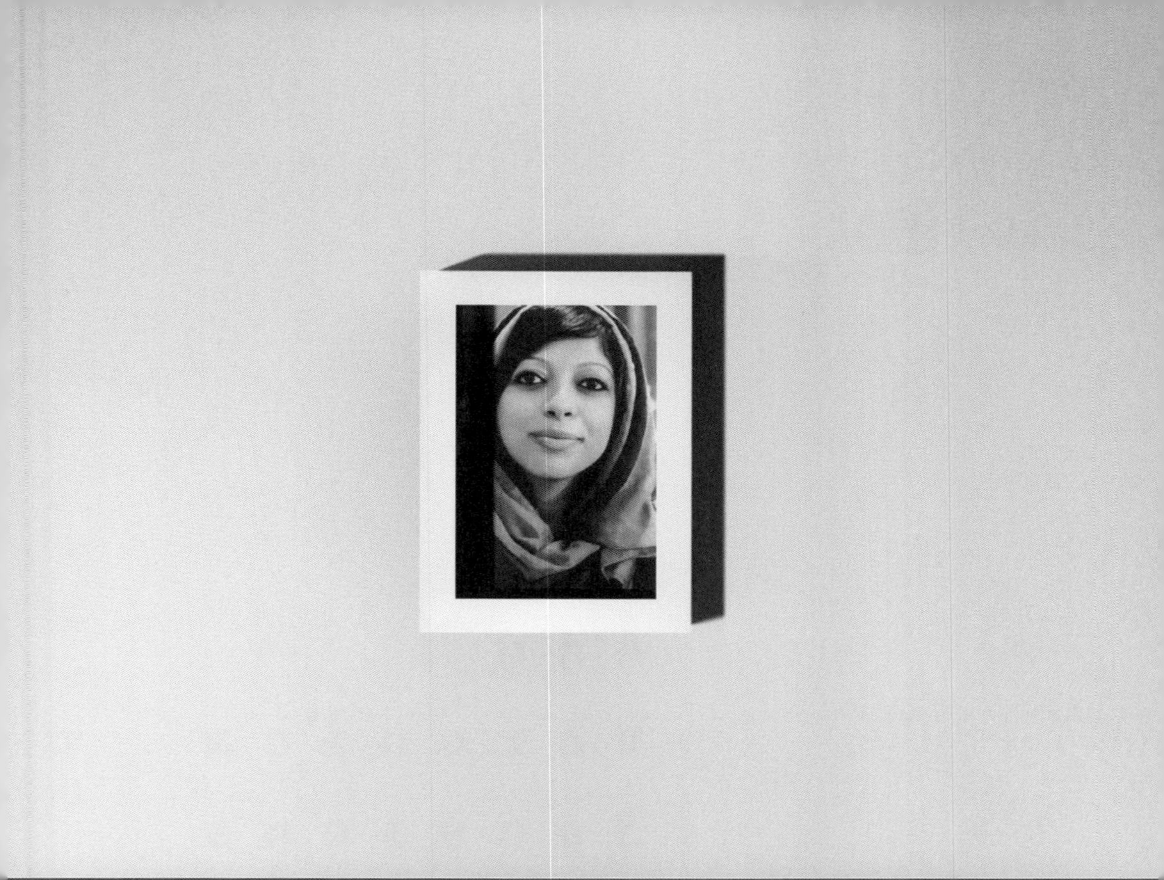

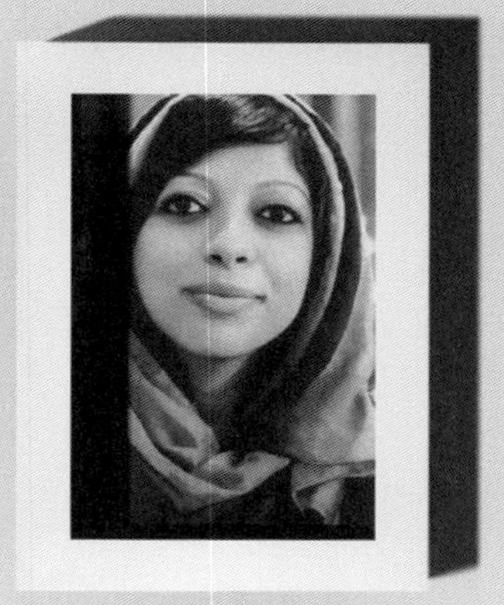

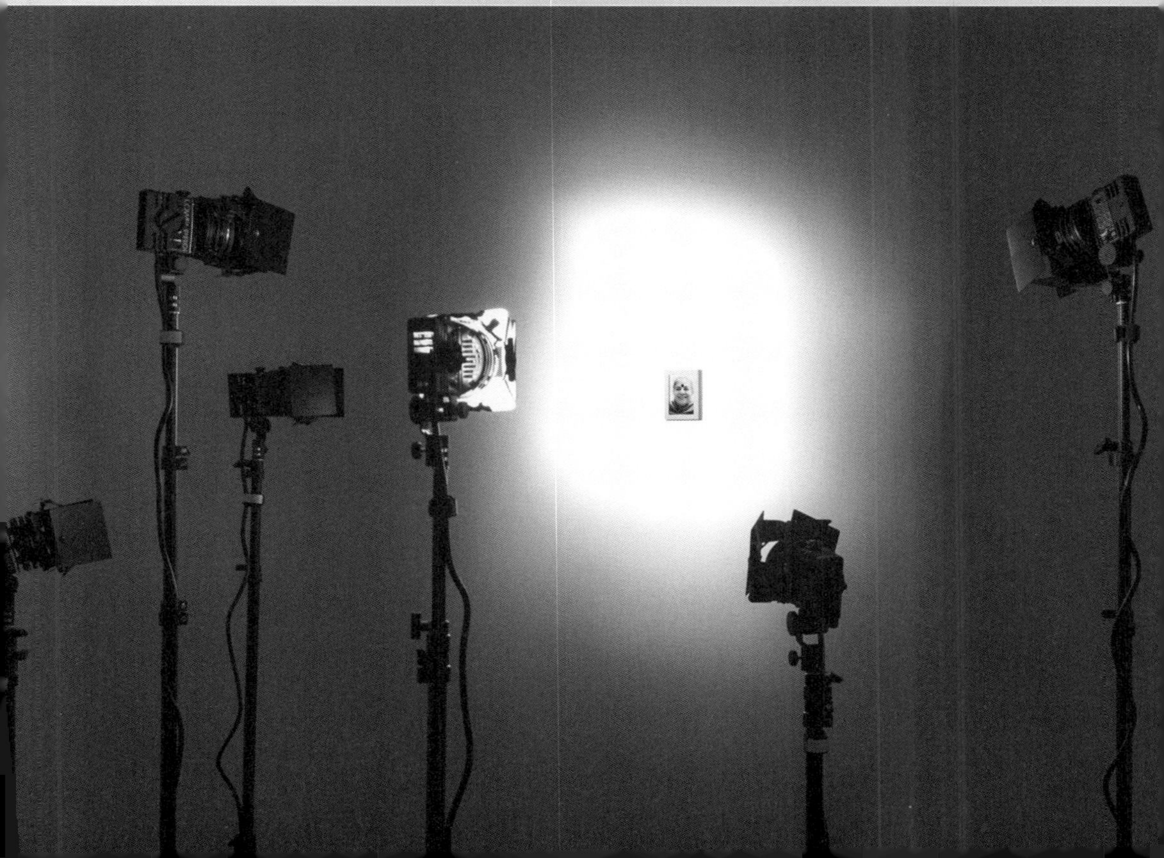

Ann Veronica Janssens

Volute
2006-2017
Micro water drops, air
Photo: Michel François

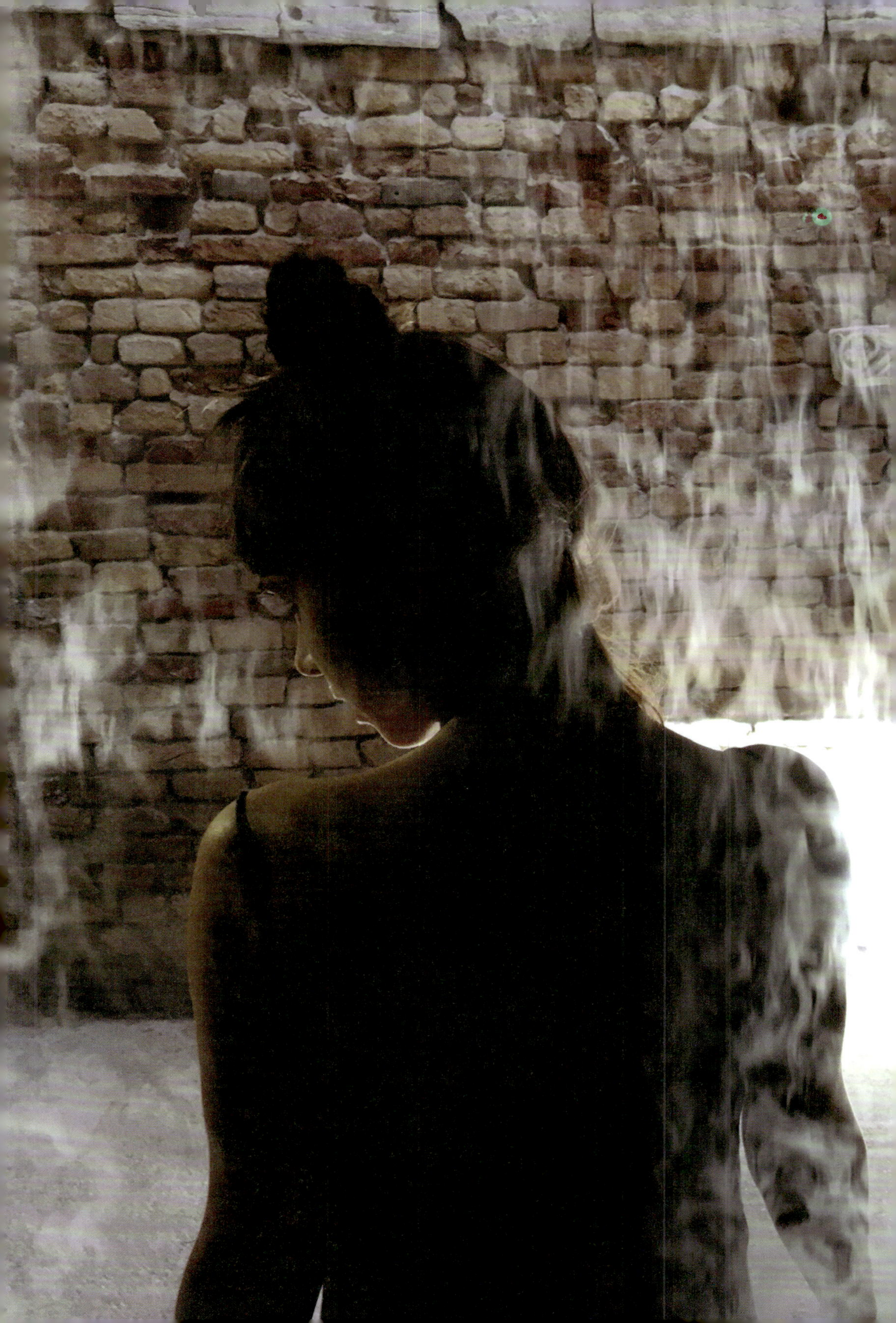

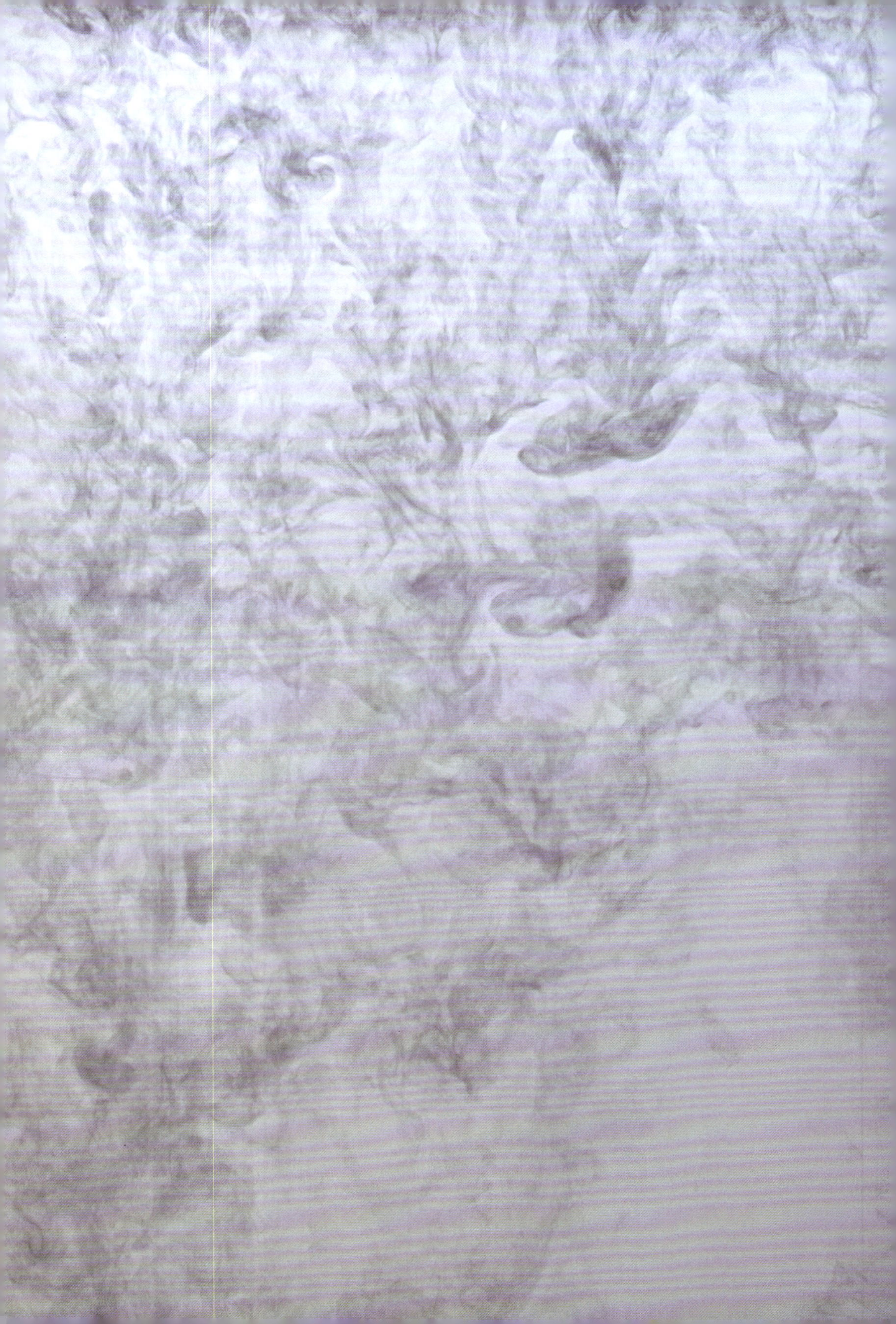

b. 1956, Folkestone, UK; lives and works in Brussels, Belgium

Ann Veronica Janssens explores the spatial and temporal world, often interrogating the limits of perception. She investigates the permeable layers of the everyday in her hypnotic installations, which require the viewer's close attention. By shifting light and movement in subtle ways, the artist allows for multiple interpretations of her work. 'I always experiment with the possibilities of rendering fluid the perception of matter or architecture, which I see as some kind of obstacle to movement and sculpture', Janssens has said. In the restaging of *Volute* (2006–19), a screen of fog envelops the viewer, pushing the formal limits of perception. The fleeting fog is, at times, barely perceptible to the naked eye, exemplifying a fleeting space between the real and the imagined. She creates the fog screen by transforming water into an opaque cloud using an ultrasound device. The work's title, *Volute*, refers to the decorative features found in the columns of classical architecture; it is also a French word for the curls of smoke that rise from a lit cigarette.

Volute
2006-2017
Micro water drops, air
Courtesy of Institut d'Art Contemporain, Villeurbanne, France
Photo: Blaise Adilon

Barbara Kasten

CONSTRUCT LB 2
1982
Image courtesy of the artist and Bortolami, New York; Thomas Dane Gallery, London; and Kadel Willborn, Dusseldorf
Artwork courtesy of the artist and Bortolami, New York

b. 1936, Chicago, USA; lives and works in Chicago

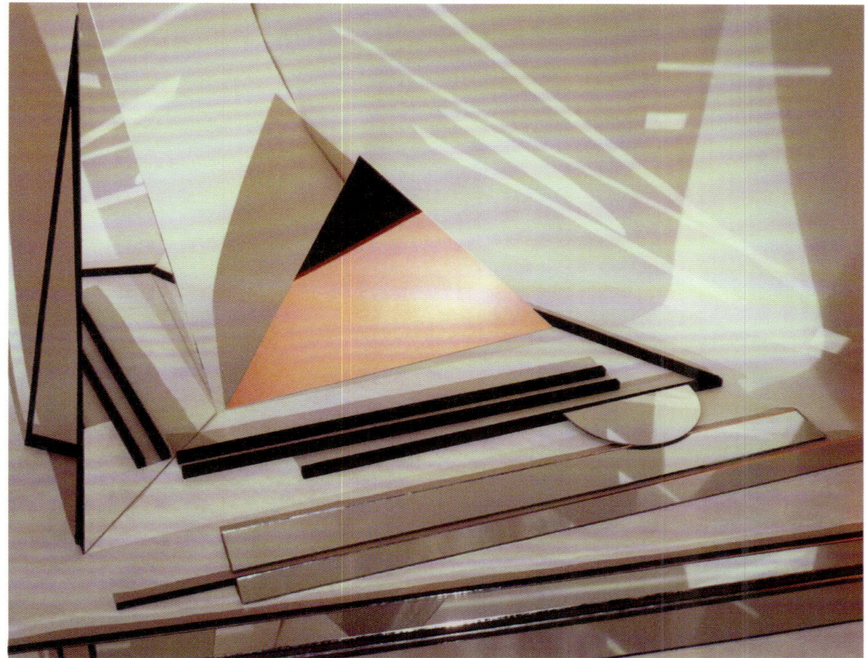

Barbara Kasten experiments with ways to integrate photography with other disciplines, such as painting and sculpture. Through the interaction of colour, form and light, she creates effects in her abstract photographs that question the nature of perception. In this survey of her works, the viewer is exposed to a variety of techniques, from cyanotypes and silver spray paint on paper to Fujiflex digital prints on acrylic. Many of these images also question photography's relationship to modernist architecture and space: carefully choreographed interiors are presented in a variety of ebullient colours, emphasising architectural motifs or details through an interplay of light and staging. Seductive hybrid forms morph into surroundings that resemble stage sets, which seem to be awaiting an absent body. In this sense, Kasten's photographs are performative objects – just like her pictures themselves – that shift in contour and texture as they are exposed to light.

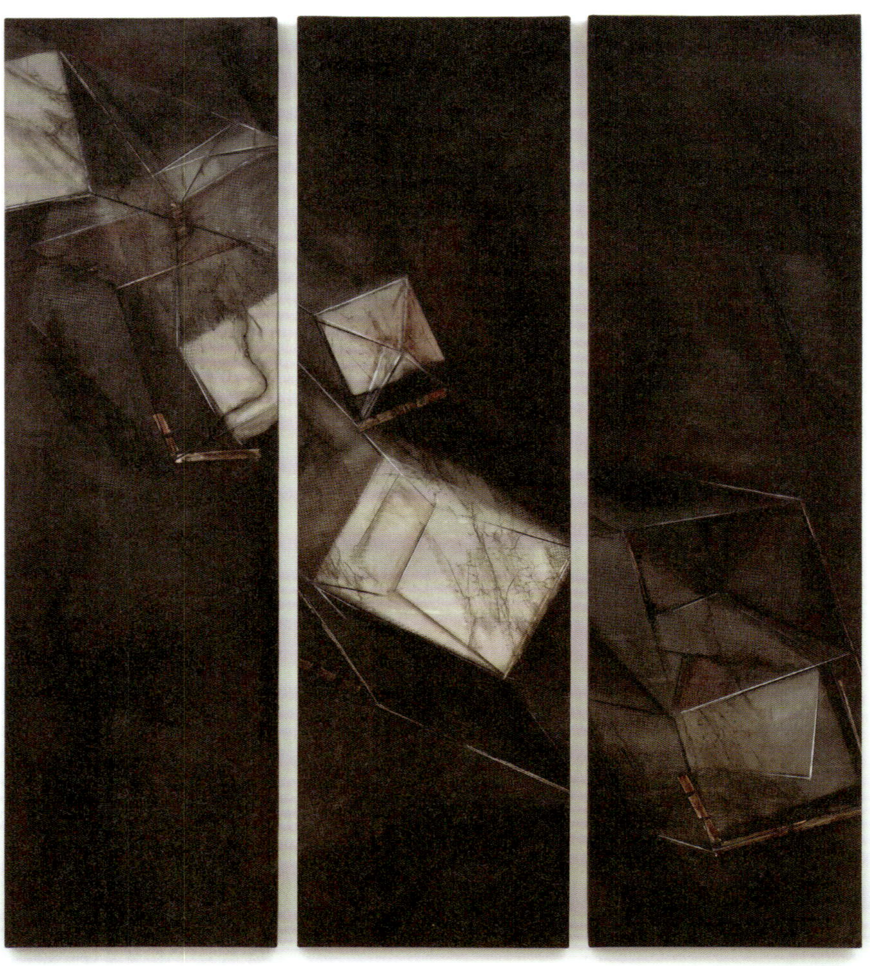

Untitled
(Photogram Painting 77-22)
1977
Image courtesy of the artist and Bortolami, New York; Thomas Dane Gallery, London; and Kadel Willborn, Dusseldorf
Artwork courtesy of the artist and Bortolami, New York

Collision 6 E
2016
Image courtesy of the artist and Bortolami, New York; Thomas Dane Gallery, London; and Kadel Willborn, Dusseldorf
Artwork courtesy of the artist and Bortolami, New York

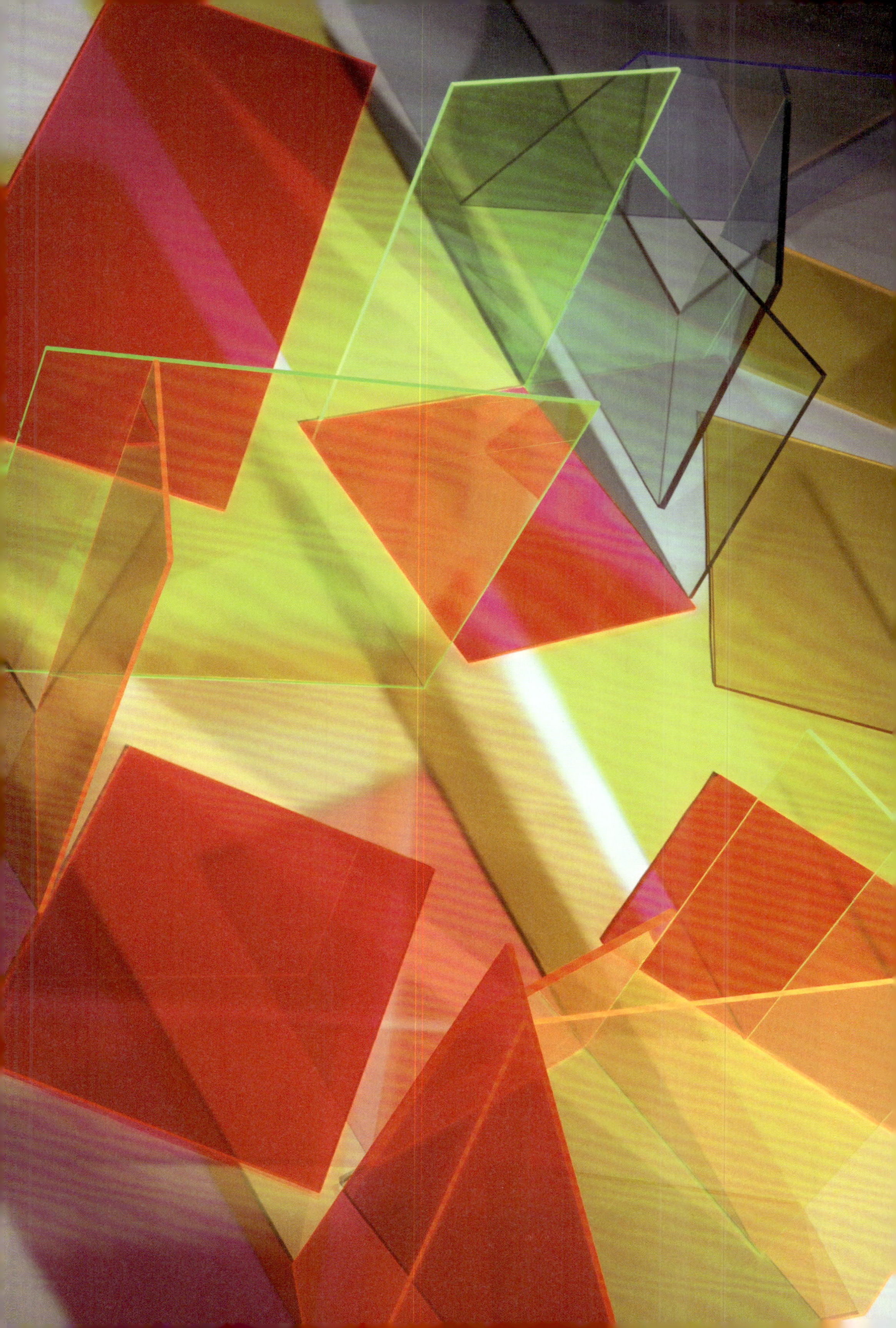

Construct 32
1986
Image courtesy of the artist and Bortolami, New York; Thomas Dane Gallery, London; and Kadel Willborn, Dusseldorf
Artwork courtesy of the artist and Bortolami, New York

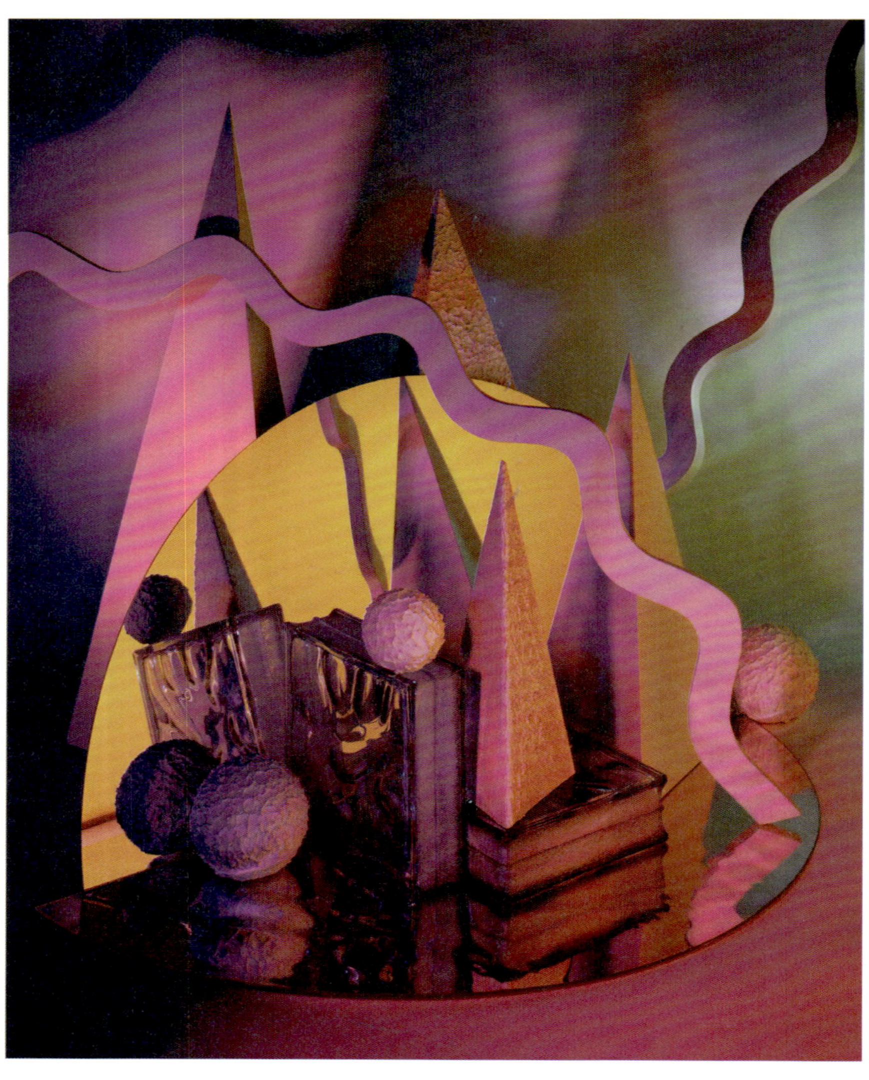

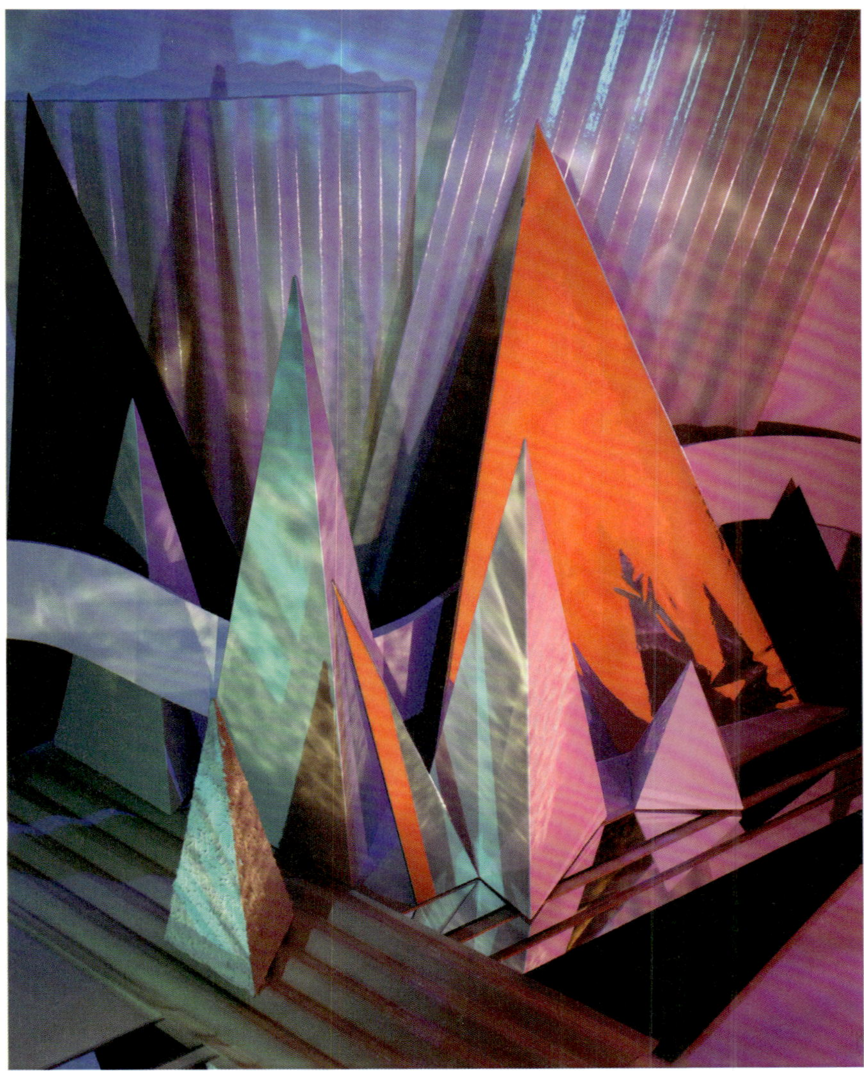

Metaphase 3
1986
Image courtesy of the artist and Bortolami, New York; Thomas Dane Gallery, London; and Kadel Willborn, Dusseldorf
Artwork courtesy of the artist and Bortolami, New York

Astrid Klein

Flycatcher III
1987/1991
Neon tubes, electric mosquito traps, steel pipe, sound
Height: 396.5, diameter ca. 100 cm
Installation view, Deichtorhallen Hamburg-Harburg, Sammlung Falckenberg, 2018
Courtesy of the artist and Sprüth Magers

Photography: Timo Ohler

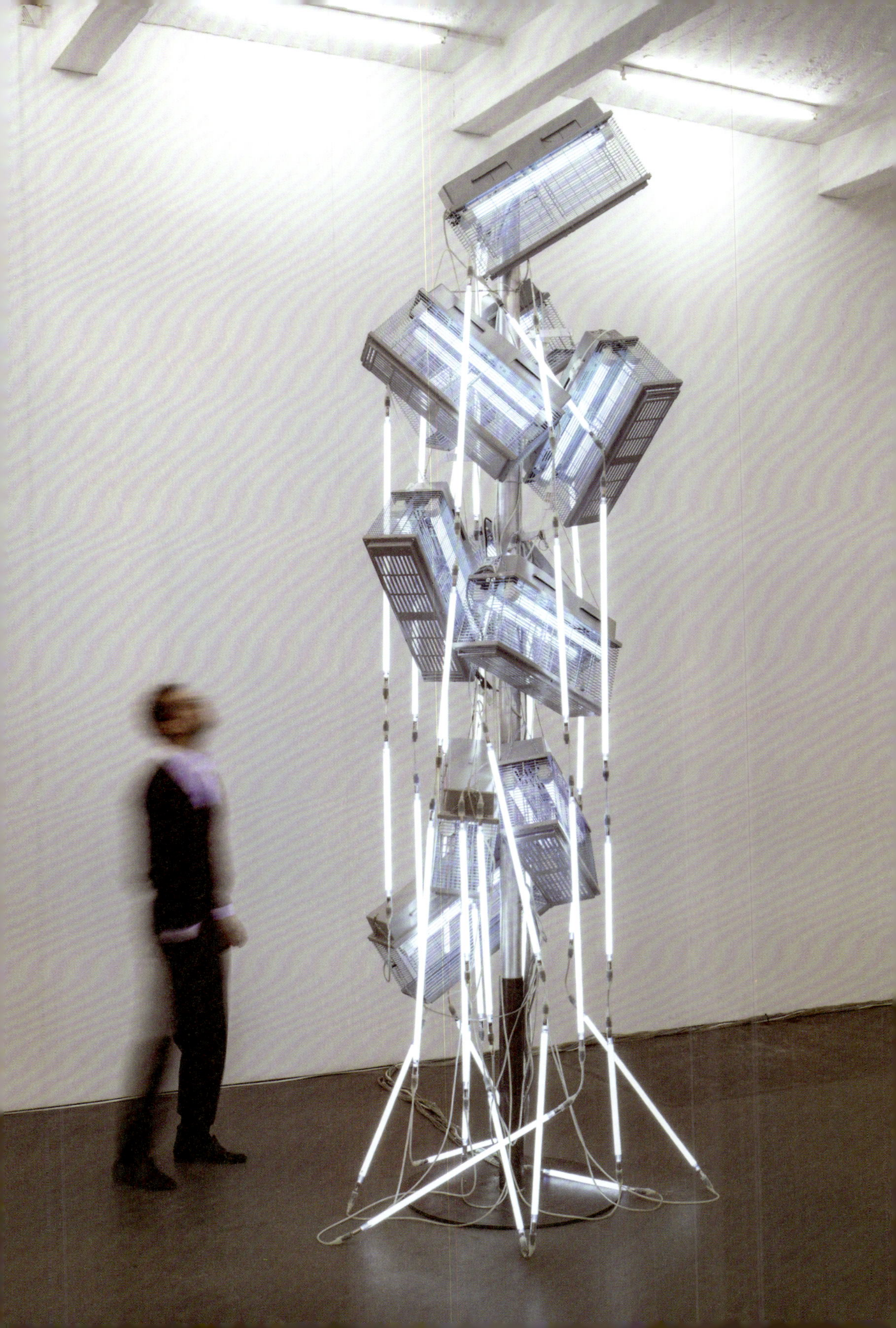

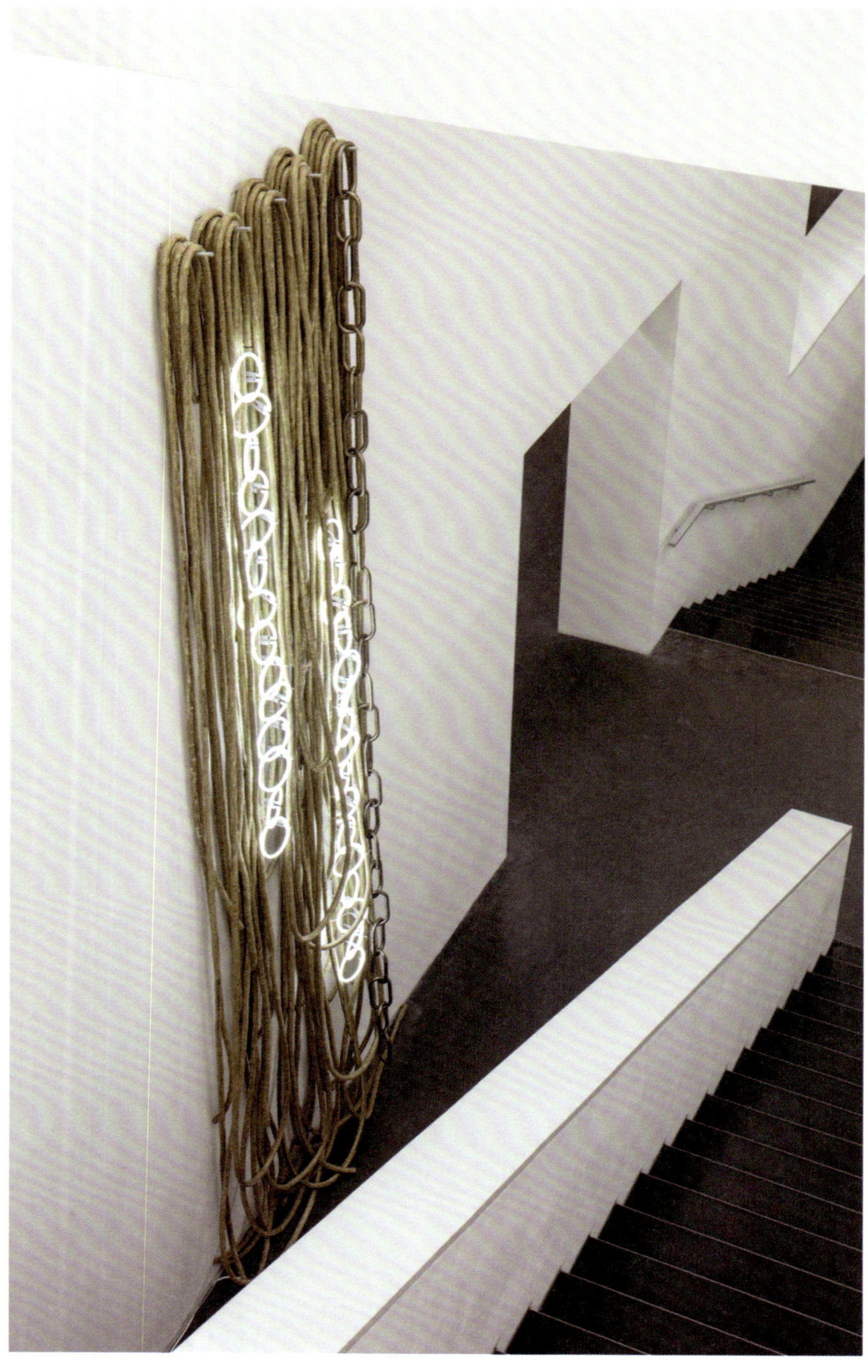

Untitled, (Better to burn out, than to fade away)
1998
Neon sculpture: rings of neon and ropes imprinted with text
Dimensions variable
Installation view, Deichtorhallen Hamburg-Harburg, Sammlung Falckenberg, 2018
Courtesy of the artist and Sprüth Magers
© Astrid Klein
Photography: Timo Ohler

Untitled, (What are you fighting for)
1988
From 'White paintings', 1988-1993
Acrylic, quartz crystal, alabaster plaster, zinc white on canvas
150 x 204.5 cm
Courtesy of the artist and Sprüth Magers
© Astrid Klein

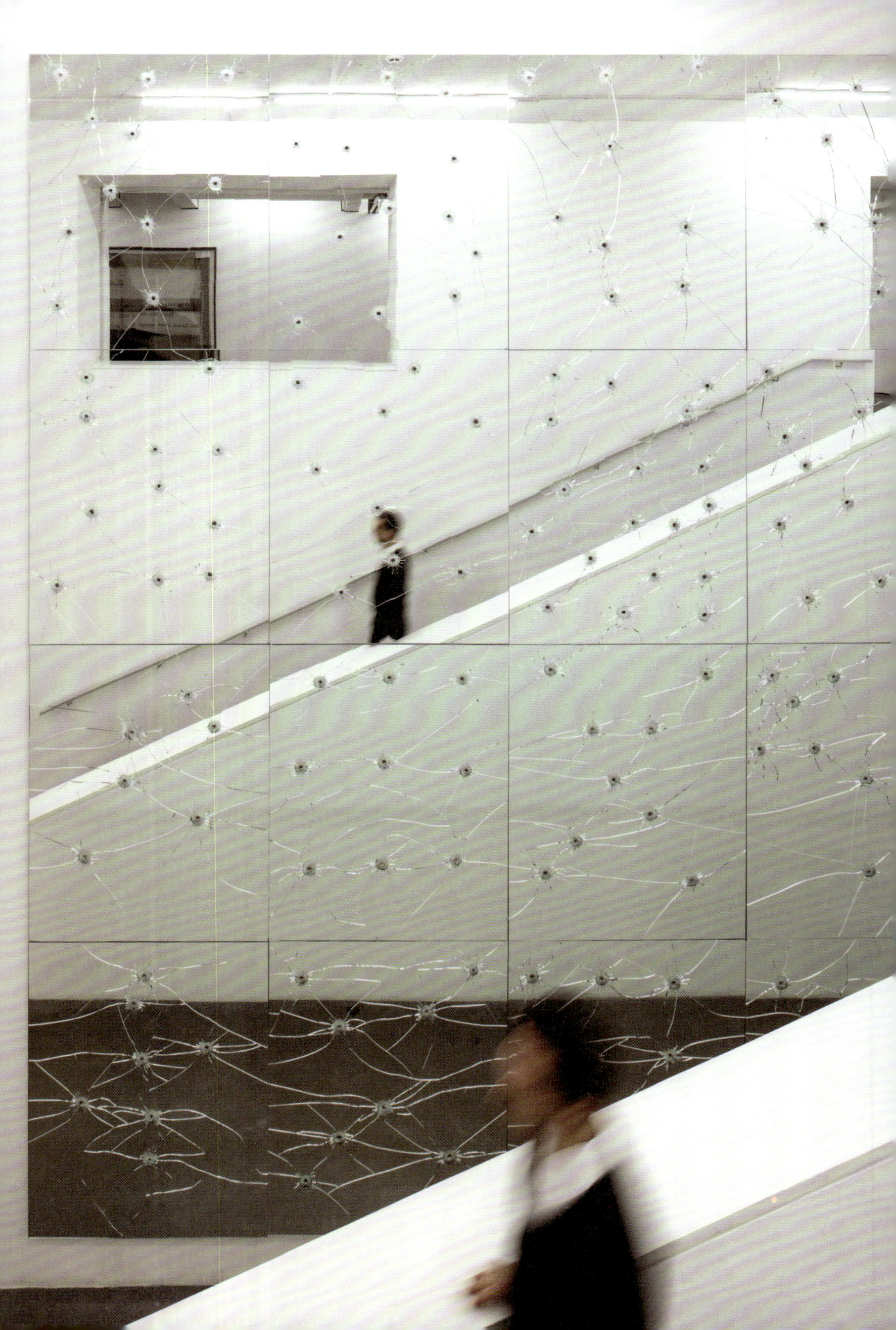

b. 1951, Cologne, Germany; lives and works in Cologne

Untitled
1993
Mirrors, bullet holes
Dimensions variable
Installation view, Deichtorhallen Hamburg-Harburg, Sammlung Falckenberg, 2018
Courtesy of the artist and Sprüth Magers
© Astrid Klein
Photography: Timo Ohler

Astrid Klein is best known for her large-format, black-and-white 'photoworks', along with her collages, paintings and neon sculptures. Since the 1970s, she has combined found photographic images and textual excerpts with drawn and painted elements to produce striking artworks. Coupling purity and elegance, Klein exhibits a seismographic sensitivity to critical contemporary issues, such as the role of women in society and notions of success and failure, as well as wider themes of remembering and forgetting, time and transience. In her neon *Flycatcher III* (1987–91), sculptural flycatchers hang in the balance, evoking a cataclysmic scenario or a bodily form abstracted. In *Untitled (Better to burn out then fade away)* (1998), a series of ropes and neon echo the Emirate of Sharjah's maritime history. With the title of the piece, the artist asks: How do we negotiate our relationship to speed in an age of acceleration? In two works from her white painting series, *What are you fighting for* (1988–92) and *Nothing to Remember* (1988–93), Klein subtly balances the banal and the sublime in order to question the limits of visibility by rendering the invisible visible. The artist incorporates textural elements, such as alabaster, crystal and plaster, into their white surfaces, engaging with the history of the white monochrome whilst exploring the limits of perception.

Marwan

Untitled
1986
Oil on canvas
195 x 114 cm
Courtesy the artist's estate
and Sfeir-Semler Gallery
Hamburg / Beirut

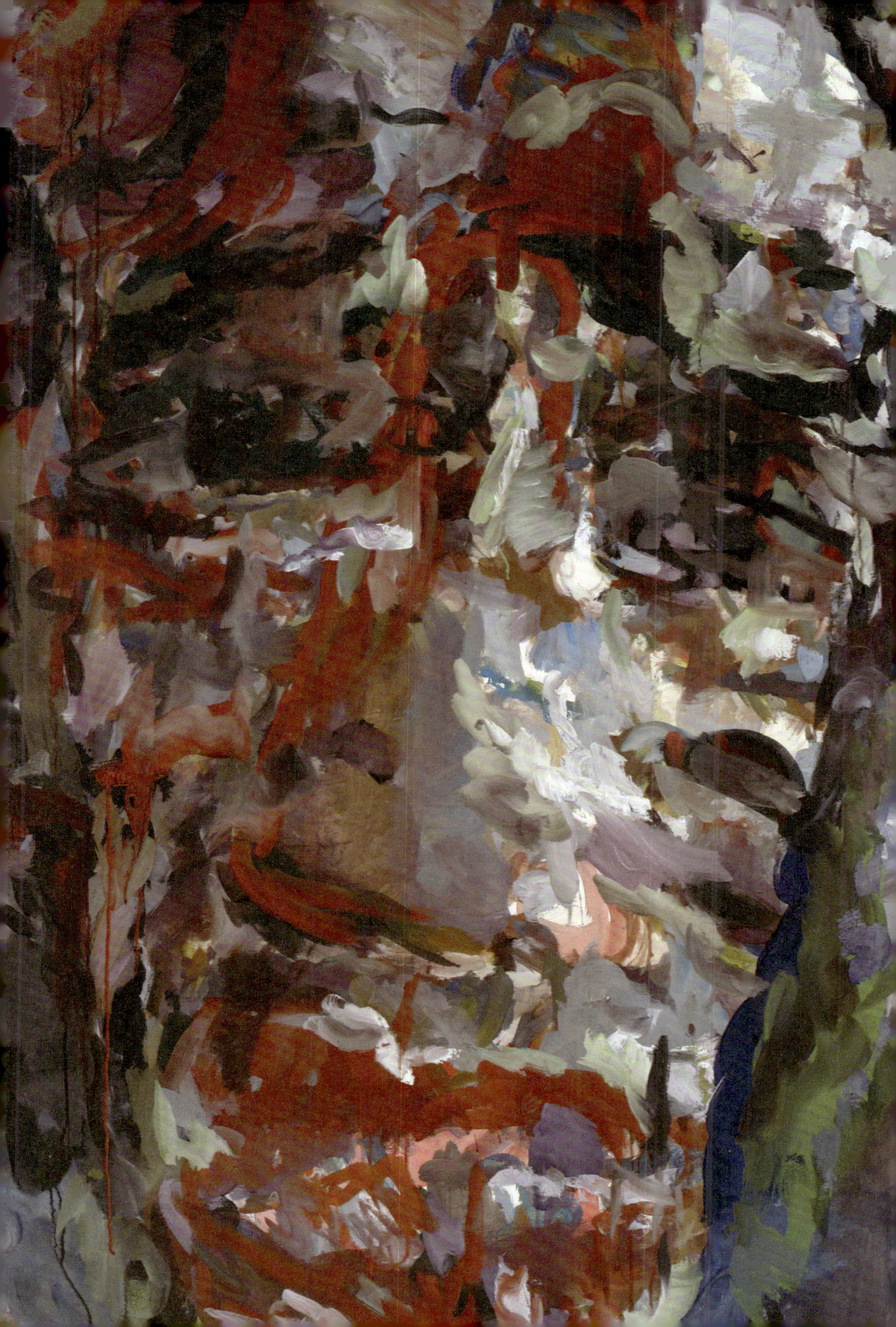

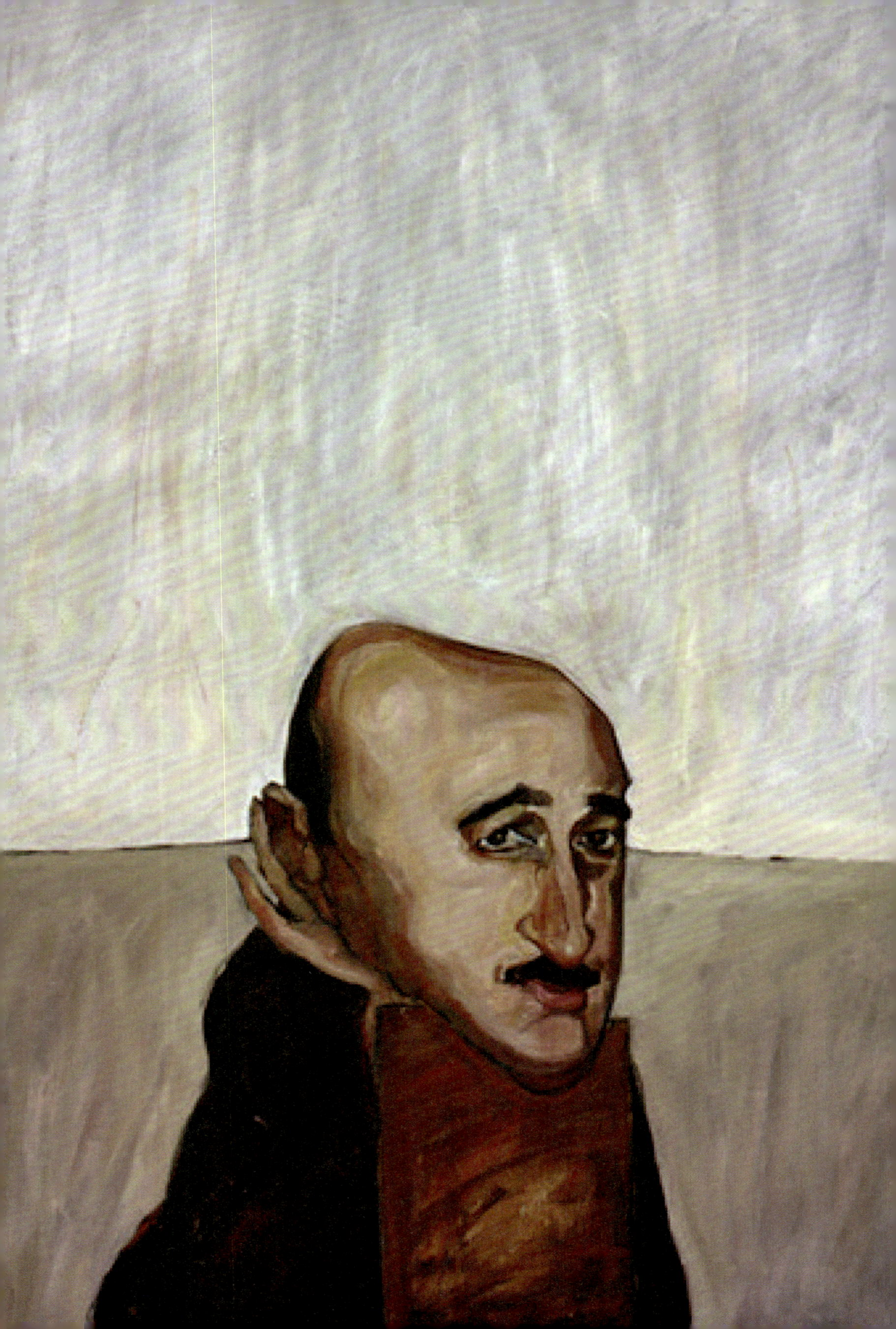

b. 1934, Damascus, Syria; d. 2016, Berlin, Germany

Marwan was a pioneering figure of Germany's new figuration movement in the 1960s. He began his career by producing large-scale expressionistic paintings in a post-surrealist style featuring strange bodies, which were often presented in compromising positions. Later in life, the artist shifted his attention to painting giant heads and faces. To look at these visages is to examine the entire history of portraiture: from discombobulated heads to abstract bodies, from caricature to surrealist wonder. These images embody and dialogue with a genealogy of composition that stretches from depictions of the Egyptian pharaohs and the Greco-Romans to the tight close-ups of the digital era. For Marwan, the face was the most expressive of all landscapes – an affective universe whose emotion required continual unfolding. This selection examines the formation of the artist's heads and their relationship to landscape through representations that are both figurative and abstract.

Munif al Razzaz
1965
Oil on canvas
195x260
Collection of Sharjah Art Foundation

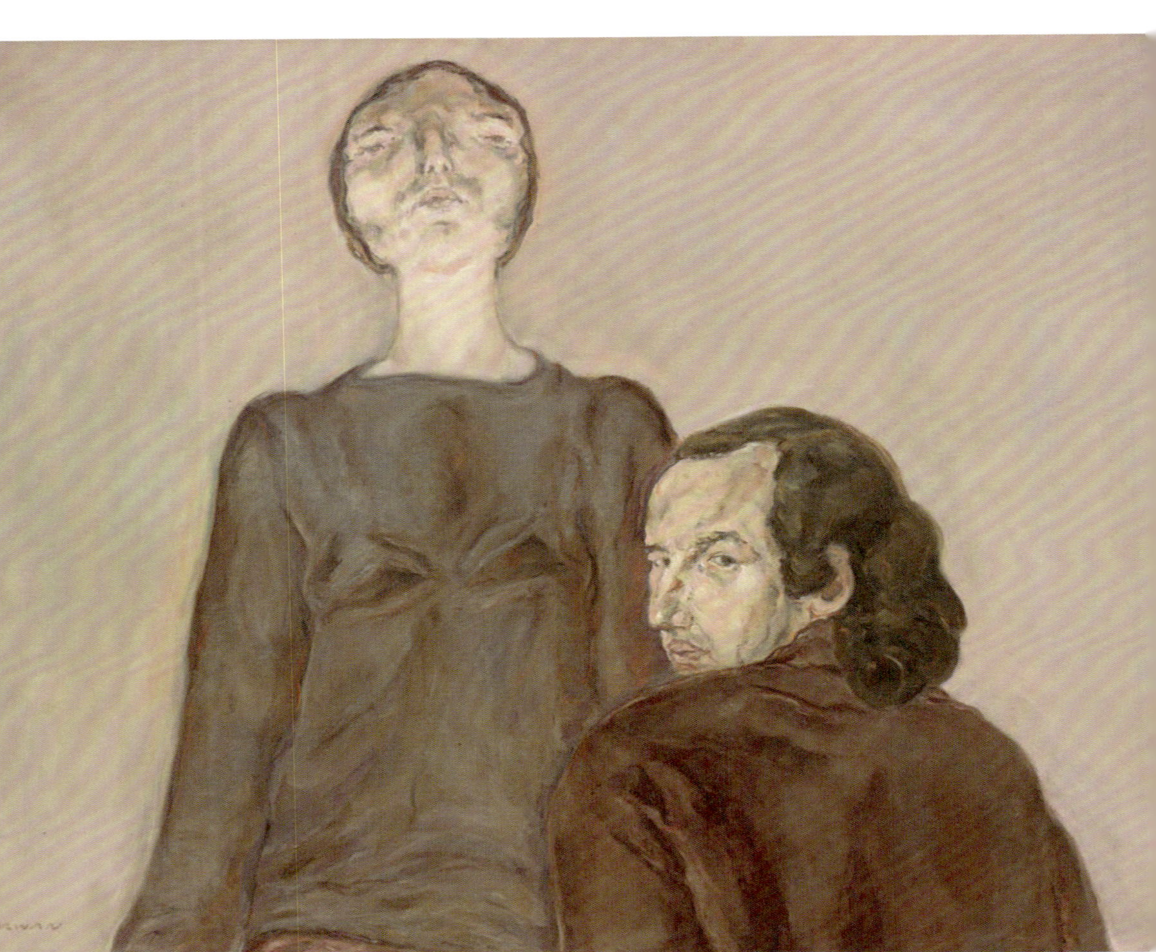

Untitled
1969
Oil on canvas
89 x 130 cm
Collection of Sharjah Art Foundation

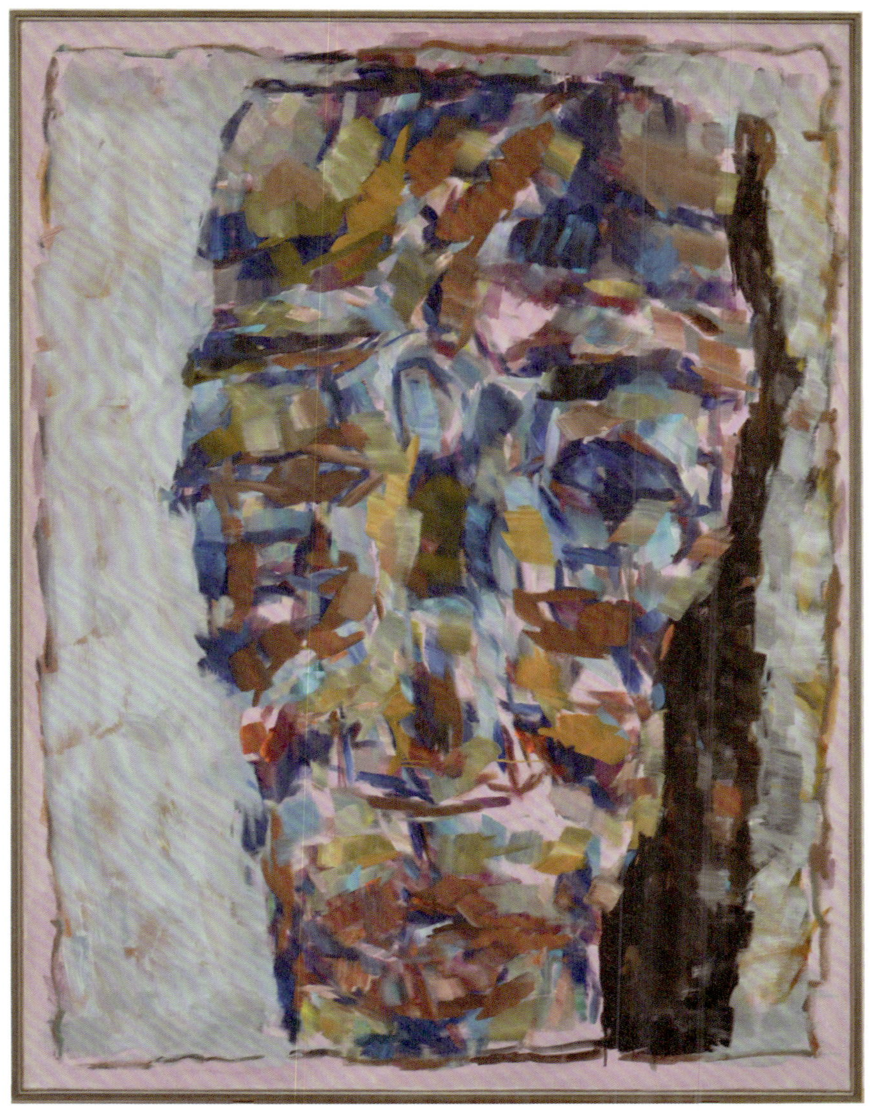

Untitled
2006
Oil on canvas
195 x 146 cm
Courtesy of the artist's estate & Sfeir-Semler Gallery, Hamburg / Beirut

Otobong Nkanga and Emeka Ogboh

Aging
ruins dreaming
only to recall
the hard chisel
from the past

Four walls
The perfect hole
Breathing through
the broken cracks

Grey Stone
The humid soil
Laying low
at absolute zero

Absolute Zero II
2017
Poetry
60 x 60 cm

Courtesy of the artist, Mendes Wood Gallery DM, Lumen Travo Gallery and Insitu Fabienne Leclerc *Gallery*

b. 1974, Kano, Nigeria / b. 1977, Enugu, Nigeria
Lives and works in Antwerp / Lives and works in Berlin and Lagos
Commissioned by Sharjah Art Foundation

For Sharjah Biennial 14, Otobong Nkanga and Emeka Ogboh collaborate on a series of multimedia interventions in the heritage house Bait Al Aboudi and the surrounding grounds. *Aging Ruins Dreaming Only to Recall the Hard Chisel from the Past* (2019) explores the land, the human (and animal) body, the organic and the inorganic, the animate and the inanimate, and the visible and the invisible, manifesting an affective ecology of prosperity and depression, hopeful beginnings and eventual demise, and the possibility of rebirth.

In the untended garden of this building, the artists have created several circular craters framed by sand mounds, and they have filled the craters with water brought in from the sea. Salt has been added to ensure that traces of saline will remain as the water evaporates over time. In close proximity to the craters, a number of speakers play a range of natural sounds, a recording of an Emirati 'rain song' performed by children in Sharjah and texts conceived from the perspectives of water, earth and trees, written and performed by Nkanga. Light-boxes rendered in the tonal shades of the sunset as well as lines of poetry describe the architecture and materiality of the building. The interplay of evaporating water and waning light recall the departure of life from Bait Al Aboudi, which now stands as a ruin, while simultaneously imbuing the courtyard enclosure with the residue of salt, the sounds of natural elements and voices, and the gradients of the sunset that signal life's inevitable return.

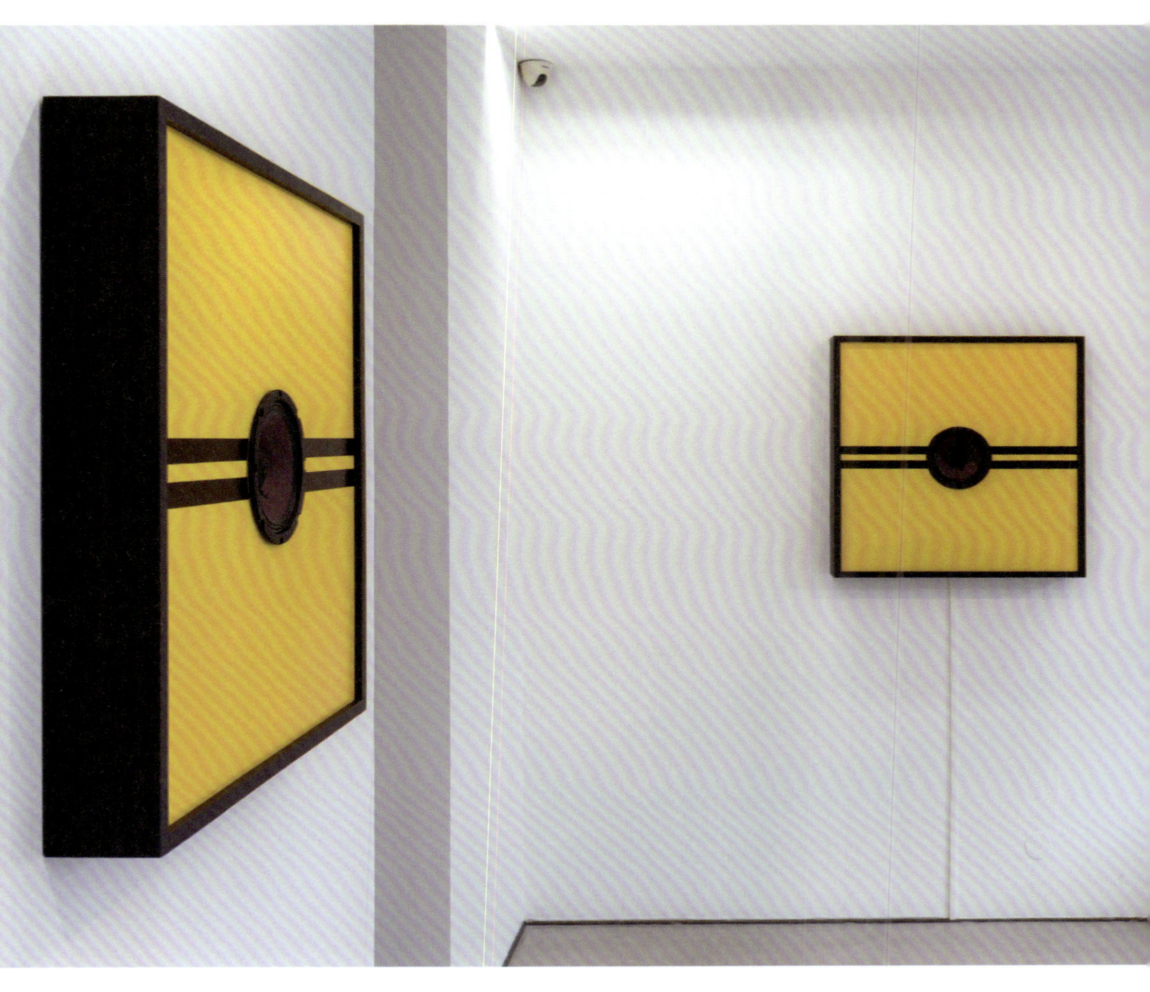

Conductor-Oshodi
2018
Portraits
Courtesy of the artist and Imane Fares gallery
Photo: TADZIO

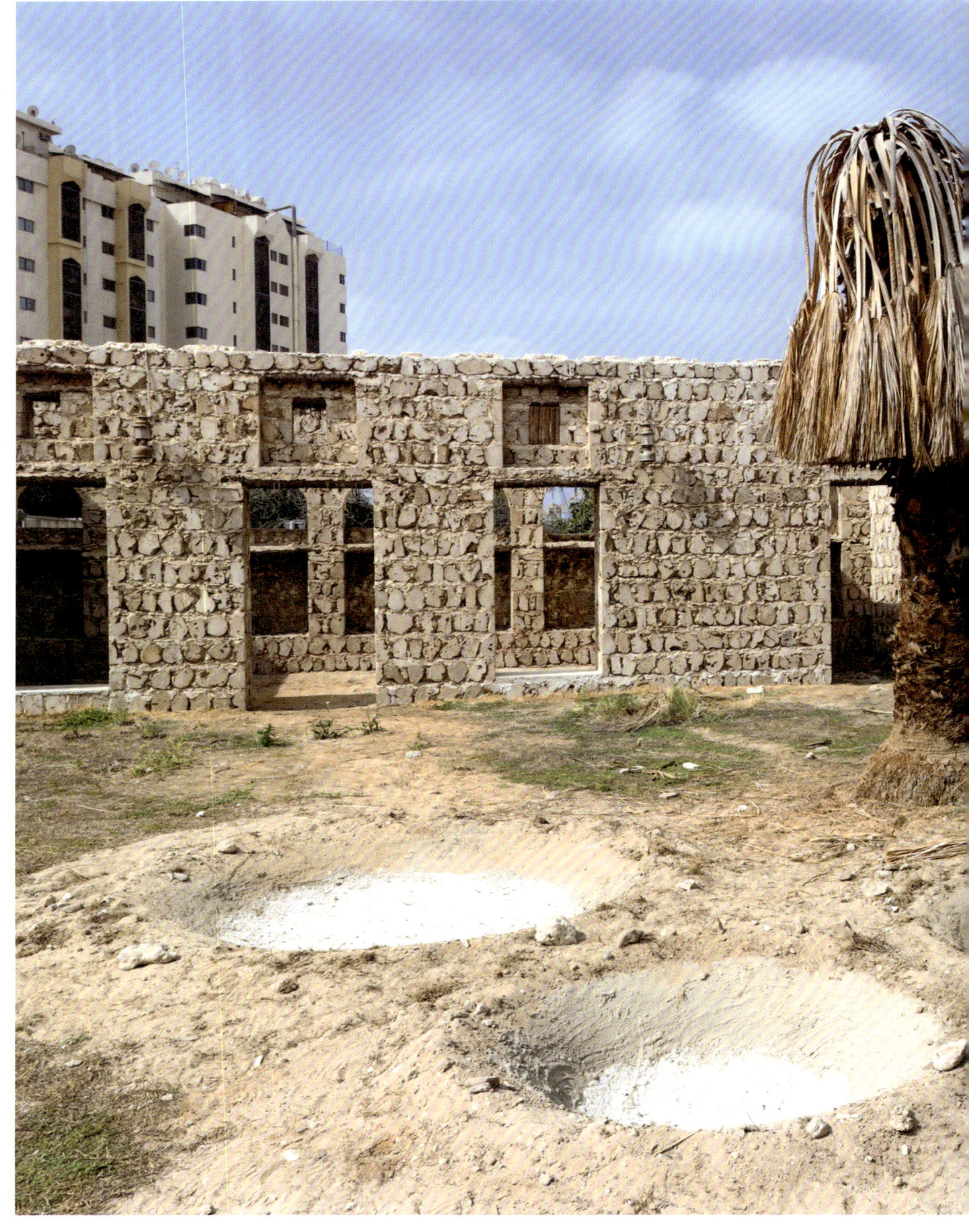

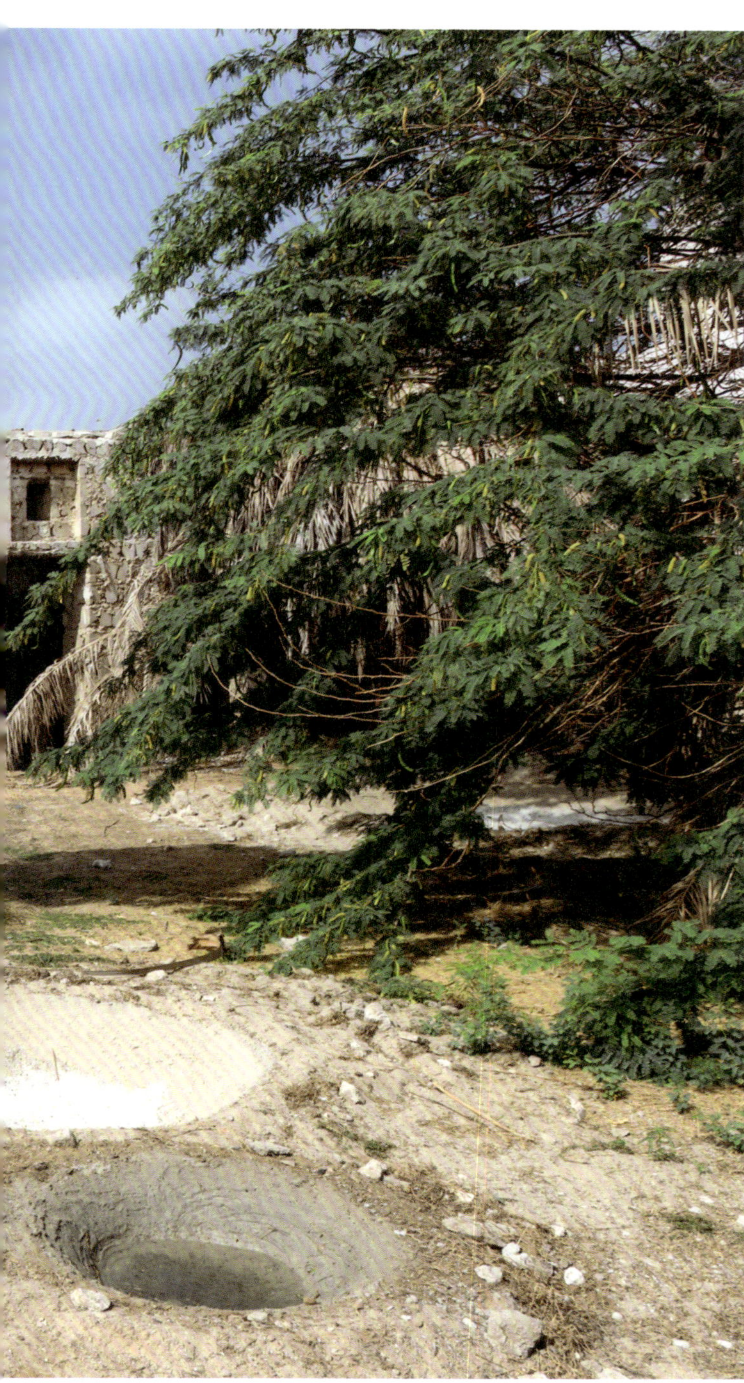

Aging ruins dreaming only to recall the hard chisel from the past
2019
Installation view Bait Aboudi
Multichannel sound installation, sculpture and light installation, poetry
Variable dimensions
Commissioned by Sharjah Art Foundation
Courtesy of Otobong Nkanga and Emeka Ogboh

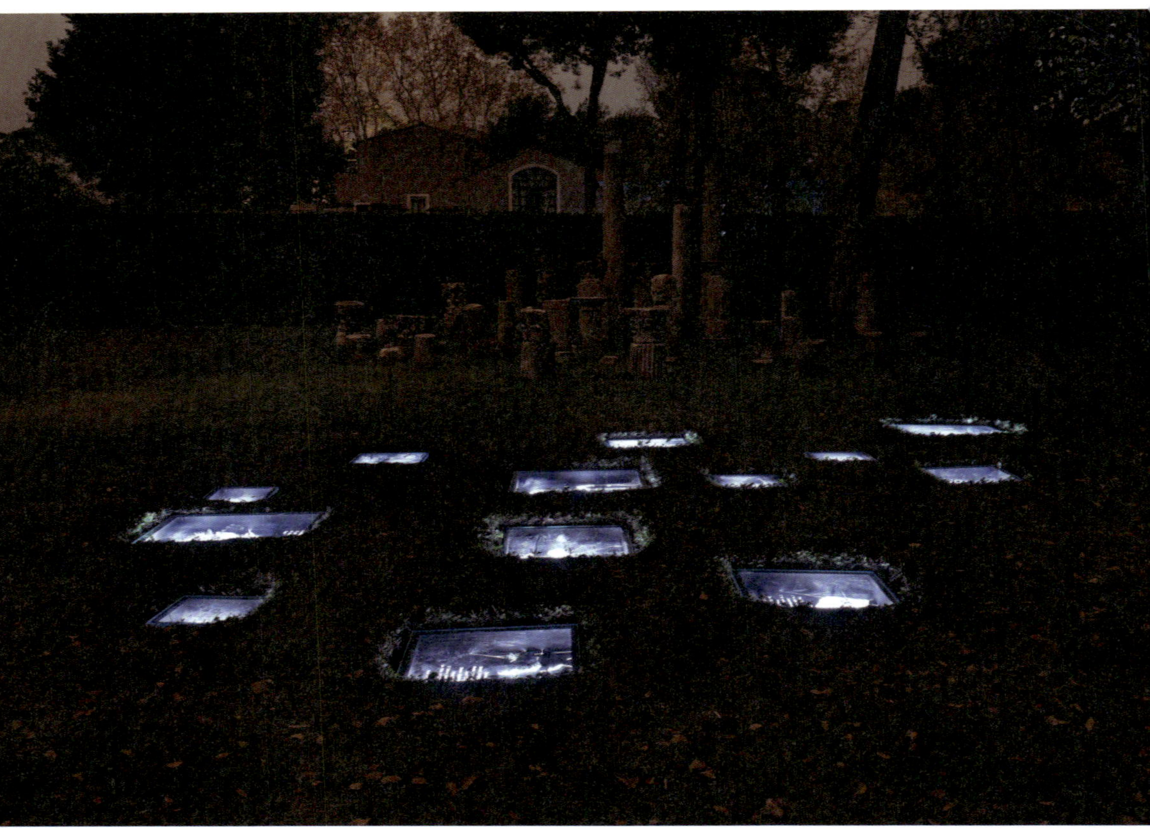

Anchoured Glow
2017
Drawing and poetry / light installation
Variable dimensions
Commissioned by Villa Medici, Rome - Open at Night, Festival of lights
Courtesy of the artist, Mendes Wood Gallery DM, Lumen Travo Gallery and Insitu Fabienne Leclerc Gallery

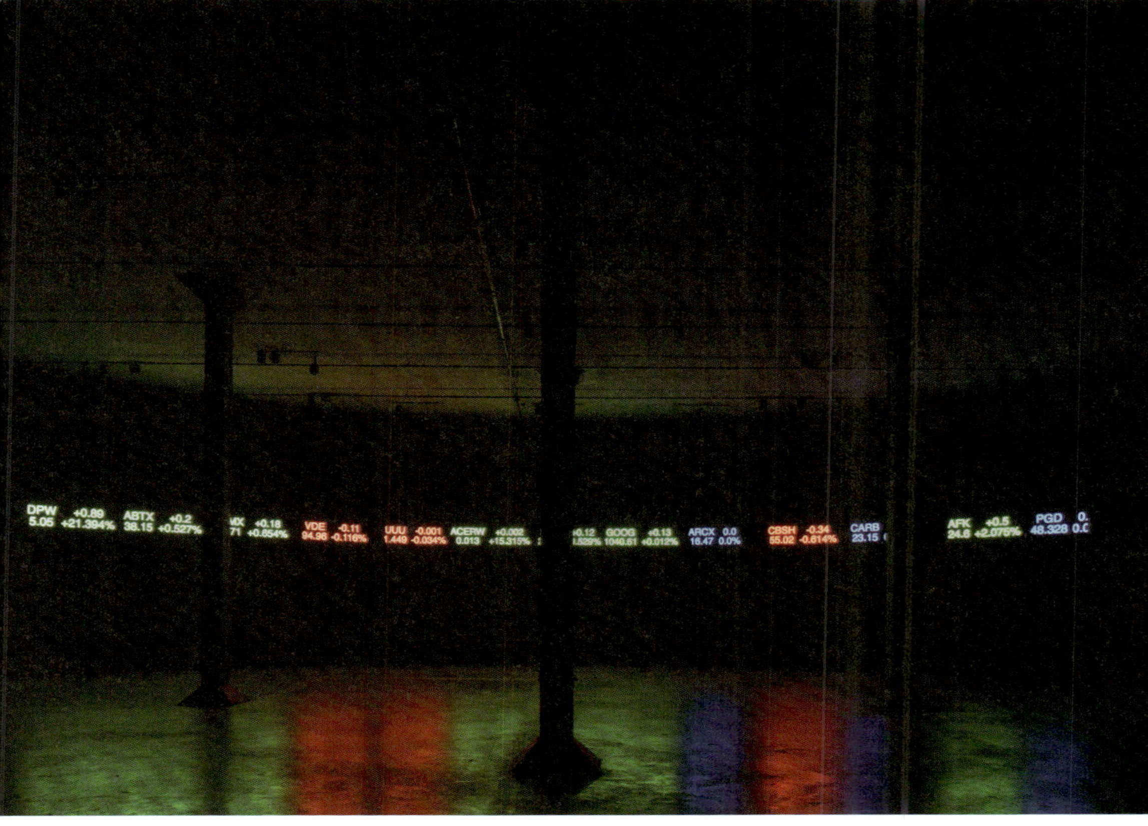

The Way Earthly Things Are Going
2017
Multichannel sound installation, real-time LED display of world stock indexes
Variable dimension
Courtesy of the artist
Photo: Tate Modern (Tate tanks)

Bruno Pacheco

Puff !!!(Sissiphilous)
2018
Oil on canvas
180 x 170 cm
Courtesy of the artist
and Hollybush Gardens
Photo: Bruno Lopes

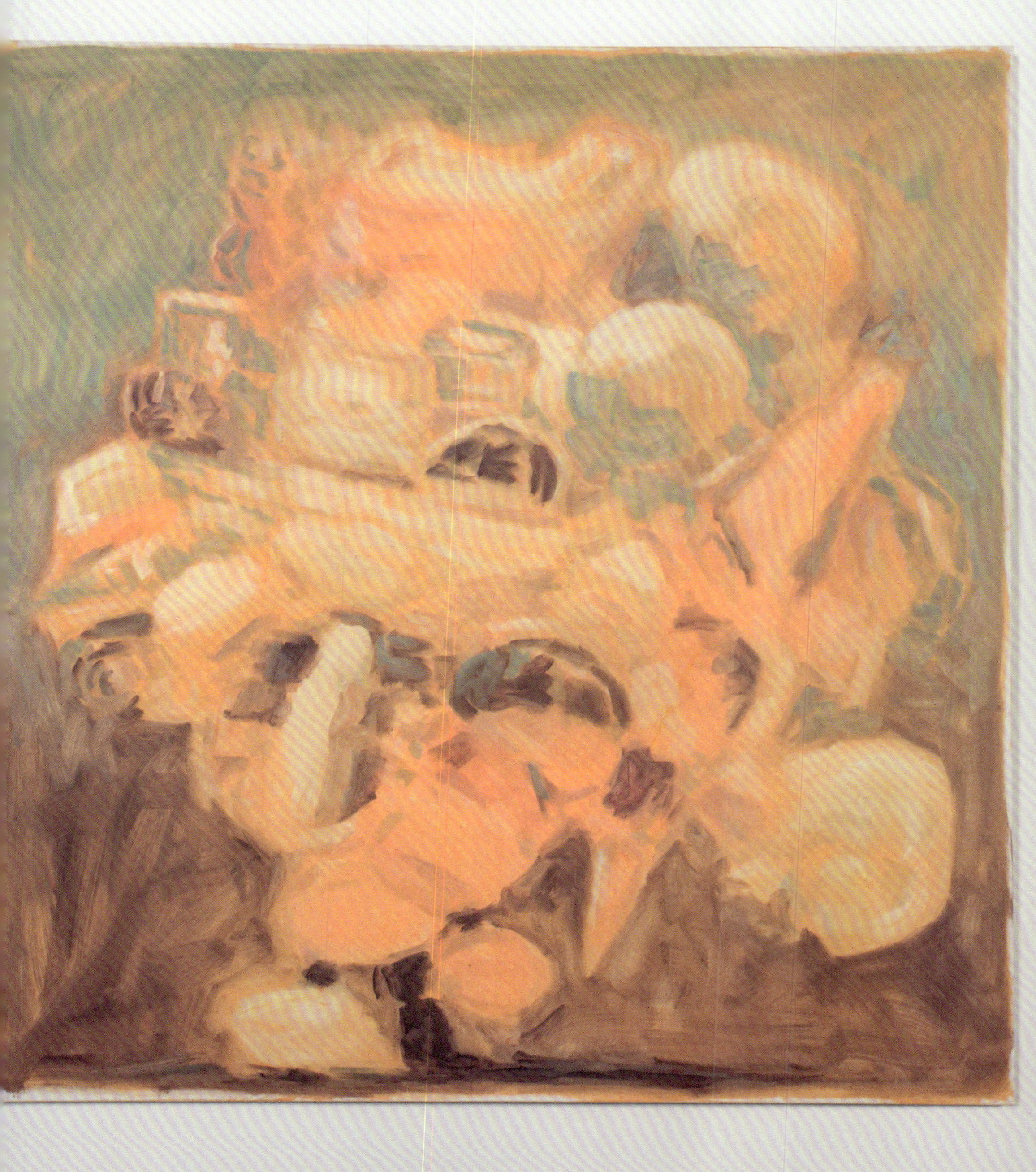

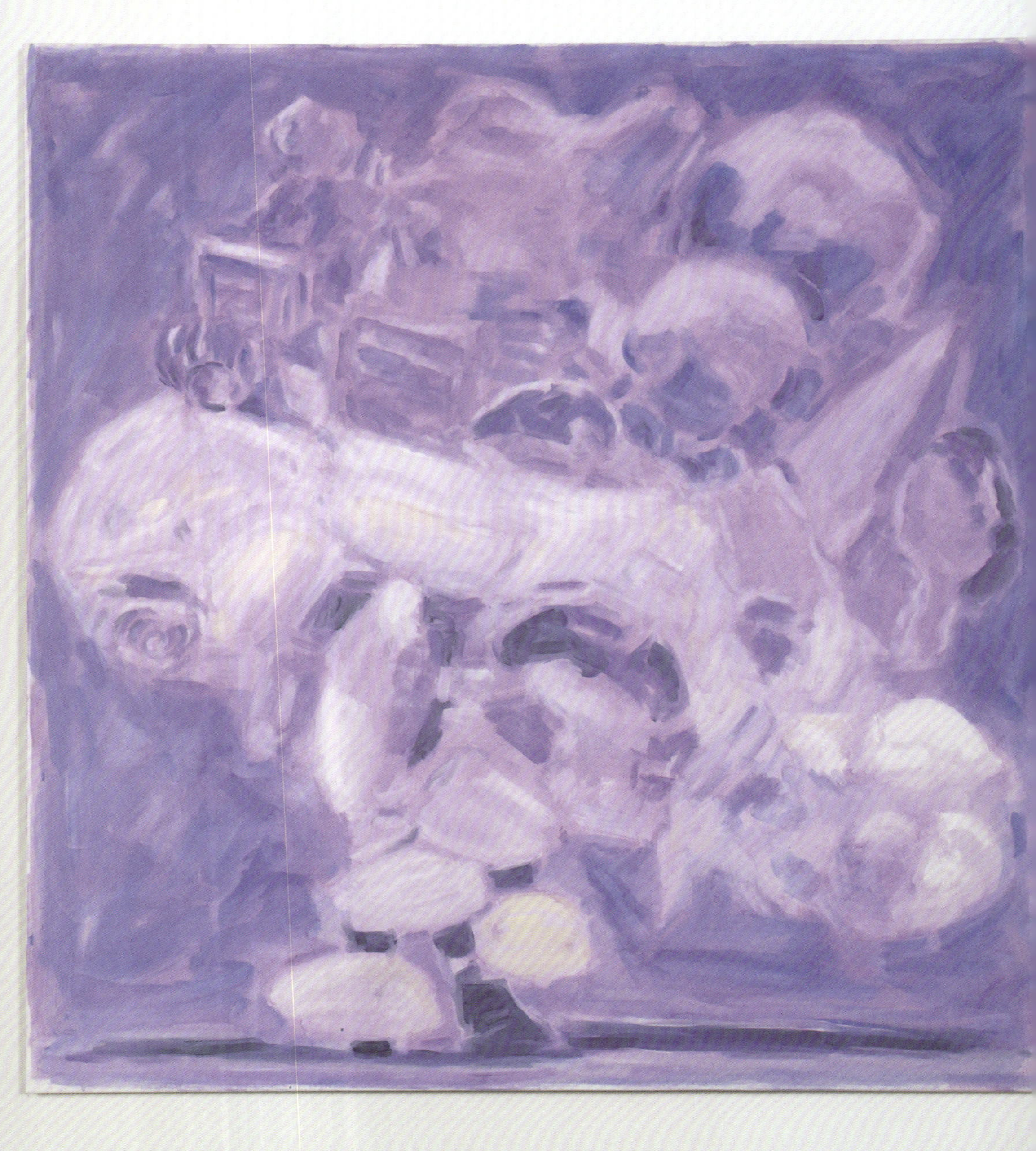

b. 1974, Lisbon, Portugal; lives and works in Lisbon, Portugal, and London, UK.
Commissioned by Sharjah Art Foundation

Bruno Pacheco's work is deeply invested in both the formal and political histories of painting. He addresses subject matter ranging from examinations of the banal to the sublime, from the singular object to the assembly of bodies in unity, as well as nature as a field of study. In *Puff! (sissiphilous)* (2018), a new suite of paintings developed for the Sharjah Biennial, the artist presents a man holding balloons who disappears amidst the shroud of circular colours until he becomes indiscernible. The works suggest the illusion of an object transforming, meta-morphing, oscillating from being a figure to an abstraction. The subject's identity is never stable. Then, as if with a pinch, the image, like the balloon, disappears – *puff*! Its weight is illusive, although at times it resembles the stone of Sisyphus from Greek mythology. The balloons' chromatic colour subtly alters, as echoed through Pacheco's dragging of wet paint, resulting in a fragmented feeling that emerges within the landscape.

Puff !!!(Sissiphilous)
2018
Oil on canvas
170 x 160 cm
Courtesy of the artist and
Hollybush Gardens
Photo: Bruno Lopes

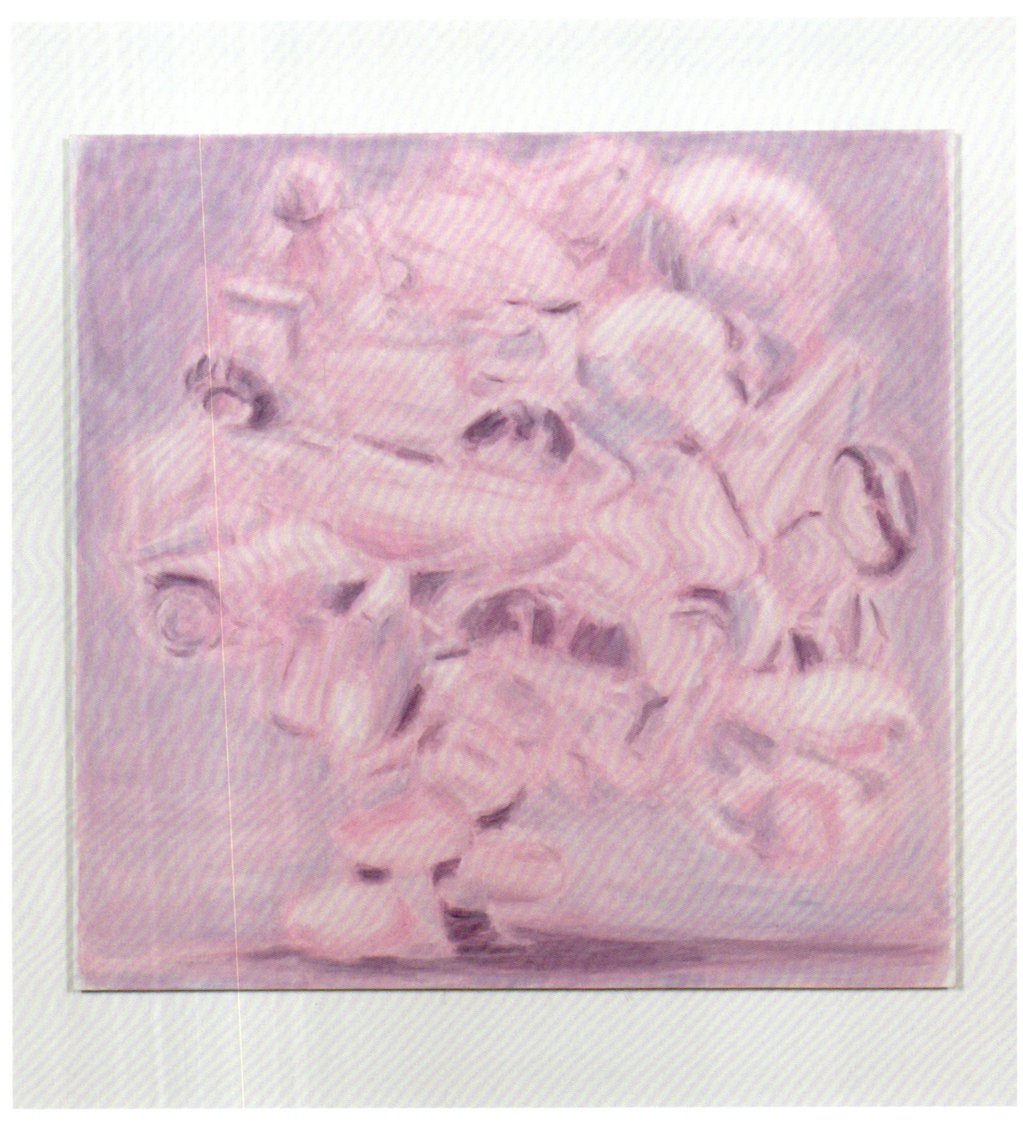

Puff !!!(Sissiphilous)
2016/2017
Oil on canvas
170 x 170 cm
Courtesy of the artist and
Hollybush Gardens
Photo: Bruno Lopes

Puff !!!(Sissiphilous)
2017/2018
Oil on canvas
180 x 160 cm
Courtesy of the artist and
Hollybush Gardens
Photo: Bruno Lopes

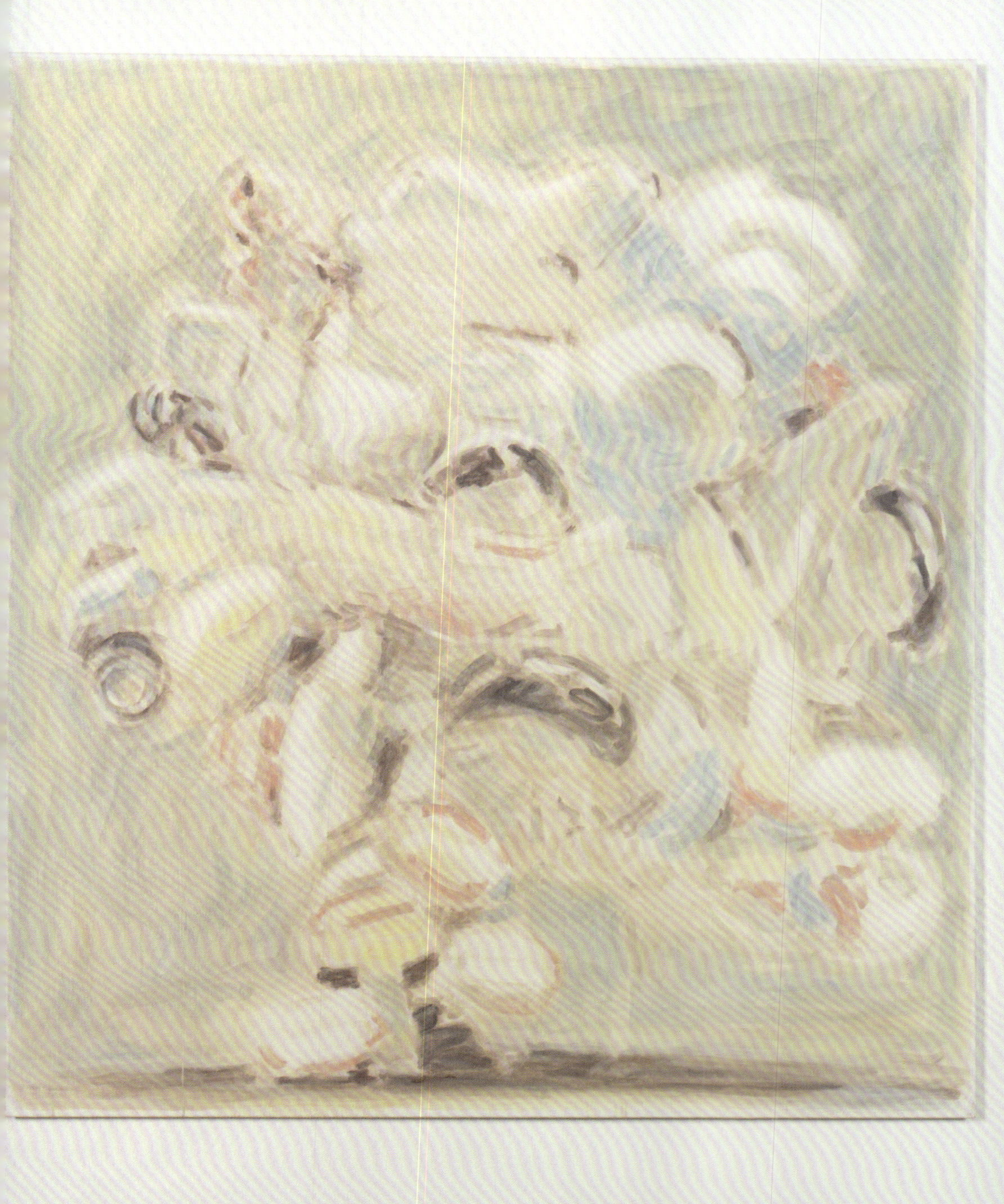

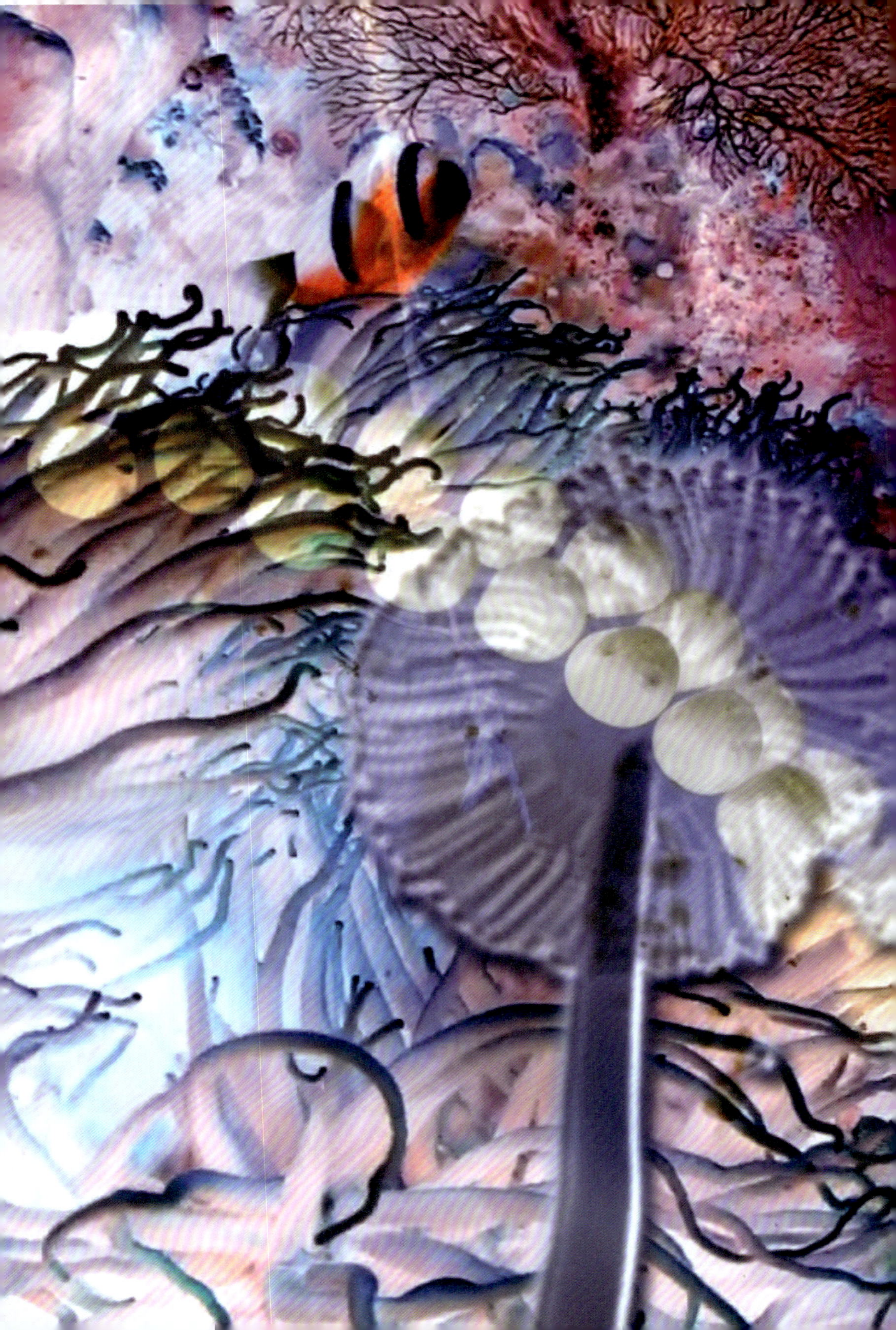

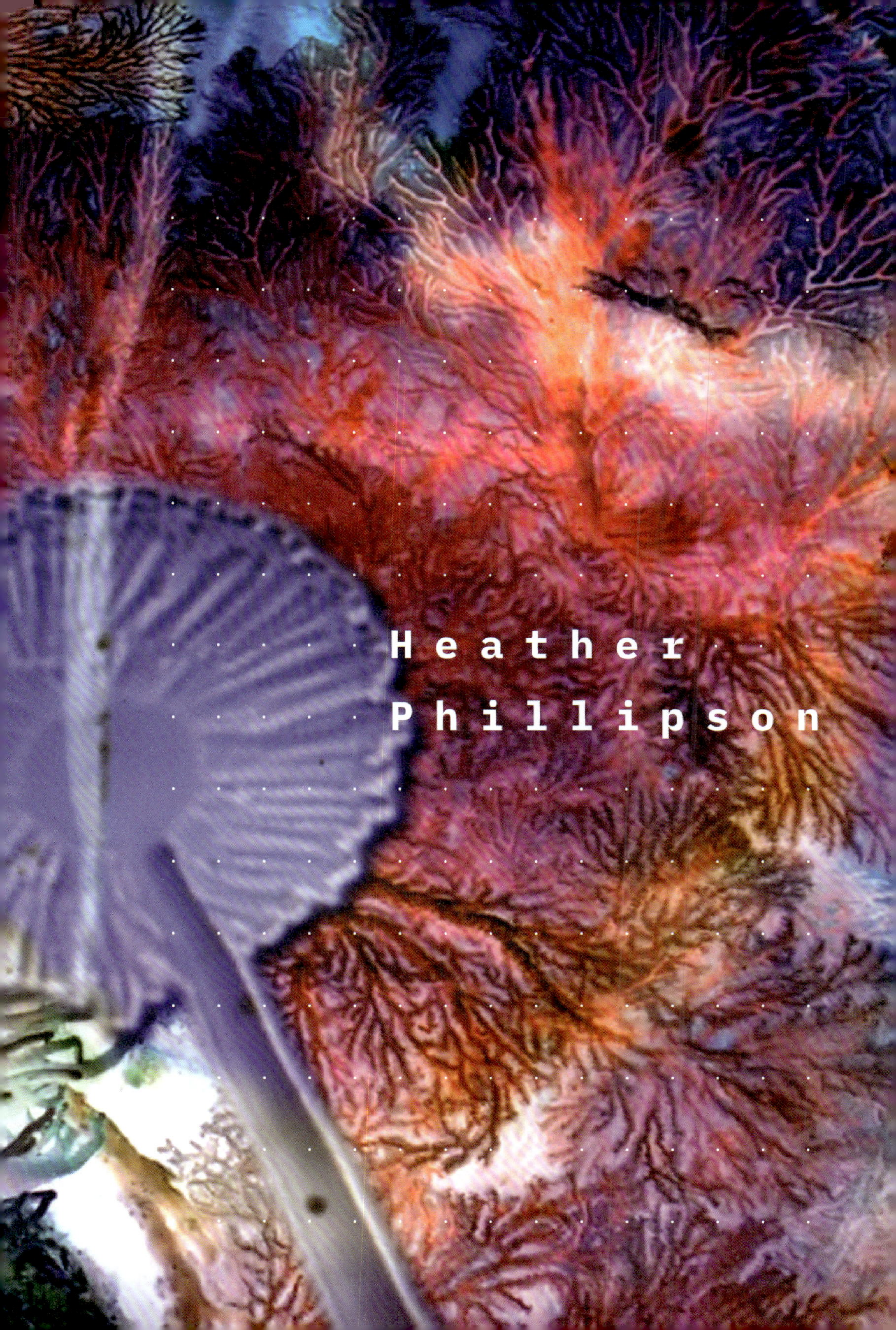
Heather
Phillipson

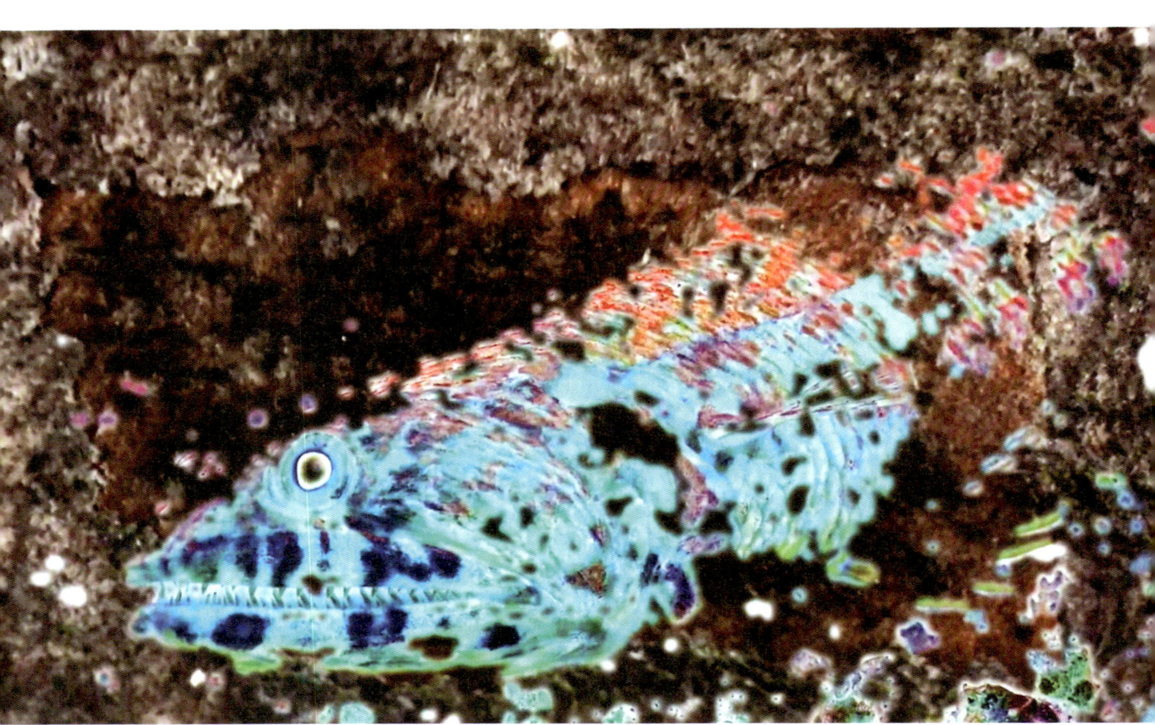

Cyclonic Palate Cleanser
2019
Still from multi-screen video
Image courtesy of the artist

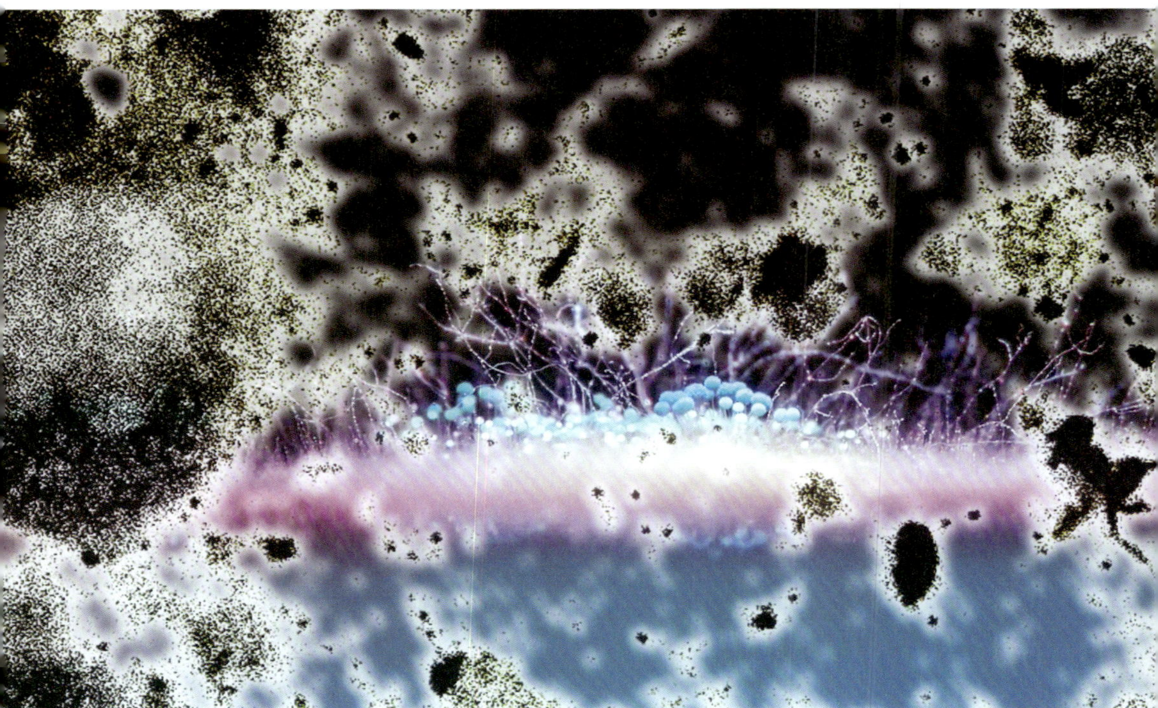

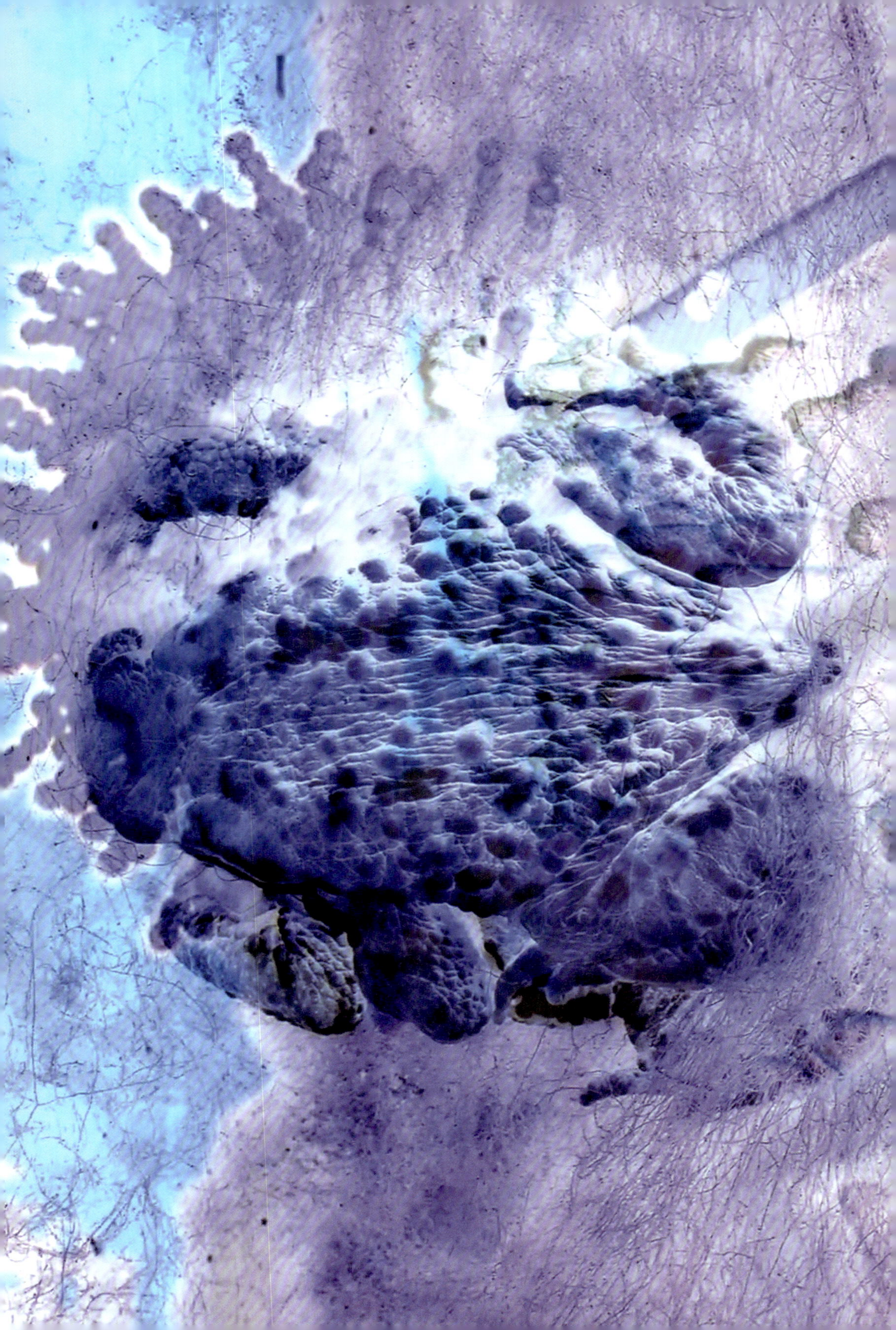

b. 1978, London, UK; lives and works in London
Commissioned by Sharjah Art Foundation

Heather Phillipson is a poet and an artist who uses a wide variety of media to reflect on the emotions that we experience every day. Inflected with a wry sense of humour, her work asks political questions about the state of consciousness that has emerged in the present era. In her new commission, *Cyclonic Palette Cleanser* (2019), the artist creates contrasting climates using Bait Al Makrani's parallel spaces. Conceived as two regions – one hot and dry, the other cold and moist – both rooms are inhabited by lumpen and molten forms. The artist explores what grows and dies in the heat and what thrives or becomes extinct in the cold. Adopting a texture and tone of 'roughness, excreting, dripping, melting and spreading', Phillipson's sculptural forms are accompanied by a series of crescendoing video loops. The courtyard itself, in turn, develops into a 'palette cleanser' – a breather for inhalation and exhalation. This in-between site, however, where warmth and damp meet, transforms into a breeding ground for mould, which is associated with respiratory and immune problems, and is therefore called the 'sick building syndrome'. As such, black mould becomes a recurring interloper, creeping across the spaces and making them both sickly bodies. Bait Al Makrani thus morphs into a triptych of atmospheres that meet and discharge in the middle.

Cyclonic Palate Cleanser
2019
Still from multi-screen video
Image courtesy of the artist

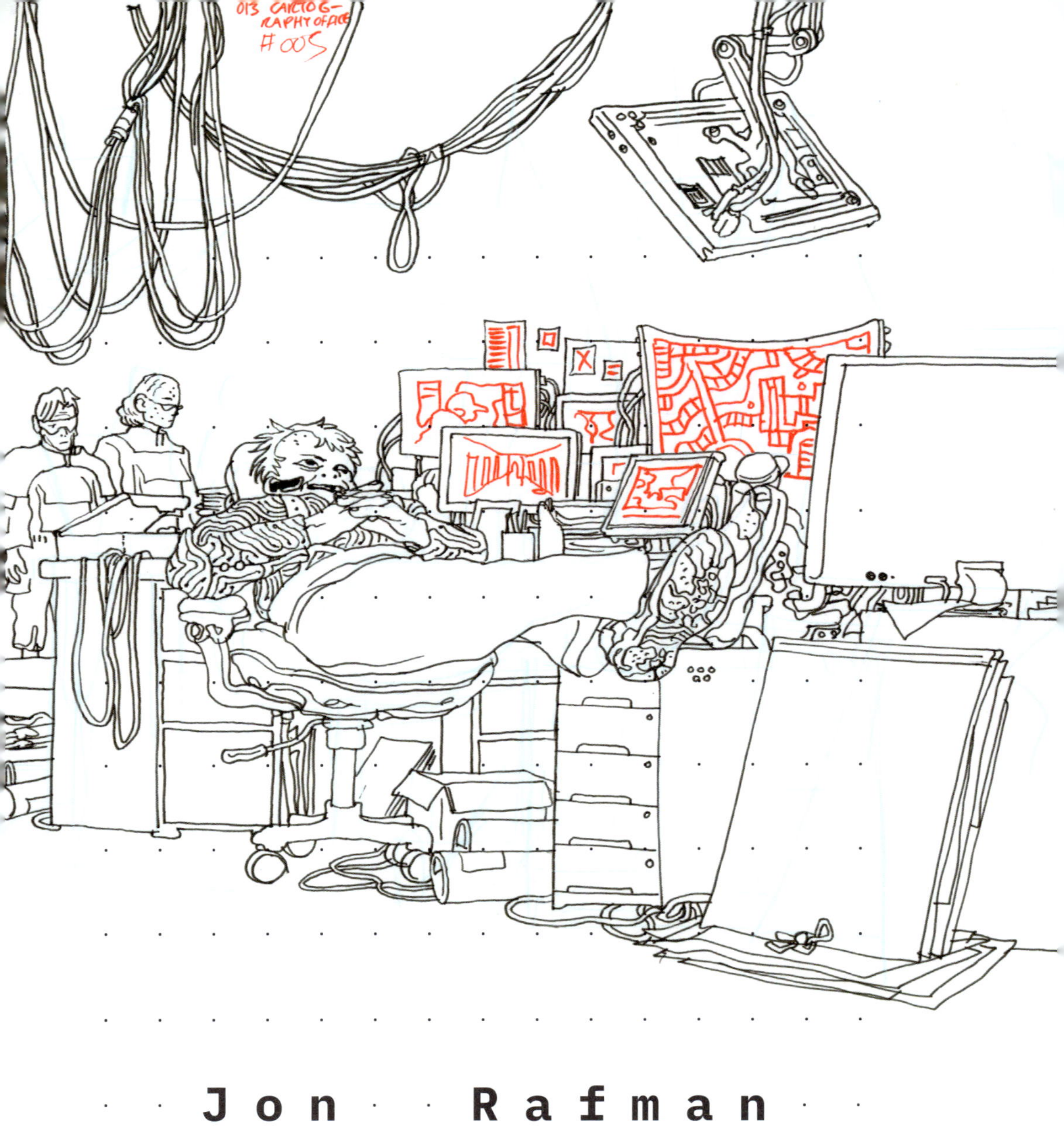

Jon Rafman

b. 1981, Montreal, Canada; lives and works in Montreal
Commissioned by Sharjah Art Foundation with the support of Canada Council for the Arts

In his sculptures, videos and immersive installations, Jon Rafman explores the paradoxes of post-modernity. His work highlights the impact that hyper-accelerated late-capitalist existence has on the human psyche.

Jon Rafman's Sharjah Biennial 14 commission, the illustrated scroll *Punctured Sky* (2019), created in collaboration with comic book artist Connor Willumsen, follows Penelope, a young woman held captive by a violent dog-worshipping organization that is part American college fraternity and part 1970s-inspired death cult. The group forces Penelope, alongside its other captives, to participate in horrific hazing ceremonies. Pushed to desperation by these grotesque rituals, Penelope escapes and traverses a wasteland, ending up in a cyberpunk megalopolis. She begins a mysterious new job as cartographer that sends her to the farthest reaches of this vast city. Penelope soon questions whether she has exchanged one hell for another, as the endless urban sprawl turns out to be an inescapable ever-expanding living entity.

Punctured Sky
2019
Mixed Media
Dimensions variable
Illustrations by Connor Willumsen

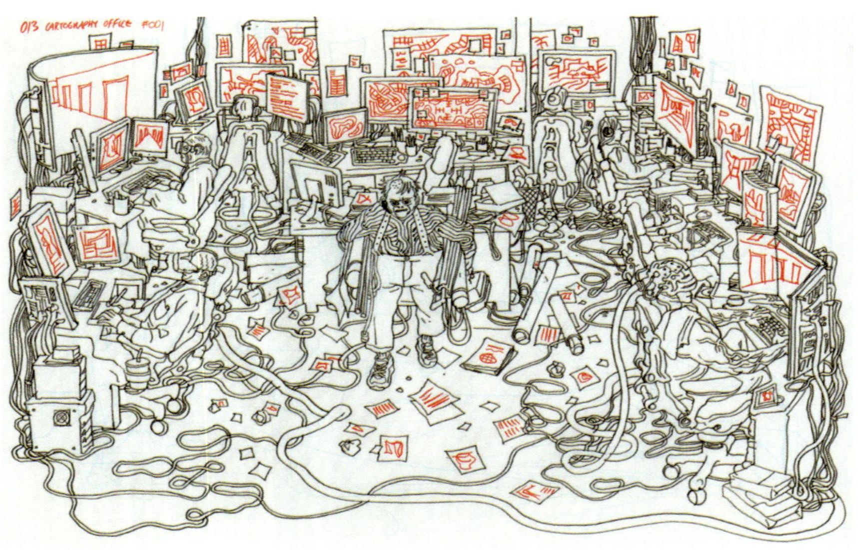
013 CARTOGRAPHY OFFICE #001

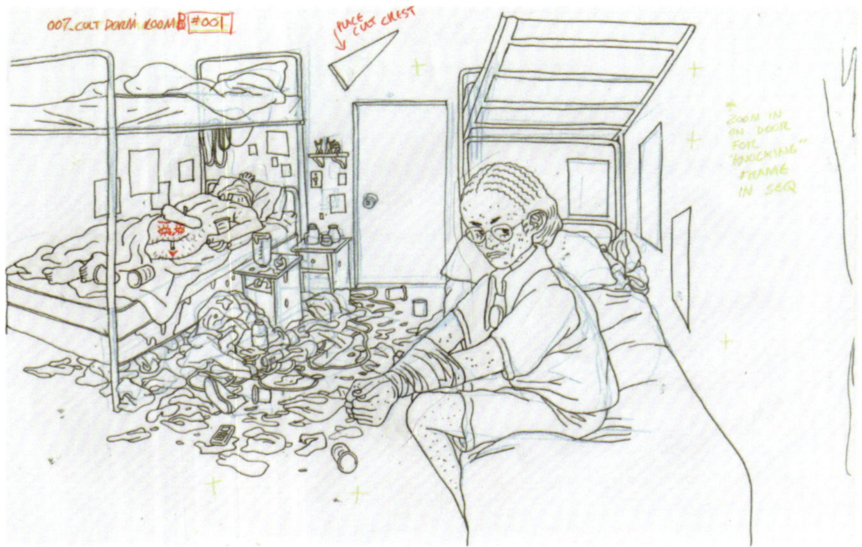
007_CULT DORM ROOM B #001
PLACE CULT CREST
ZOOM IN ON DOOR FOR "KNOCKING" FRAME IN SEQ

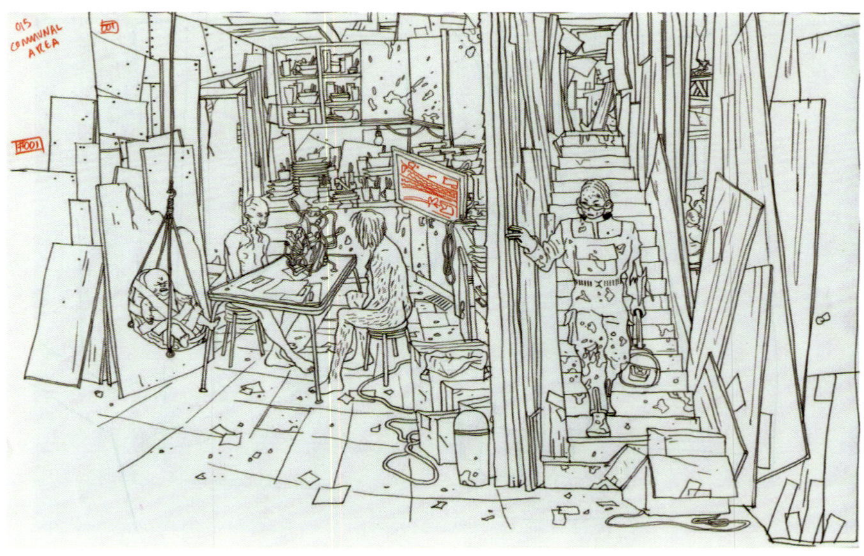

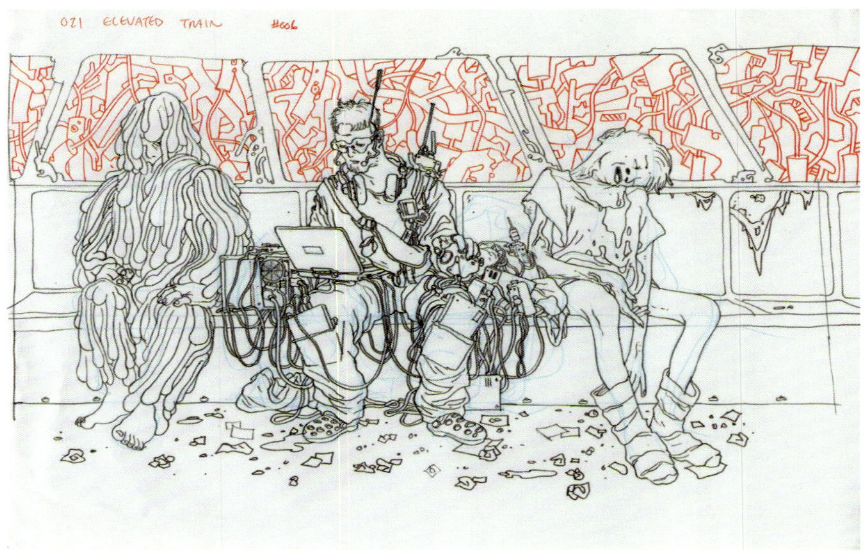

Punctured Sky
2019
Mixed Media
Dimensions variable
Illustrations by Connor Willumsen

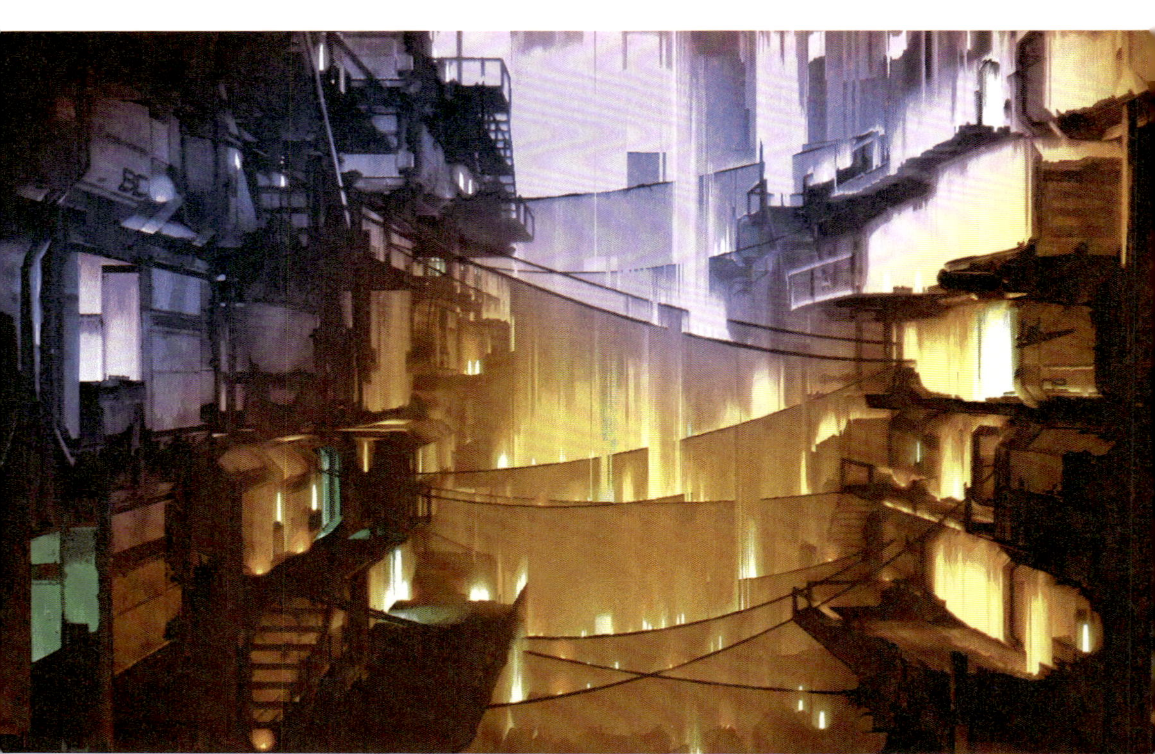

Legendary Reality
2017
Single-channel video
Runtime 15:43 min

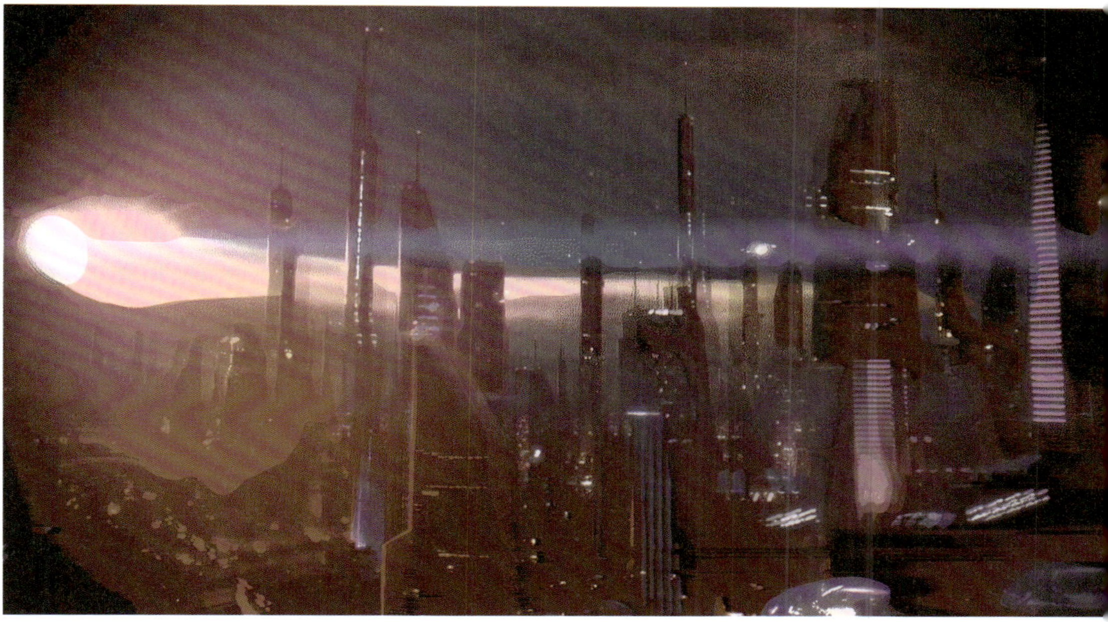

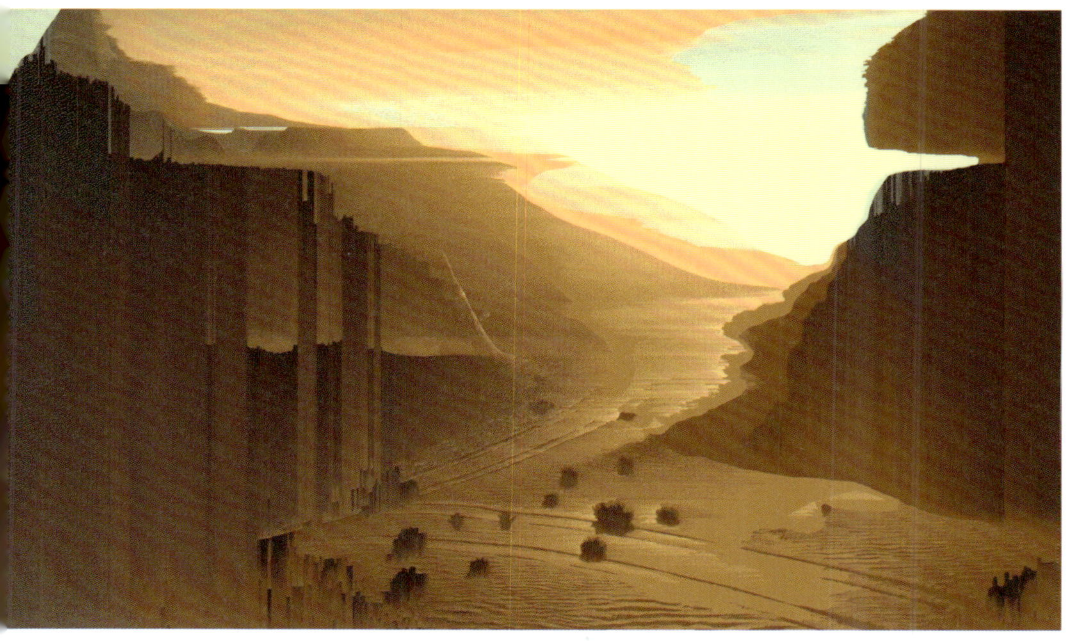

Michael Rakowitz

G.I. 'HOSTAGE' IS A REAL DOLL

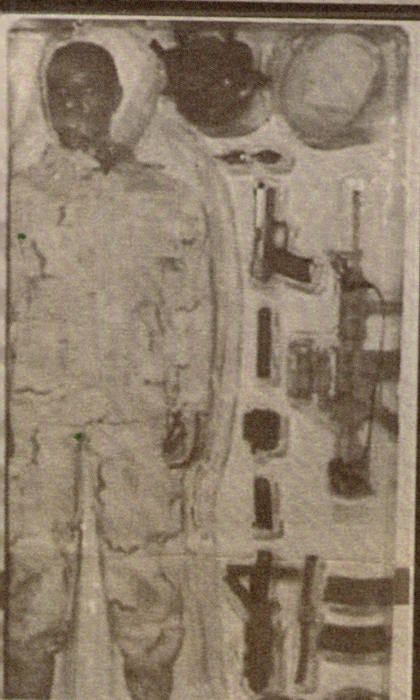

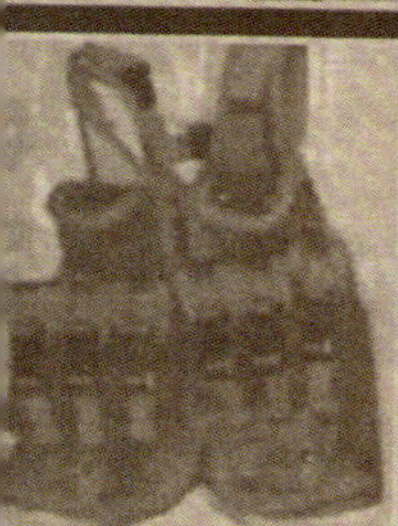

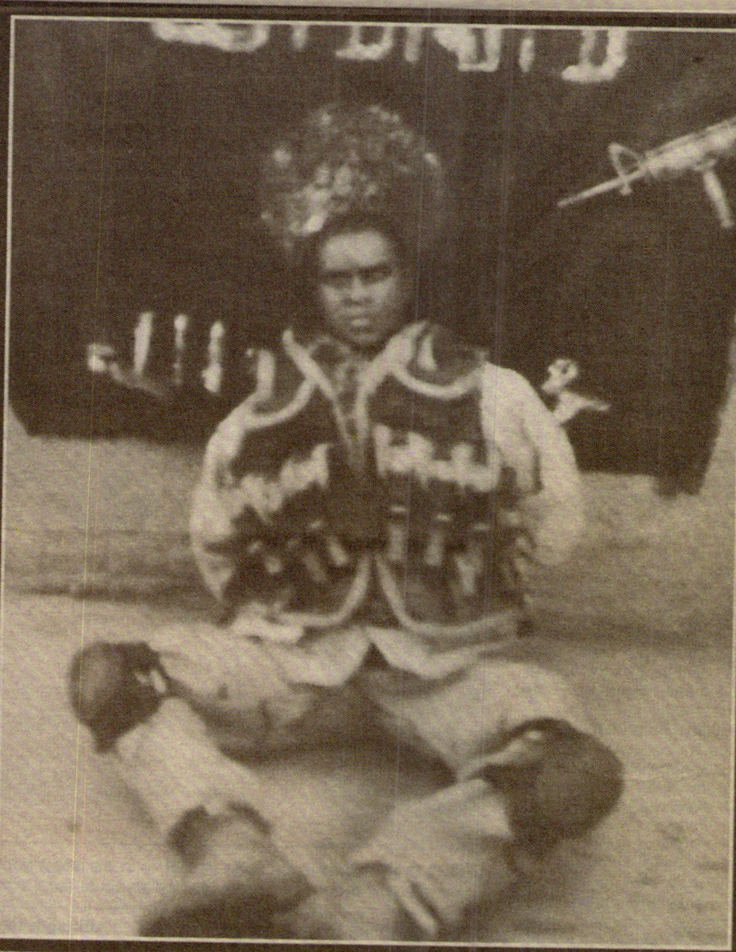

DUMMY: The "hostage GI" proudly displayed on a terrorist Web site turns out to be "Cody" the action figure (above and left), complete with toy gun aimed at his head.

aq kidnap 'victim' a toy soldier

NILES LATHEM
t Correspondent

HINGTON — Mas- orist Abu Musab al- , meet your new — "Cody" the ac- re.

wake of historic s and top-level ter- called the Mujahedeen Squadrons on the terrorist group Ansar al-Islam's Web site.

A photo on the site appeared to show an African-American soldier sitting on a floor with a gun pointed at his head in front of a banner with the

as being one of their popular action figures — called "Cody." It's sold on U.S. military bases in Kuwait.

"It is our doll. To me, it definitely looks like it is," said Dragon Models spokesman Liam Cusak.

"Everything the guy is

bility for at least two other kidnappings. In this instance, they threatened to cut off the soldier's head in 72 hours if male and female prisoners were not released from U.S. prisons.

But military officials quickly realized that no soldiers were missing

terrorism expert Rita Katz, who studies Islamic extremist Web sites.

Meanwhile, Iraqi President Ghazi al-Yawer said yesterday that it's too soon to start talking about the withdrawal of real American soldiers from Iraq, de-

b. 1973, New York, USA; lives and works in Chicago

Michael Rakowitz explores recent contested social, political and cultural histories. Drawing on his experience of growing up with an Iraqi mother and an American father, the artist has developed a body of work that delves into history and popular culture, often using his own family's biography as a starting point. His illustrated objects, installations and interventions invite viewers to contemplate their complicit relationship to the political world around them, recognising that hospitality and hostility are interlinked. In his film *The Ballad of Special Ops Cody* (2017), Rakowitz tells the peculiar tale of an American soldier named John Adam, who has been captured by an Islamic religious group that predates ISIS. However, on close investigation, it turns out that the protagonist is none other than Special Ops

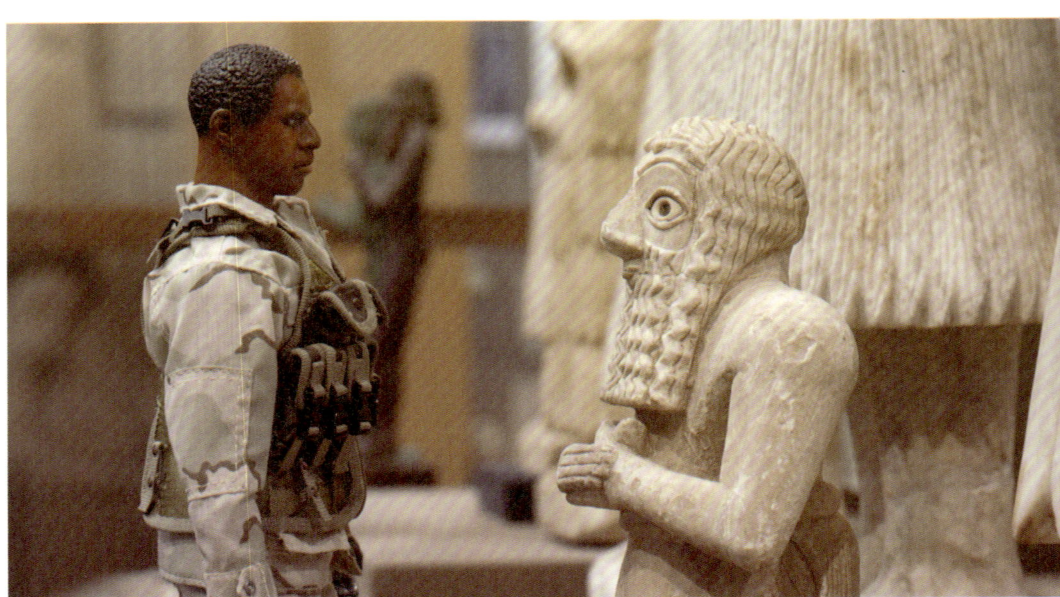

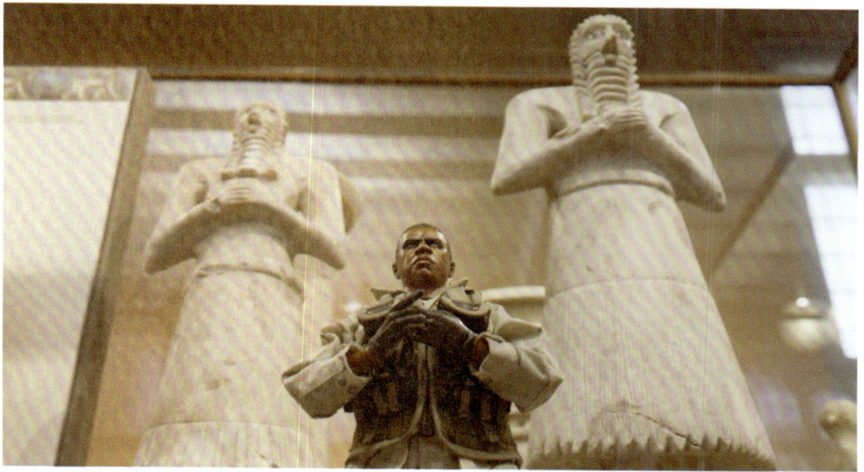

The Ballad of Special Ops Cody
2017
Video stills
Courtesy of the artist, Al Ma'mal Foundation for Contemporary Art, Jerusalem, and Contemporary Art Museum Palestine.

Cody, a souvenir action figure depicting a US infantryman. Rendered in exacting detail in both African American and Caucasian likenesses, the toys were available for sale exclusively on US Army bases in Kuwait and Iraq, and were often sent home, as a kind of surrogate, to children whose fathers were fighting in the war. Rakowitz obtained one of these dolls for this hoax and rendered it alive through a stop-motion animation movie filmed at the Oriental Institute at the University of Chicago, an institution that has had a relationship with the National Museum of Iraq since it was founded in the 1930s. In Rakowitz's film, Special Ops Cody enters the Oriental Institute's vitrines that hold Mesopotamian votive statues taken by the West. The ancient works represent another kind of hostage: one meant to be left behind as a surrogate by worshippers visiting temples, praying eternally with hands clasped in the visitors' stead after they left the sanctuary of their deities. The film is voiced by an American female Iraq War veteran who embodies Cody with life.

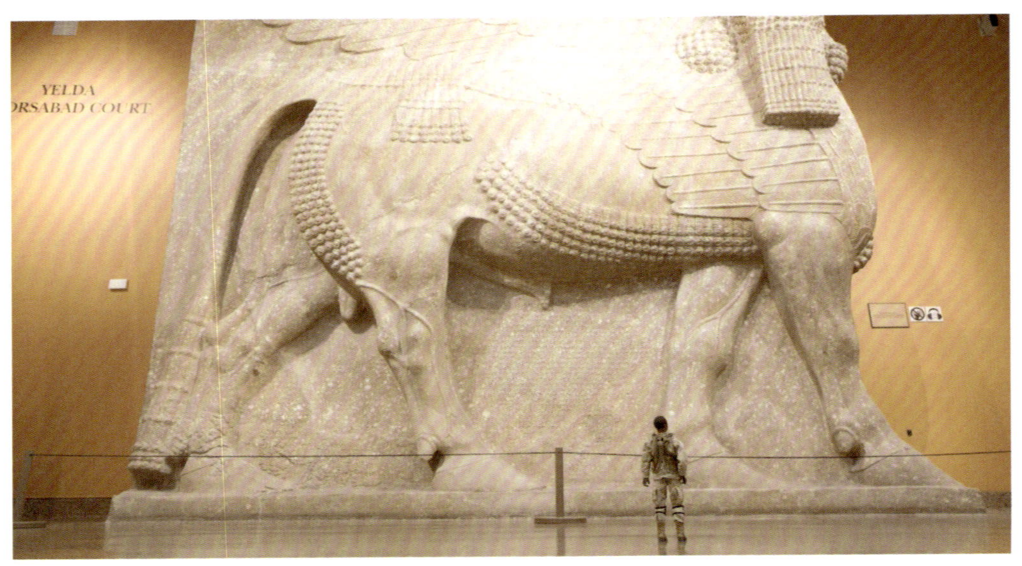
YELDA

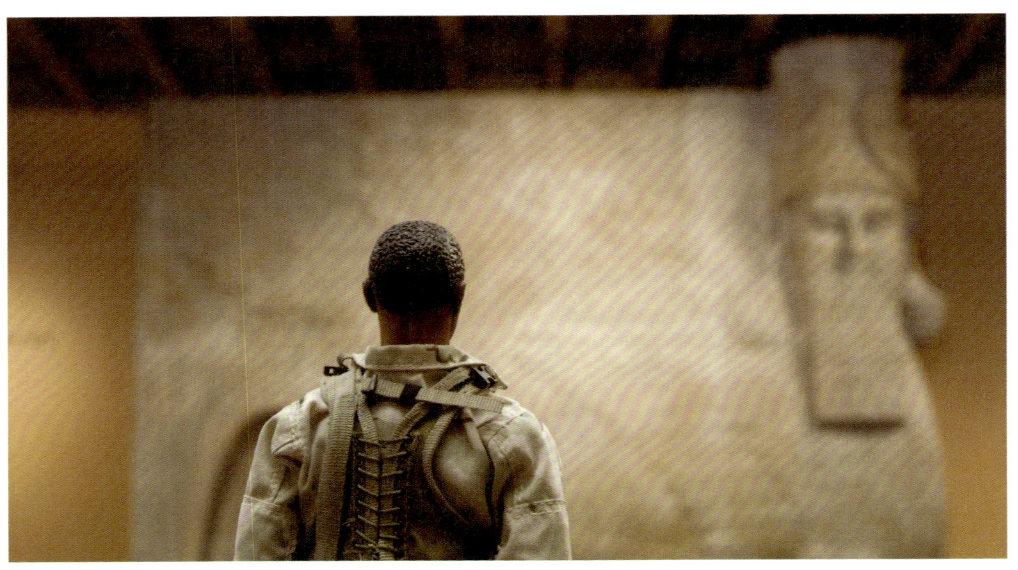

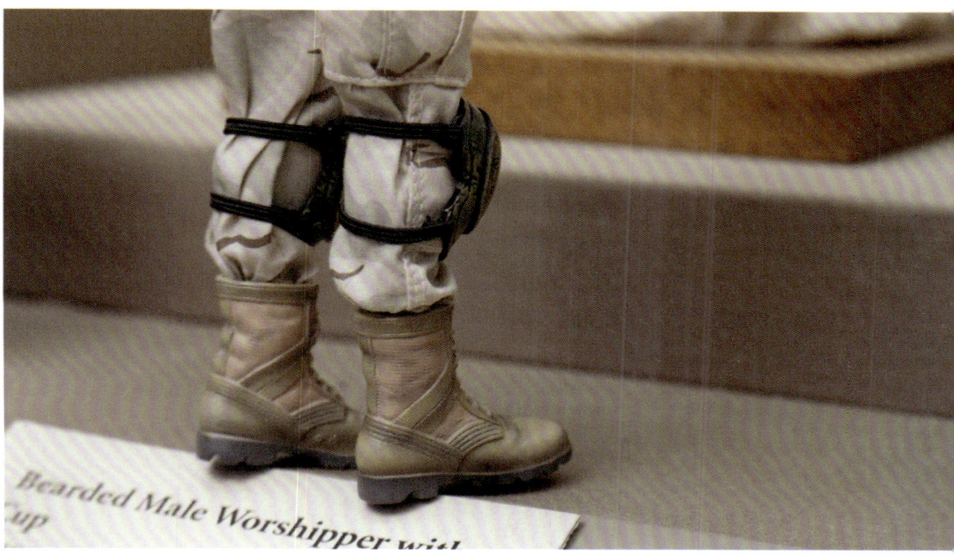

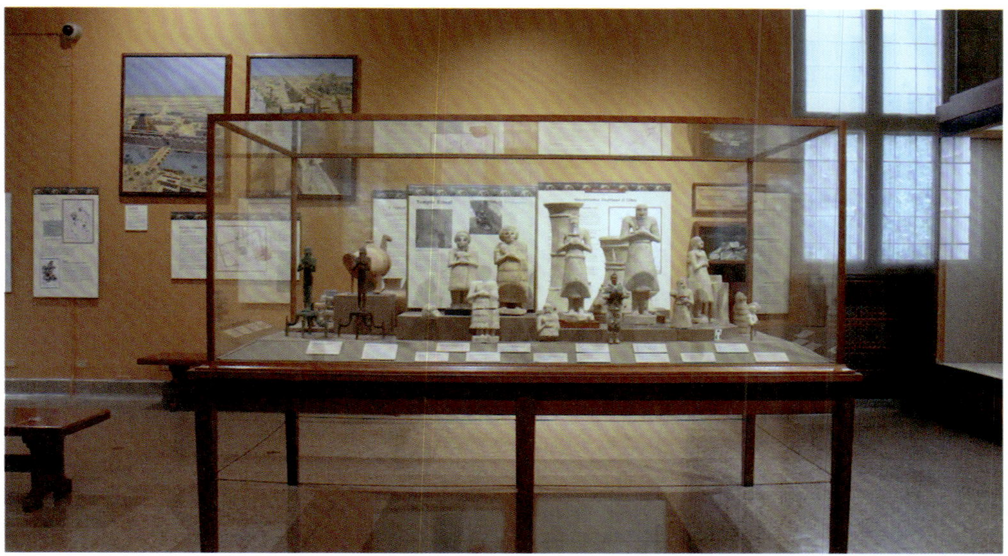

The Ballad of Special Ops Cody
2017
Video stills
Courtesy of the artist, Al Ma'mal Foundation for Contemporary Art, Jerusalem, and Contemporary Art Museum Palestine.

P a m e l a

R o s e n k r a n z

b. 1979, Uri, Switzerland; lives and works in Zurich
Commissioned by Sharjah Art Foundation
Supported by Pro Helvetia and Stiftung Erna und curt Burgauer.

Pamela Rosenkranz melds a multiplicity of materials that stem from the high-tech, consumer and pharmaceutical industries. Her work primarily reflects how science transforms the meaning of humanity as well as the relationship between nature and culture. The artist presents *Healer* (2019), a new commission in which an algorithmic snake lives, breathes, sleeps and dreams in the sun-drenched courtyard of Sharjah's Bait Al Serkal. Rosenkranz's immersive installation combines the most recent advancements in biorobotics with the far-reaching symbolic power of the snake. The project grew out of her research interest in the field of robotics, referencing 'snakebots', whose capabilities vary in size and range. Some are small enough for surgical means; others undertake search-and-rescue missions; large ones conduct scientific research in contaminated areas and perform deep-water tasks, such as maintaining oil-drilling platforms. The snakebot in *Healer* is defined by three main criteria: its locomotion resembles that of a real snake, it bears the visual appearance of a snake that has transformed into a robot and it is programmable to mimic 'natural' behaviour. In the Fertile Crescent, the earliest written documents tell of the deep-rooted connection we share with this animal. Symbolising the essence of the origins of the world in Babylon and ancient Egypt, the beginning and the end of time, the snake spans the history of human existence, connecting the present world with the past. The snake is both a harbinger – a representative of the divine in the course of cultural evolution – and a technical tool from which to learn. In times of rapidly advancing technology, the snake's fatal weapon, its venom, has been reappropriated as a life force. Yet the reptile's exceptional ability to survive can also be interpreted as a symbol of future catastrophic events that point to a time after human existence. In Sharjah, the snake thus becomes an anthropomorphic creature that acts as a metaphor for healing in the broadest sense.

Healer
2019
Research material for concept genesis
Courtesy of the artist

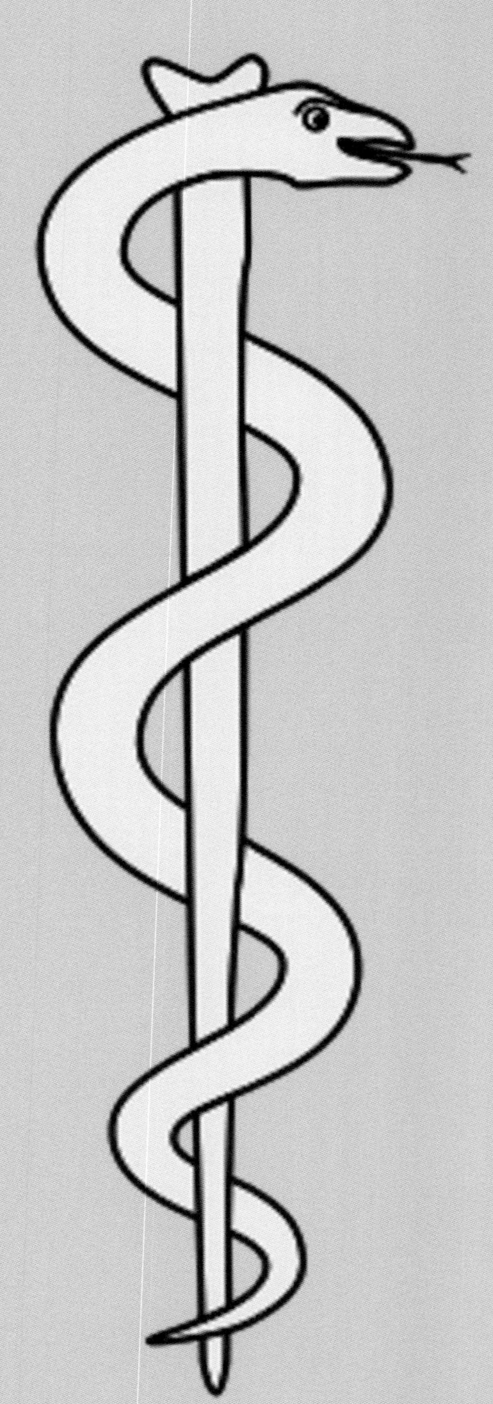

Hrair

Sarkissian

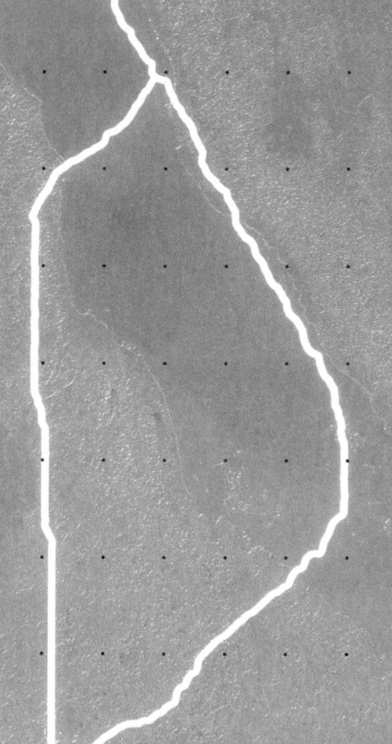

b. 1973, Damascus, Syria; lives and works in London, UK

Hrair Sarkissian works with photography, video, sculpture and installation to reveal the hidden facets of life, especially those specific to the Middle East. Often employing documentary techniques, his photographs and sculptures are eloquent expressions of a hidden paradox that exists between beauty and the concealed violence of specific surroundings.

In *Final Flight* (2018–19), the artist examines the northern bald ibis, one of the rarest birds in the world. After having been declared extinct from the wild in 1989, a surviving colony of seven was discovered in 2002, with help from the local Bedouin population, in the Syrian Desert near Palmyra. They were the last-known living descendants of the ibises depicted 5,200 years ago in rock inscriptions containing some of the oldest Egyptian monumental hieroglyphs ever unearthed. The tiny new colony was intensively studied and protected until war broke out in Syria; it then disappeared again, around the time Palmyra was destroyed in 2014. Here, Sarkissian presents a series of seven skulls of northern bald ibises, along with an aluminium map representing their winter migration path from Syria to Ethiopia. The skulls are 3-D printed facsimiles of a specimen preserved in, and lent by, an ornithologist in Southern Spain.

Horizon (2016) traces one of the shortest and therefore most popular refugee sea routes: from Kaş, on the south-western shore of Turkey, across the Mycale Strait, to the island of Megisti on the south-eastern edge of Greece. The sea is a place where visions are born, memories appear and landmarks disappear. Although this route is one of the shortest in terms of distance, it is also the beginning of a longer journey into the unknown. Capturing this path across the Mediterranean from above, Sarkissian evokes the danger that refugees face when surrounded by water; he thus also shows the dark, mysterious and unpredictable depths of the sea. Only uncertainty accompanies the migrants, as they hold on to just one line: the horizon. This line divides the blues of the water and the sky, the up and the down. It illustrates how close the future is, and provides a starting point

Final Flight
2018
Milled relief on aluminium plate
125 x 230 x 0.6 cm
Courtesy of the artist

for building hopes and dreams – a refuge for escaping the darkness of the present, whilst holding on to the memories of the past. Once the water has been crossed, the experience of the sea is no longer the same. Two-channel video, HD; 6 min., 58 sec.

Residue (2019) is based on a pile of gelatin silver negatives [1] that Sarkissian discovered a few years ago in the corner of a second-hand photography shop in Damascus. Stuffed in a dusty white plastic bag swung on a tripod, they were hidden from sight, waiting to rot from neglect. To the shopkeeper, they were 'rubbish'; for the artist, they comprised a treasure trove. These negatives date from the 1950s to the 1970s, and form part of a photographic archive compiled by an anonymous photographer. The images are studio portraits, mostly of women, but there are also depictions of men. Some of them show signs of fading and aging, from having been kept without any care; but others managed to survive and withstand the test of time. Perhaps these images are not unique in their photographic quality, but the individuals depicted in them certainly are. The subjects do not tell us much about themselves, but they hint at the world they created and the time in which they lived. Overall, the characteristics of an era that has evaporated from the present prevail in these works. They also tell us something about our own world, and ask questions about the future. For *Residue*, Sarkissian selected one image out of the pile: a head-and-shoulder portrait of a woman in the prime of her life, looking far into the unknown, not realising that one day in the future her image might be within our gaze. The artist scanned this image (original size: 9 x 12 cm) with a 3-D scanner and recreated it in exactly the same proportions, but significantly enlarged (approximately two metres high), keeping the exact same deteriorated texture of both the front and back surfaces. When looking at this woman, the viewer is distracted by the deterioration of the gelatin layer, with its scratches and dusty surface. These elements prevent us from seeing the photograph's subject and force us either to excavate more details from within the image, or to let our imaginations wander. They also make us look at the work's wounded surface and see the loss – not just of the life – of this particular woman. We also witness the loss of the time in which she lived; not with nostalgia, but with the awareness of what our shared future holds: the wounds of what has become of her world today.

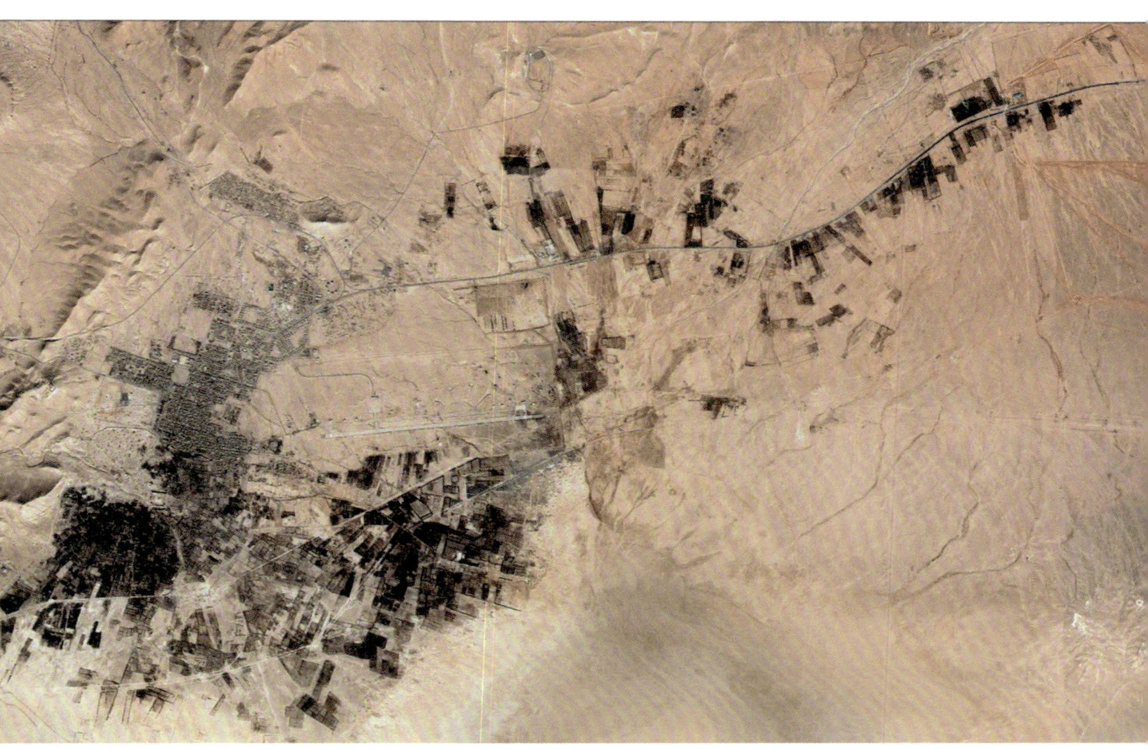

Final Flight
2018
Courtesy of the artist

1 A gelatin silver negative on film is a negative on a plastic film support – either cellulose nitrate, cellulose acetate or polyester – with a layer of gelatin holding silver particles that form the image. The sensitised film is manufactured in standard camera formats, either as multiple-image rolls or as single-image sheets.

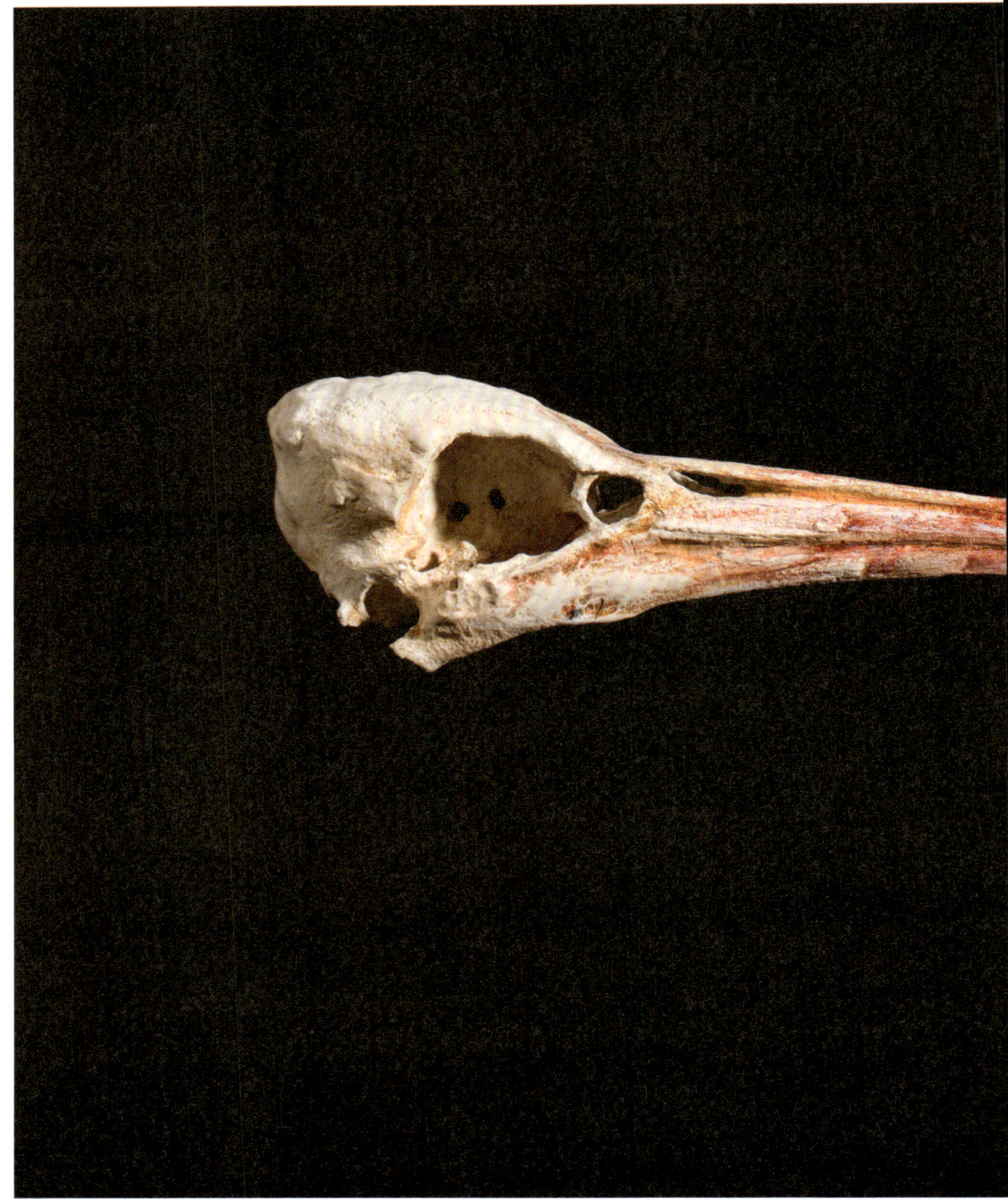

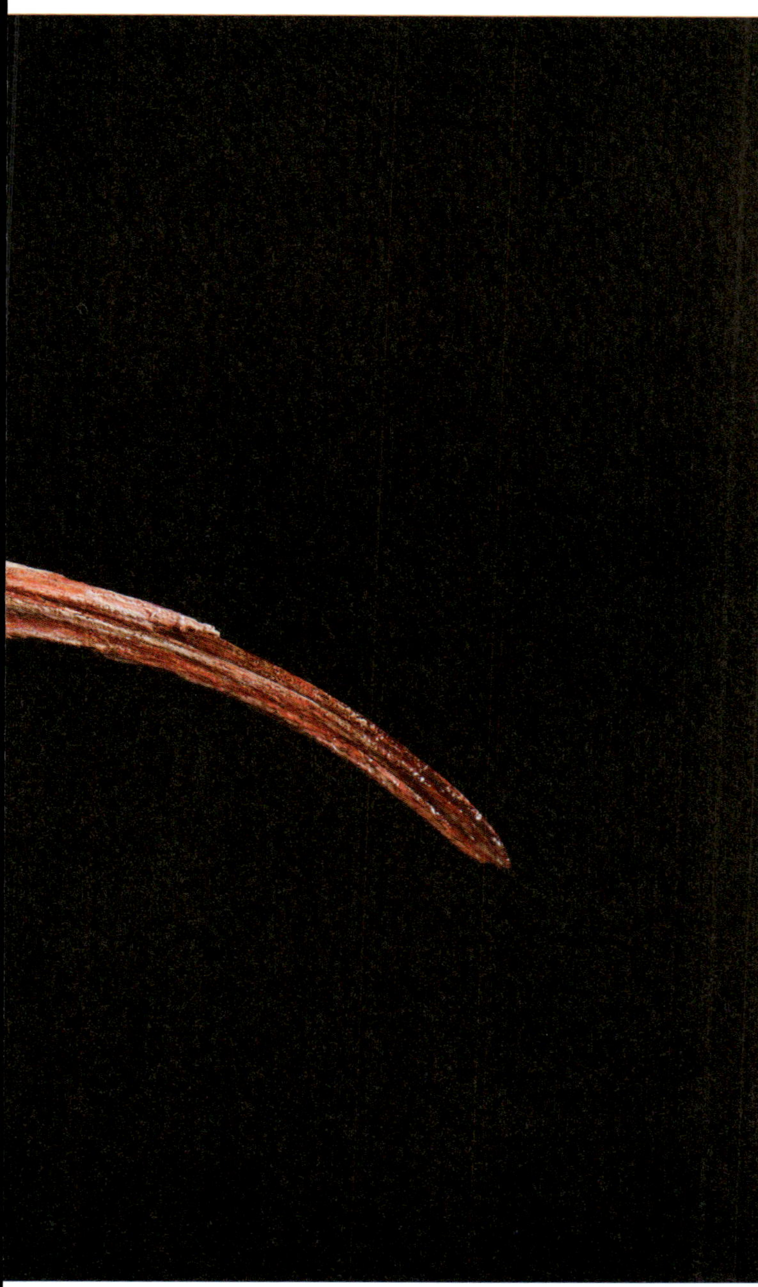

Final Flight
2018
Hand painted resin/bone cast
of a 3D-model skull
26 x 6 x 5 cm
Courtesy of the artist

Anwar Jalal Shemza

Abstract Writing
1965
Pyrography on wood
104 x 77 cm
Courtesy and copyright the
Estate of Anwar Jalal Shemza

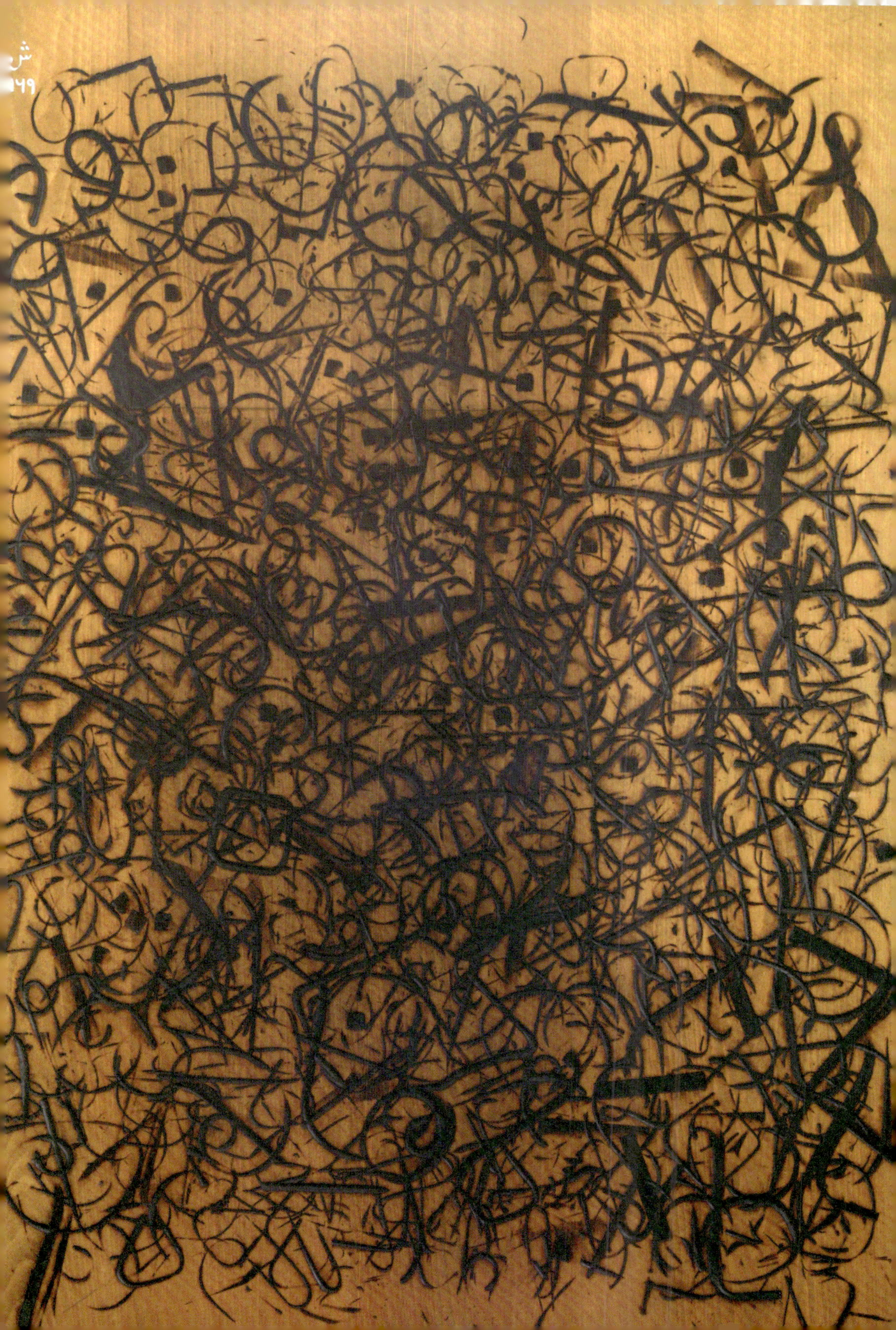
ش
١٦٩

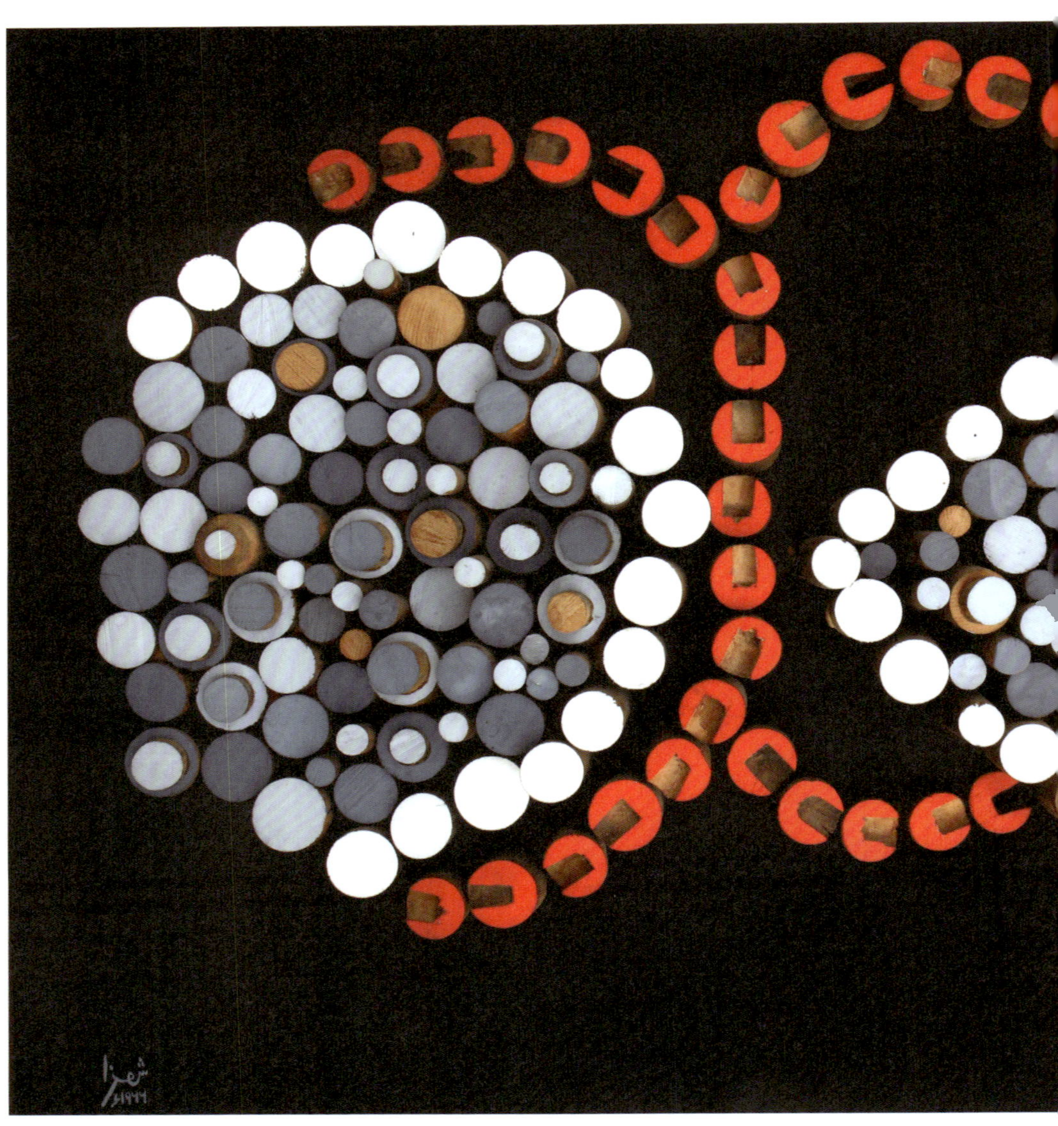

Untitled
1966
Wood on chipboard and matt emulsion paint
61 x 76 cm
Courtesy and copyright the Estate of Anwar Jalal Shemza

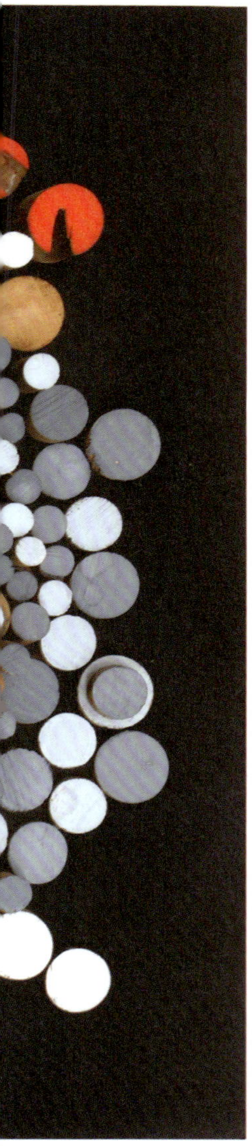

b. 1928, Simla, India; d. 1985, United Kingdom

Born to Kashmiri and Punjabi parents, Anwar Jalal Shemza attended the Mayo School of Art in Lahore, Pakistan. By 1956, he was an established artist and writer in the country, when he relocated to the United Kingdom to study at London's Slade School of Fine Art. This move marked a significant change in his life and practice. Flabbergasted by a statement by famed art historian E. H. Gombrich – who characterised Islamic art as purely 'functional' in a lecture attended by Shemza – the artist abandoned his previous work and embarked on a journey to create a dramatically different style and visual language. The bold abstractions in this suite of works represent this pivotal development for the artist, whose diasporic perspective allowed him to explore modernism through the double prism of Islamic and Western aesthetics. Throughout his career, Shemza's visual vocabulary drew on an array of deeply studied and lived experiences, from carpet patterns and calligraphic forms to the environments around him; from the Mughal architecture of Lahore to the rural landscapes of Stafford in England. In the formalist compositions of the artworks exhibited, these layered elements are distilled into an intensive exploration of geometric abstraction and pattern, built up mostly using just two simple forms: the square and the circle. As Shemza once wrote – inscribed in Urdu script on the surface of another painting from this period, yet incredibly relevant here – 'One circle, one square, one problem, one life is not enough to solve it' (*One to Nine and One to Seven*, 1962).

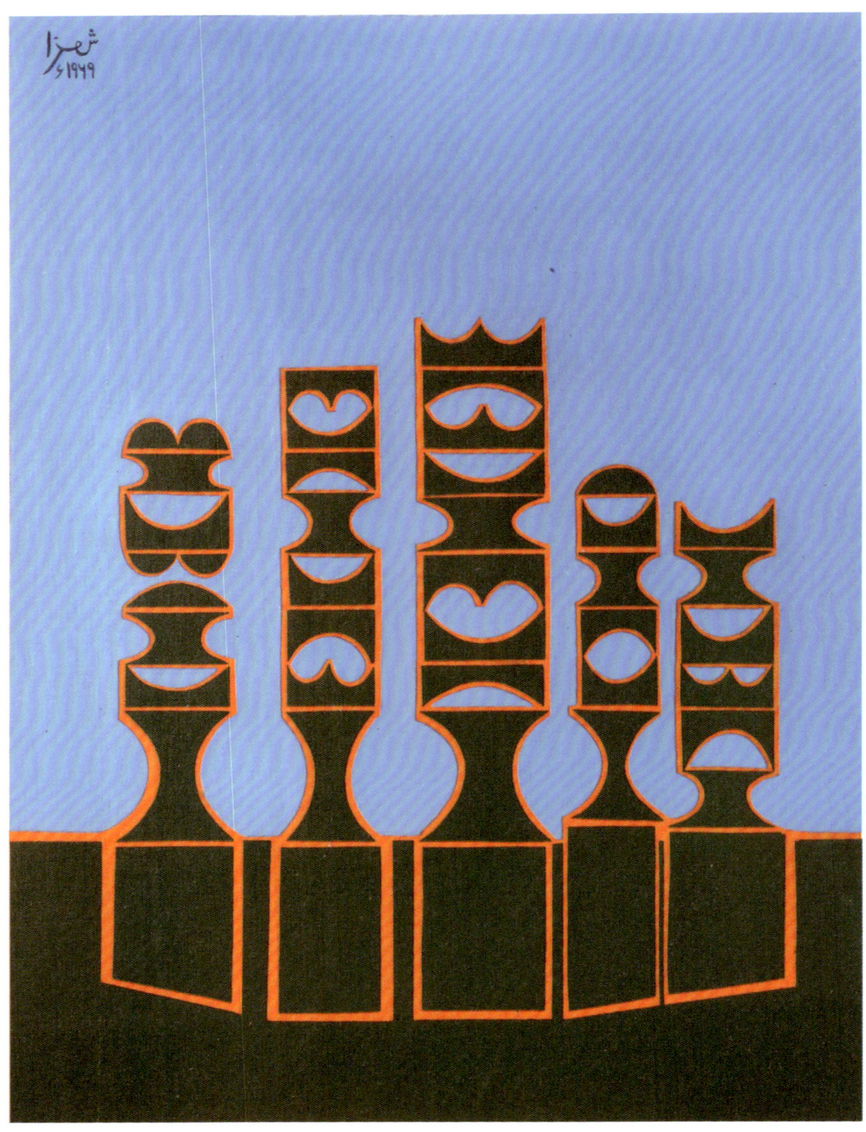

Chessmen
1969
Oil on silkscreen and cotton cloth
60 x 46 cm
Courtesy and copyright the Estate of Anwar Jalal Shemza

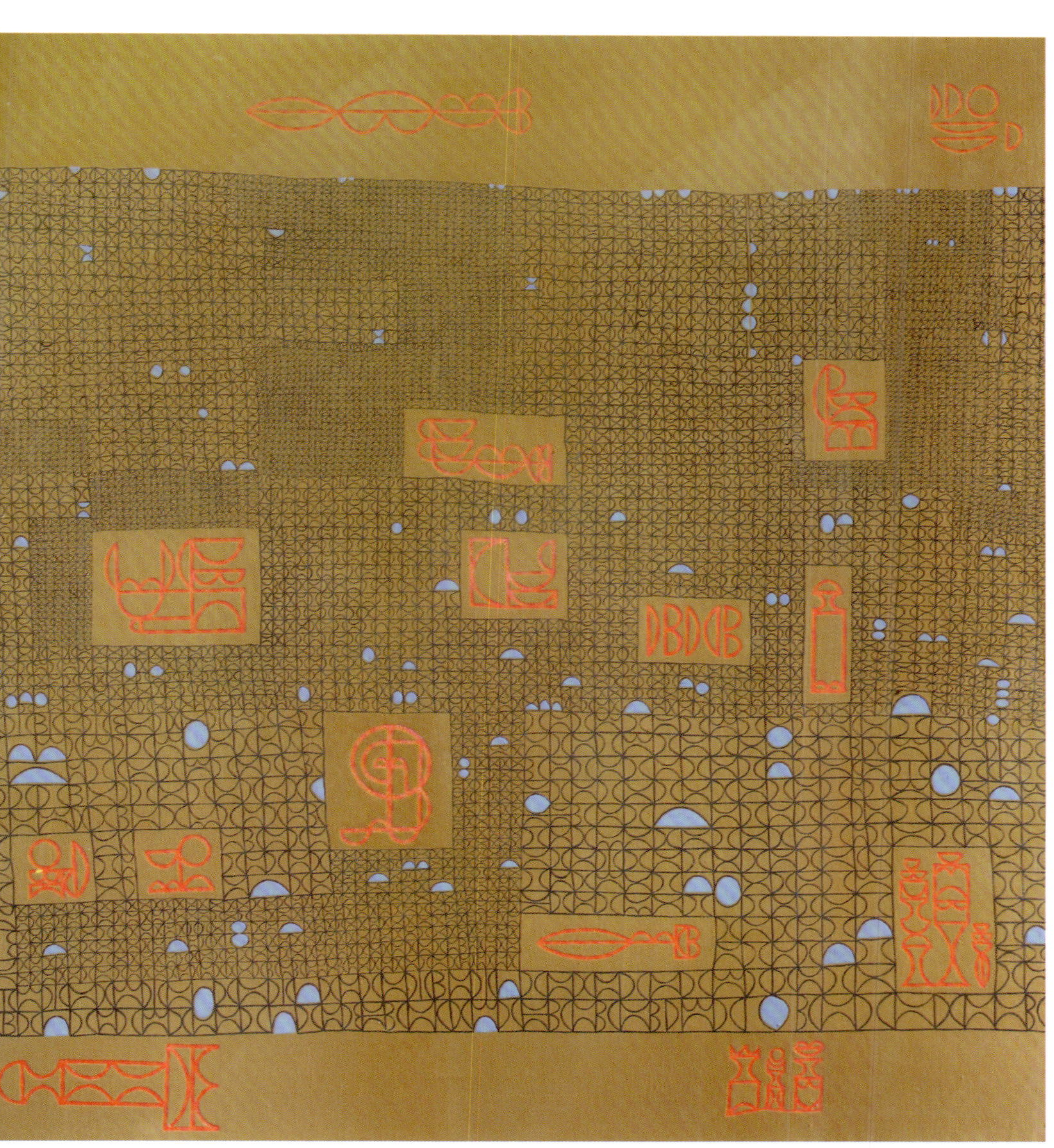

Love Letter 2
1969
Oil on canvas
91.5 x 91 cm
Courtesy and copyright the
Estate of Anwar Jalal Shemza

Kemang Wa Lehulere

b. 1984, Cape Town; lives and works in Cape Town

In a self-described 'protest against forgetting', Kemang Wa Lehulere exhibits a conceptual conversation between himself and self-taught South African artist Gladys Mgudlandlu (ca. 1920–1979), the first black woman to stage regular gallery exhibitions under apartheid. She frequently painted birds, and was thus known as the 'Bird Lady'.

Wa Lehulere uses collaboration, reinterpretation, re-presentation and quotation as artistic modes to investigate recent history and events receding in collective memory. He works to materialise these narratives through his sculptures, drawings and videos, pinpointing individual occurrences and personal accounts to reveal and situate the tensions between national history and national subject.

My Apologies to Time (2016) is wrought from old school desks that Wa Lehulere converted into birdhouses and connected through an interlacing system of steel pipes. The African grey parrot central to the composition is known for its ability to mimic not only human speech, but also the calls of other animals. This ability to repeat while lacking the faculty to understand reflects the tendency of institutions of learning to function as ideological instruments of conditioning rather than foundations for critical thought. Birdhouses, often simultaneously protective breeding sites and domestic cages, offer commentary on the friction between safety and imprisonment.

For *Does this mirror have a memory* (2015), Wa Lehulere asked Sophia Lehulere, his aunt who had visited Gladys Mgudlandlu's house as a child, to draw Mgudlandlu's paintings from memory. In a roving statement on collectivity, Wa Lehulere juxtaposes his aunt's chalk representations with original works by Mgudlandlu, which he purchased at auction.
Homeless Song #3: The Bird Lady in Nine Layers of Time (2015) foregrounds the act of excavation. Wa Lehulere documents the chipping away of paint and plaster to uncover murals painted by Mgudlandlu at her house in

Homeless Song 3: the bird lady in 9 layers of time
2015
Digital video
Duration 9 min 57 sec
Courtesy of Stevenson, Cape Town and Johannesburg

Photo: Mario Todeschini

Gugulethu. The discovery is not just a revelation, but a visualised metaphor for how black artists were historically sidelined and, later, forgotten.

Wa Lehulere's exhibitions thread the life stories and works of late artists such as Mgudlandlu as a means to question the mechanics of museology and canon, as well as a way to examine the effects of sanctioned histories and policies on individuals from marginalised groups. Especially with Mgudlandlu – an artist who died in the township where Wa Lehulere was raised – such collaborations question change and stasis between past and present. In the context of this particular biennale, *Leaving the Echo Chamber*, they also prompt new ways of destabilising archives and imagining futurity.

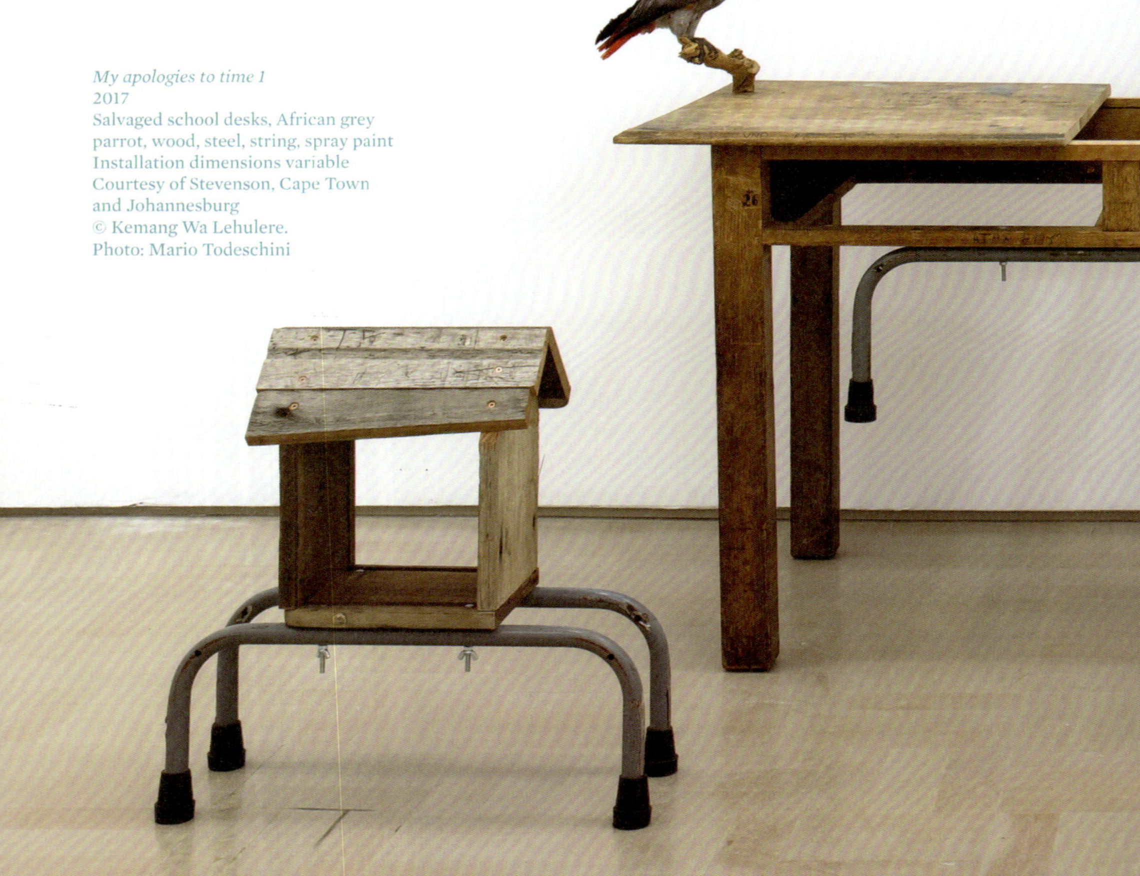

My apologies to time 1
2017
Salvaged school desks, African grey parrot, wood, steel, string, spray paint
Installation dimensions variable
Courtesy of Stevenson, Cape Town and Johannesburg

Photo: Mario Todeschini

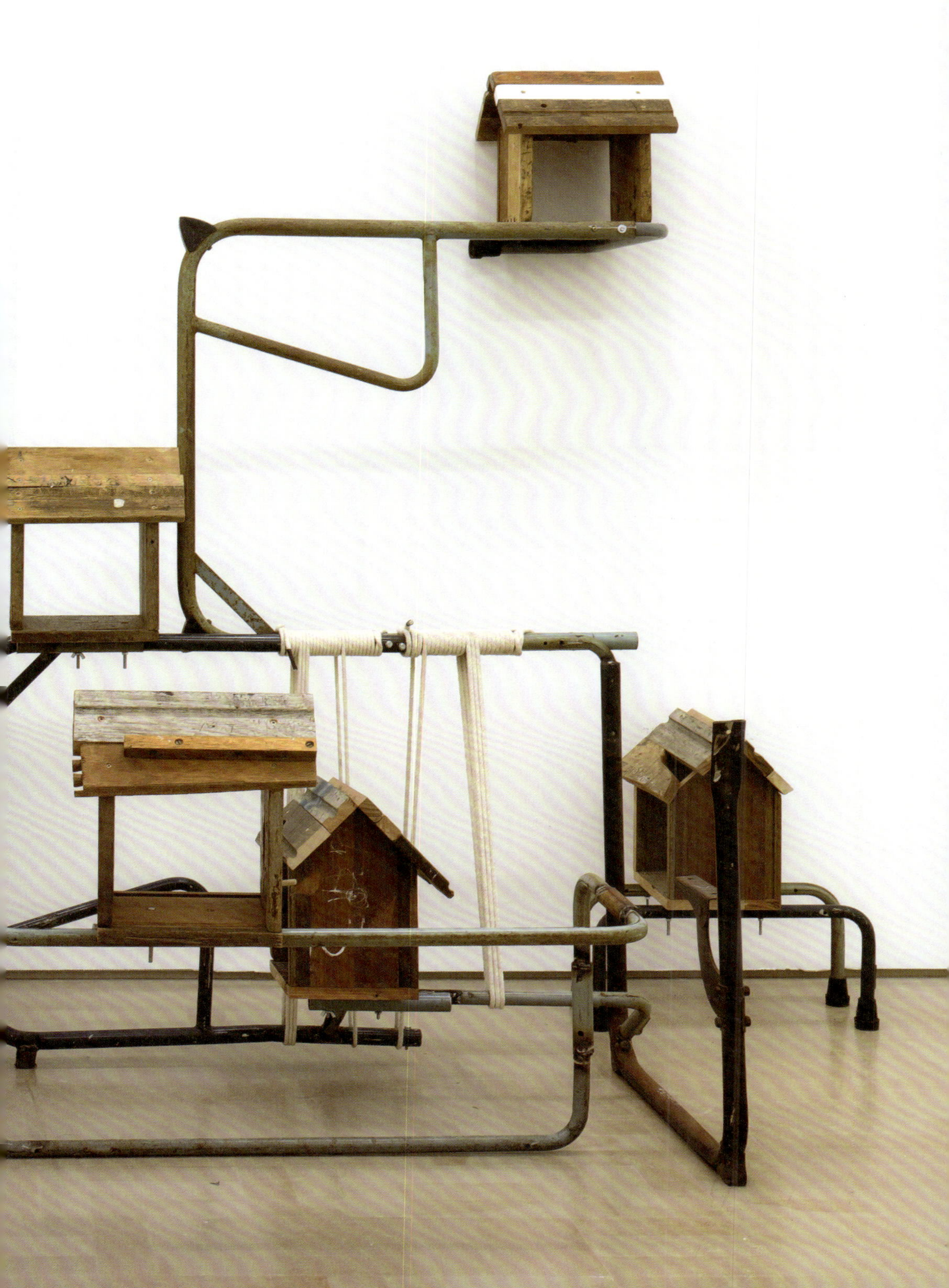

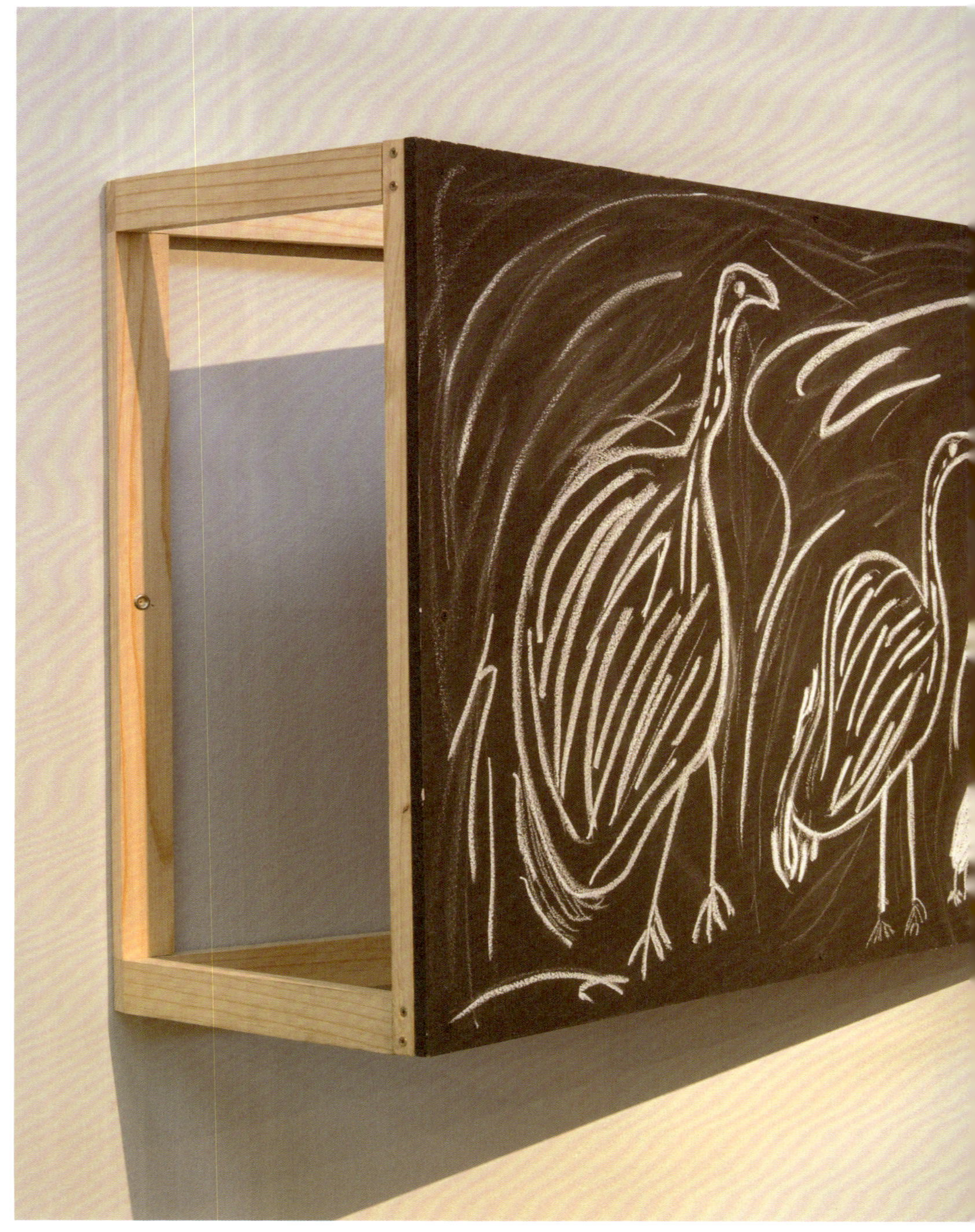

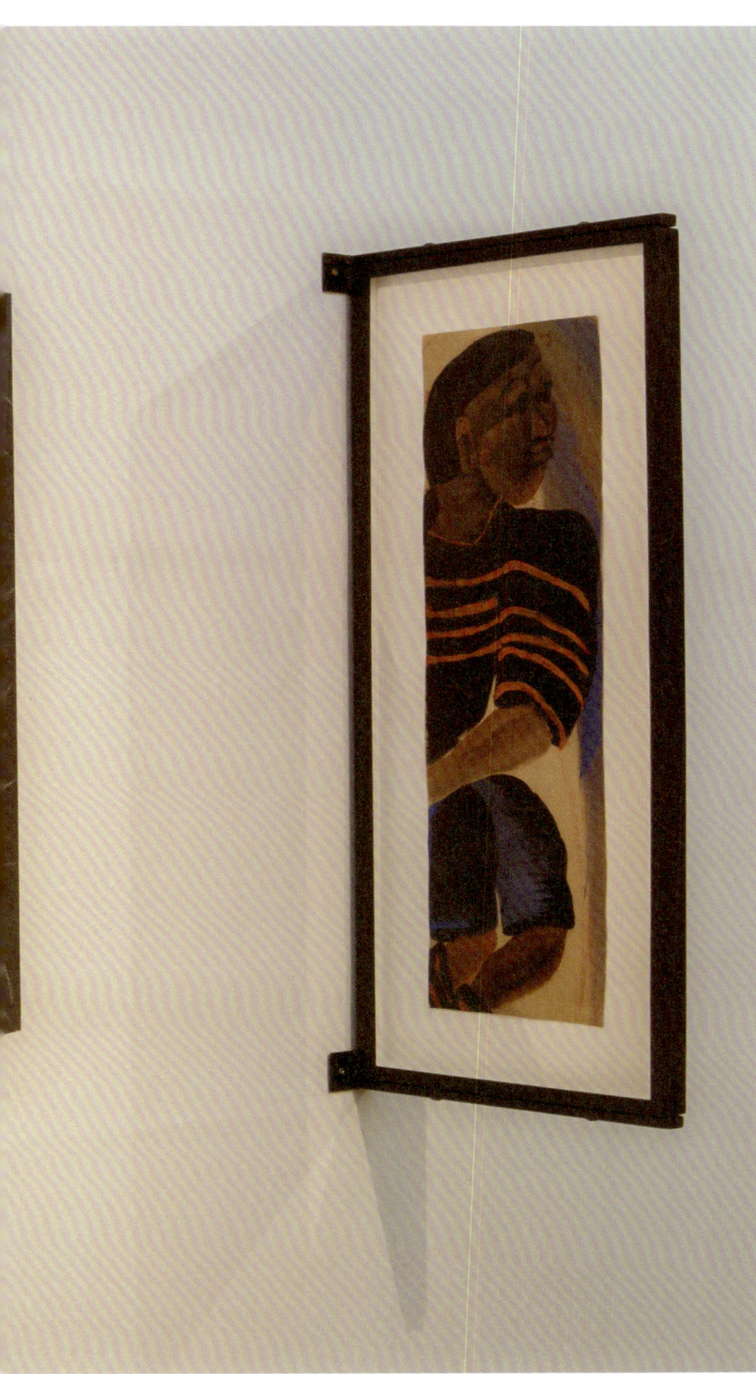

Does this mirror have a memory 12
2015
Drawing in collaboration with Sophia Lehulere
chalk on blackboard
70 x 100 cm

Untitled
Painting by Gladys Mgudlandlu
undated, gouache on paper, recto and verso
72 x 22 cm

Courtesy of Stevenson, Cape Town and Johannesburg

Photo: Mario Todeschini

M u n e e m W a s i f

b. 1983, Dhaka, Bangladesh; lives and works in Dhaka

Munem Wasif's stark black-and-white photography and films investigate complex social and political issues with a traditional, humanistic language, by getting close to their subjects, both physically and psychologically. Expressionistic in style and long-term in method, the artist frequently experiments beyond tradition, testing the possibilities of fiction by borrowing a familiar documentary language. He is also often interested in the concepts of 'documents' and 'archives' as well as their influence on addressing politically and geographically complex issues. At the heart of Wasif's installation in Sharjah Biennial 14 is a film titled *Machine Matter* (2017), which opens with images of decrepit metal scraps in abandoned jute factories in Bangladesh. Known as the 'golden fibre', jute is specific to the artist's native country, where it once connected Bengal's peasant smallholders to global capital; jute has been used as packaging material in world trade since the nineteenth century, before artificial fibres and shipping containers came into play. In his film, workers' faces are absent, but, as Tanzib Wahab states, Wasif 'transfer[s] the wrinkles [of the body] to the machines' in the factory. Through long, silent shots of waiting, the artist's film takes us on a journey to an 'unclaimed death'. His installation is a rumination on modernism and the disappearance of industry as well as the livelihoods industry engenders and exploits.

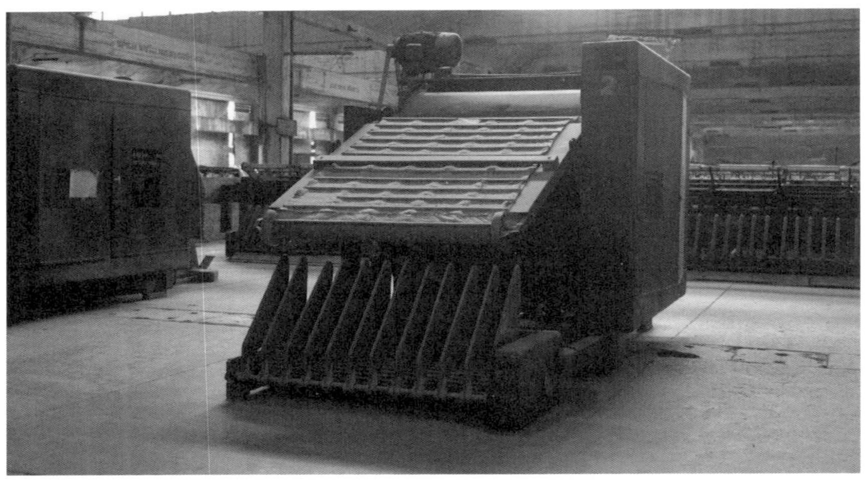

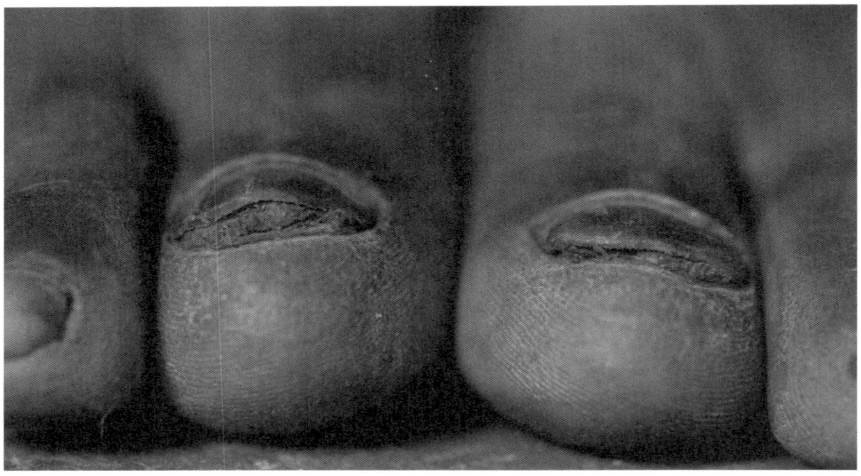

Machine Matter
2017
Video still, single-channel, 14m05s, black and white, stereo, loop
Courtesy of the artist
Production: Kauser Haider
Assistant Cinematographer: Ferdous Ahmad, Samsul Alam Helal, Joe Paul Cyriac
Camera Assistant: Rajin Monir, Shudir Chandra Das, Tajul Khan, Joy
Sound Design: Saddul Islam
Color Grading: Saibal Rabbi Jitu

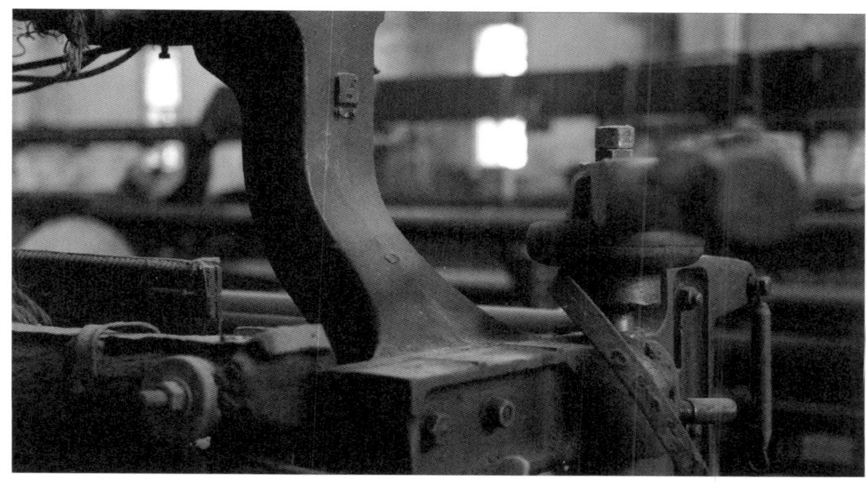

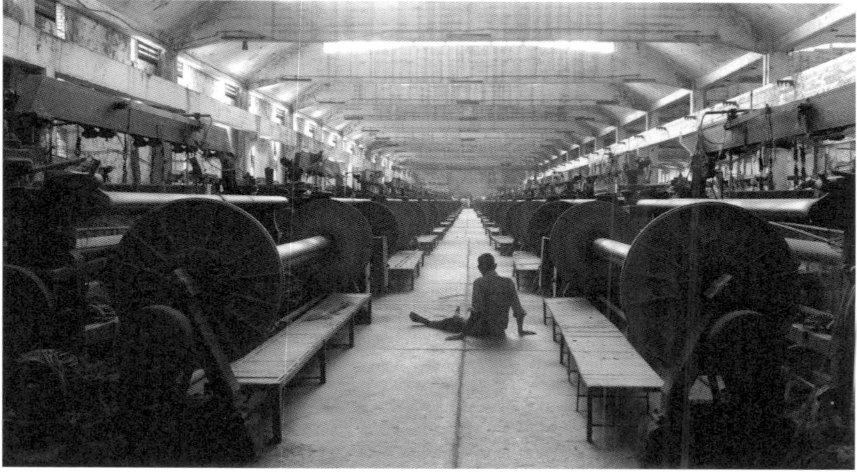

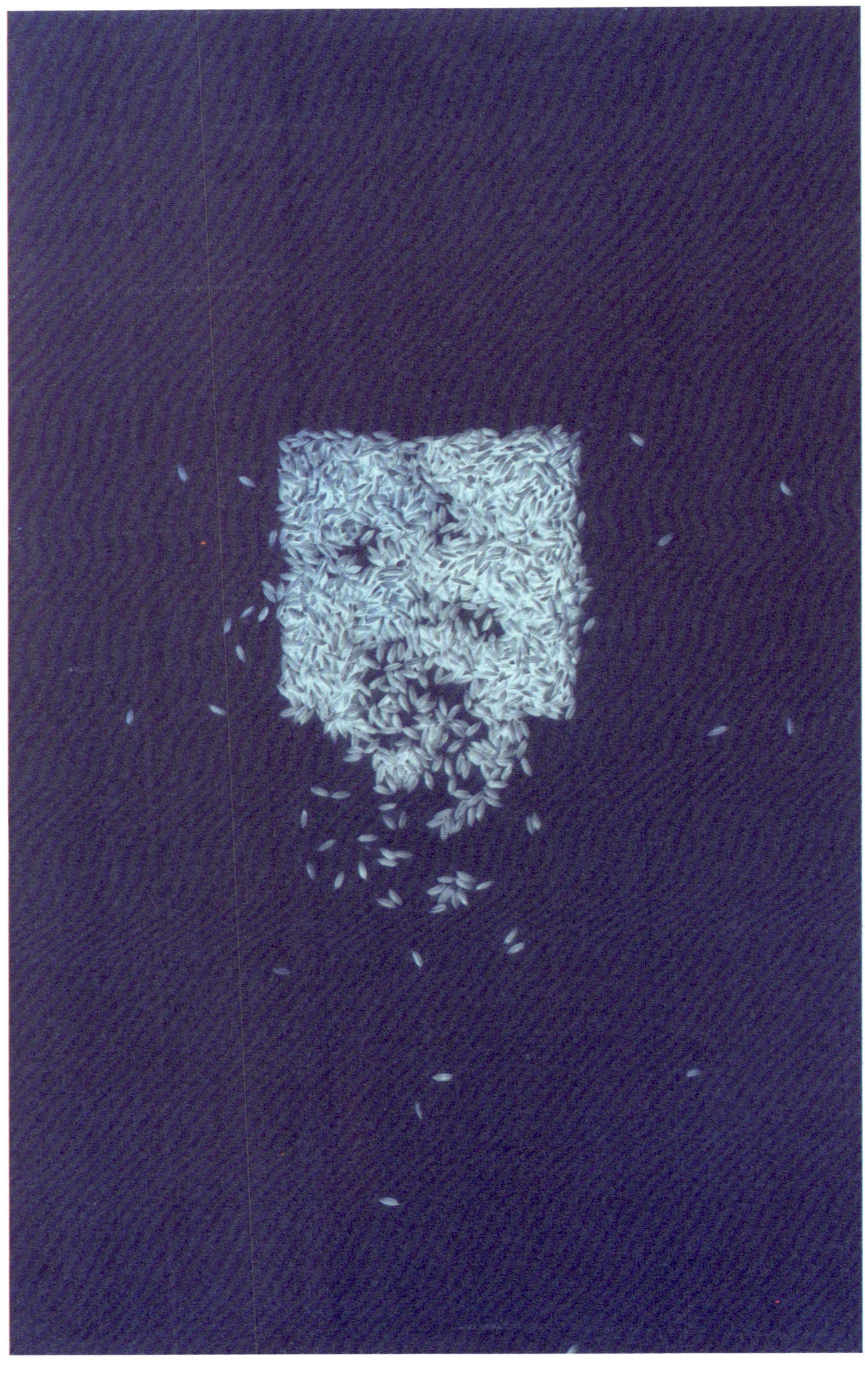

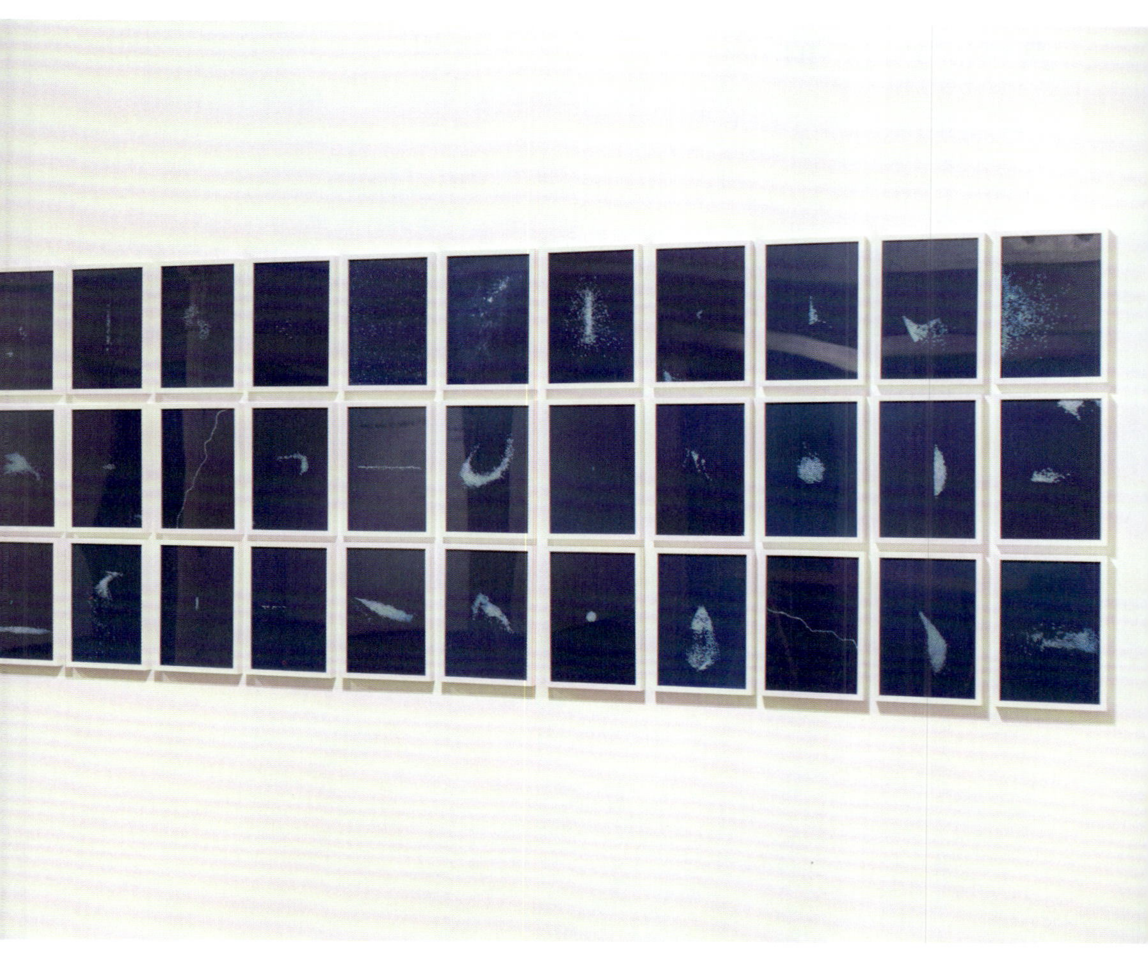

Seeds Shall Set Us Free
2017
Cyanotype prints on acid free paper
Courtesy of the artist

Akram Zaatari

b. 1966, Sidon, Lebanon; lives and works in Beirut

Commissioned by Sharjah Art Foundation with the generous support of Barjeel Art Foundation, Elie Khoury Art Foundation, General Directorate for Security Support, Fujifilm ME and KT Drones

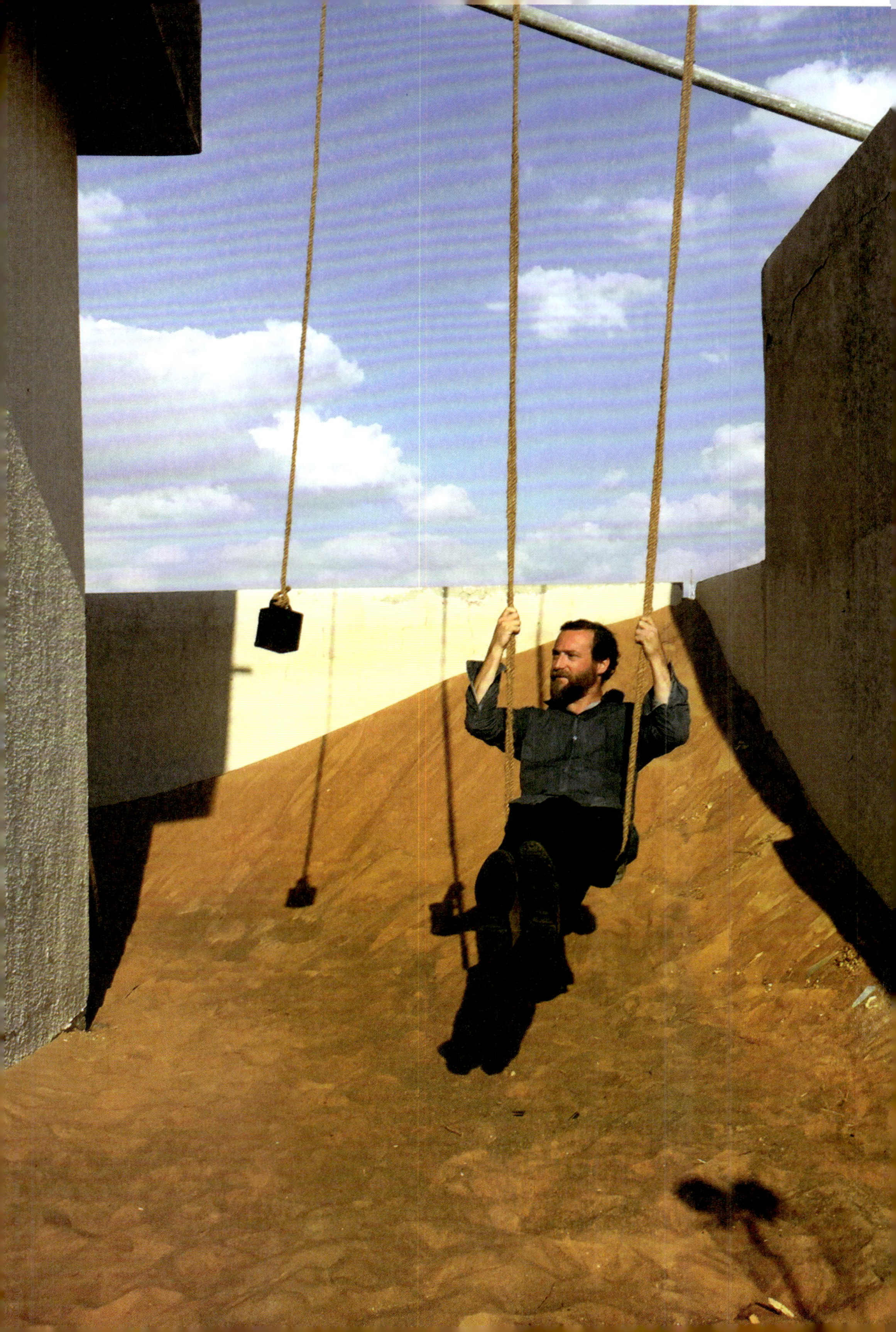

Akram Zaatari's videos, films, photographic installations and publications excavate past landscapes and reorganizes the finds in his own present narratives. His Sharjah Biennial 14 work, *The Landing* (2019), takes as its starting point Shaabiyat Al Ghurayfah, a public housing project built for descendants of Al Kutby tribe (pronounced 'Ketby') in Al Madam, Sharjah in the early 1980s. In 1994, the families moved to new housing in the vicinity, leaving their old houses to be covered slowly in shifting sands. Today Shaabiyyat Al Ghurayfah looks like ancient ruins.

The Landing consists of a feature-length film presented in the gallery along with documentary components. In the film, Sharif Sehnaoui, Abed Kobeissy and Ali Hout are stuck in the desert. Their moves, their communication, their discovery of location take the form of an acoustic exploration of space. A repertoire of simple gestures playfully engages with structure, space, threshold, verticality and perspective. Their acts resonate with artist Hassan Sharif's early performances, such as *Swing*, *Digging and Standing*, and *Recording Stones* (all 1983), which were staged in the UAE desert outside urban centres. Cables, sewage pipes, tubes, shovels, kitchen tools, electric air blowers and even a helicopter landing on site are all deployed in this film for their sonic rather than narrative potential—creating refractions, confrontations and transformations in a broken narrative. Also included in this work is a video produced from audio interviews with Rashed Ben Khelfan, a former resident of Al Ghurayfah, and his son-in-law Muhayyar Ali Rashed, in which they reflect on life in Al Madam during the first ten years after the country's unification. In the accompanying installation, a car featured in the film has been placed partway between the gallery and its courtyard, transgressed by the gallery's glass façade, a transparent barrier between inside and outside. Finally, a recent photograph shows Shaabiyyat Al Ghurayfah today, filled with visiting tourists and families.

The Landing (video still)
2019
Video, color, 61 minutes, aspect: 1:2.39 surround sound Courtesy of the artist and Sfeir-Semler Gallery, Hamburg / Beirut

A film by: Akram Zaatari
Cast/Performance: Sharif Sehnaoui, Abed Kobeissy, Ali Hout
Cinematography: Talal Khoury
Sound: Victor Bresse
Editing: Rita Mounzer, Lucid
Color Grading: Belal Hibri
Line production: Lara Checkerjian, Ginger Beirut

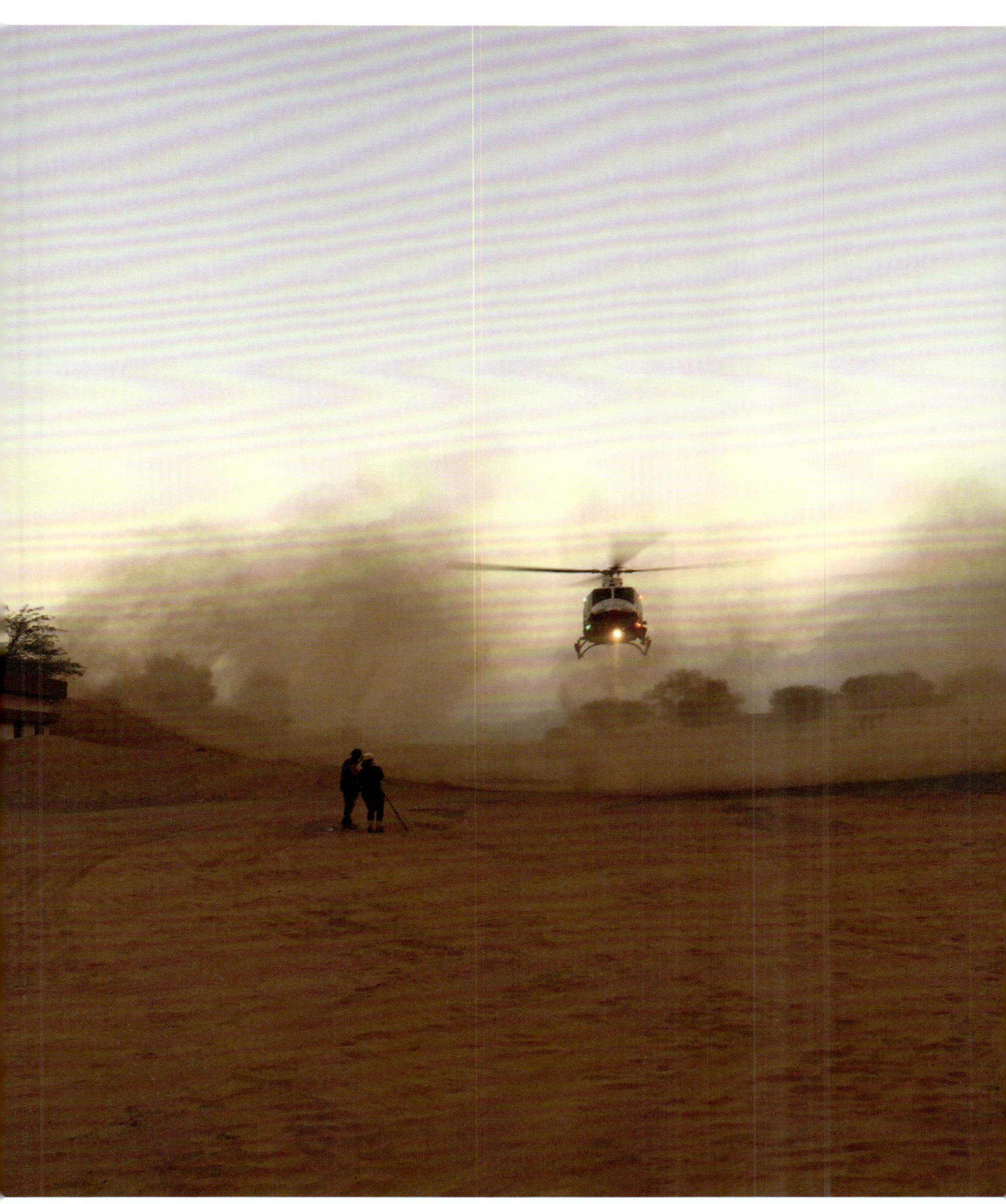

M a k i n g N e w T i m e M a

k i n g N e w T i m e M a k i

n g N e w T i m e M a k i n g

N e w T i m e M a k i n g N e

w T i m e M a k i n g N e w T

i m e M a k i n g N e w T i m

e M a k i n g N e w T i m e M

a k i n g N e w T i m e M a k

i n g N e w T i m e M a k i n

g N e w T i m e M a k i n g N

e w T i m e M a k i n g N e w

T i m e M a k i n g N e w T i

m e M a k i n g N e w T i m e

M a k i n g N e w T i m e M a

k i n g N e w T i m e M a k i

n g N e w T i m e M a k i n g
N e w T i m e M a k i n g N e
w T i m e M a k i n g N e w T
i m e M a k i n g **T h e** N e w
T i m e M a k i n g N e w T i
m e M a k i n g N e w T i m e
M a k i n g N e w T i m e M a
k i n g **U n k n o w i n g** N e
w T i m e M a k i n g N e w T
i m e M a k i n g **X** N e w T i
m e M a k i n g N e w T i m e
M a k i n g N e w T i m e M a
k i n g N e w T i m e M a k i
n g N e w T i m e M a k i n g

(Weave the Future Golden over Dark Days)

'The irreducible price of learning is realizing that you do not know'.
—James Baldwin

It is the summer solstice, and I have made lone pilgrimage to a sacred well.

The cement around it is stained red from iron oxide, and I join a procession of people waiting to drink from it. When my turn comes, I squat beside the font and place my lips to the stream of water issuing from the mouth of a stone lion.

It tastes like blood.
But I immediately feel better.
Probably, I just need to take some Vitamin D.
But *what if* it really is magic?

I feel sheepish about this superstitious compulsion. I don't think of myself as the kind who drinks the Neopagan Kool-Aid – but here I am, sucking magic water out of a statue's mouth and doing *wudu* in the white water of Avalon. This is no better than the blind acceptance of 'alternative facts' swirling around the echo chamber of our non-consensual reality. Right?

Frankly, I am embarrassed about the comfort that consulting a clairvoyant or visiting a *shawafa* gives me these days. I worry that it's just the beginning of my participation in a deliberate, collective unknowing.

On this day, like every other, my feed is full of bad news from the United States. 'Tender age shelter' is a phrase now. An MSNBC pundit weeps on TV, just like in *Five Years*.[1] I am focused on America because, as with the consumption fuelling our future's demise, it has an outsized grip on the narrative of our collective, global fate. I have been reading a one-quid copy of the essay *Dark Days* by James Baldwin. Unlike the American exile, whose book I carry in my pocket today, I do not have any love for America. However, as Baldwin writes in this famous *Esquire* essay, I do 'insist on the right to criticize her perpetually'.

America has done us all a real bad wrong.

It has sown profound discord and turned into an inescapable den of white supremacy and environmental destruction.

Not far from the sacred waters, there is a place offering 'Sound Healing and Chakra Tuning'. I look in, through the window. It's a hanging garden of wind chimes. The place is shut. Solstice is a holiday here. So, there is no one to give me a sonic colonic or access my inner wisdom with a gong bath.

There is, however, a stranger with dirty-dishwater dreadlocks. I sit beside them at the bus stop. A card floats into my peripheral vision. 'Someone told me to give this to you'. I notice that people here make gestures like these with blithe gravitas. It is difficult to question. 'Who told you?' I ask. She shrugs. Bangles jangling. And walks away in a cloud of Nag Champa. I look at the laminated card. It reads, 'WEAVE THE FUTURE GOLDEN' in all caps. It features some kind of orientalist goddess emerging from a watercolour smog in a graceful swirl.

I look it up.

It's from a deck called the Kuan Yin Oracle set. Wikipedia tells me this goddess's name means 'the One Who Perceives the Sounds of the World' and saves sentient beings from suffering and ignorance.

How fucking auspicious. It's a sign. I'm sure of it!

I use it as a bookmark whilst I finish *Dark Days*. Reading this tract of social criticism and personal essay feels relevant to me at this moment as it probably did in 1980. The words leap up. True and vital. Un-aged on the page.

A frequent refrain across all of Baldwin's writing is the necessity of individuals and nations to confront the past with brutal honestly in order to achieve total freedom. Part of that is accepting one's responsibility and agency in the state of one's affairs. Not, perhaps, throwing up one's hands into the air and waiting for the divine to take over.

Now I know, for some, that the ideas of fate and chance and objects, like crystal balls and ouija boards, are all just pretty tools for scrying one's own feels.

But emotions are as real as the weather.

And they are unknowable and out of balance right now. They are an equation with a big bold 'X' – that volatile variable over which I, for one, have little control.

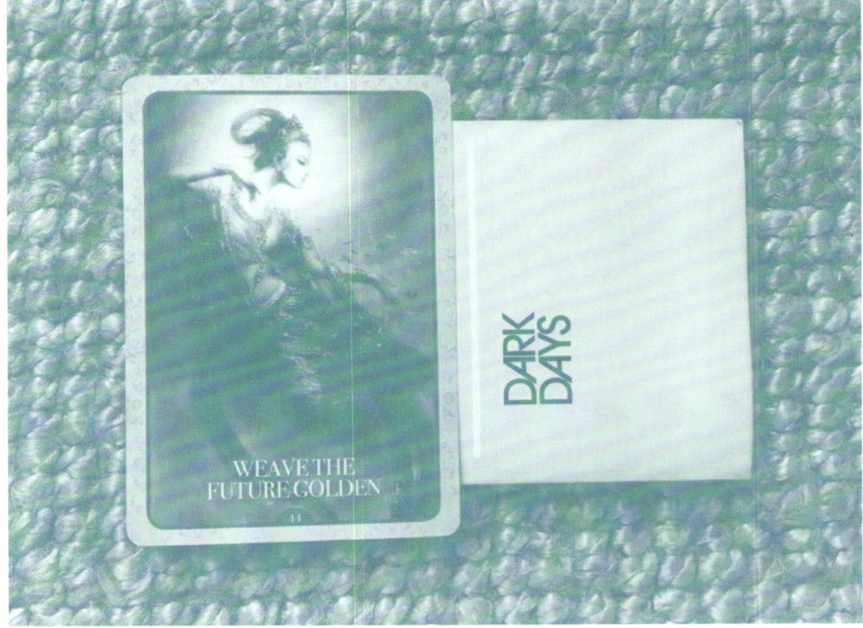

So I lay the orientalist oracle card out over the Baldwin book like a two-card cross. This is much simpler than the Celtic cross tarot or True Love spreads, but nonetheless powerful. I set about reading it. The meaning that comes to me rings as clear as a bell.

Use the tools you are given. Confront your histories with honesty. Rescue the unknowable future.

1 *News guy wept and told us, earth was really dying*
Cried so much his face was wet, then I knew he was not lying...
—'Five Years', David Bowie

N e w T i m e M a k i n g N e
w T i m e M a k i n g N e w T
i m e M a k i n g N e w T i m
e M a k i n g N e w T i m e M
a k i n g N e w T i m e M a k
i n g N e w T i m e M a k i n
g N e w T i m e M a k i n g N
e w T i m e M a k i n g N e w
T i m e M a k i n g N e w T i
m e M a k i n g N e w T i m e
M a k i n g N e w T i m e M a
k i n g N e w T i m e M a k i
n g N e w T i m e M a k i n g
N e w T i m e M a k i n g N e
w T i m e M a k i n g N e w T

imeMakingNewTim

e**Intimate**Making

NewTimeMakingNe

wTimeMakingNewT

ime**Clocks:**Makin

gNewTimeMakingN

ewTimeMakingNew

Time**A**MakingNewT

imeMakingNewTim

eMakingNewTimeM

akingNewTimeMak

ing**Provocation**N

ewMakingNewTime

MakingNewTimeMa

kingNewTimeMaki

Living through a moment of revolutionary rupture was a brutally embodied experience of time. I don't know what concept of time I had before the scale of this encounter, but certainly I took for granted a much more normative sense of the clock. Time was what I imagine it to be for most of us: a linear and neutral value by which we measure and schedule our lives. It was what I now understand to be an extension of Newton's clock – a concept of time with an arrow, and an ever moving present becoming the past; one that is the same everywhere.

The first fundamental shift in my concept of time came not in relation to the clock of physics, but to the political clock, the social clock that regulates how we live and make decisions. Within the scale and opportunities of the rupture unfolding in Egypt in 2011, now, but now, became a time to which everything had to be given. Rightly or wrongly, the openings of revolutionary time created the sense that what we could make happen now could change the future. Time itself had a different thickness. It was intoxicating, experiencing something that was the thing itself and could only otherwise be interpreted or translated. Within its raw poetry, I began to intuit the existence of three different clocks inside of me. One that existed in the day to day of present concerns; one that existed to the rhythm of generations; and one that beat arrhythmically to the unpredictable and swirling storms of revolutionary change.

I began to think that these forms of time were clocks to whose rhythms we could give dominance in the here and now, and I felt in them a hierarchy. Each level up compromised the levels below. To live for the revolutionary anti-clock was to interpret the world and make decisions within it that might seriously disrupt the ebbs and flows of generational time, and certainly to live for this clock was in direct opposition to the world of the everyday. Generational time was closer to a kind of love within family – the stories that unfold over three or four generations, sometimes measuring traumas and how we liberate ourselves from them, other times enacting continuity. Meanwhile the clock of the working hour, to which everyone has become tied institutionally, was a clock that fought against us, it seemed. To be bound by its logic, was to privilege a definition of today over a future that might come.

I pictured each clock as intersecting waves. The first as small and frequent; the second as wide but even enough; and the third beyond the graph, intervening when it became visible like a resonant charge that could collapse all linear conceptions of time and make other presents, futures and pasts absolutely tangible: architectures and archetypes. Memories could be encountered from the future, retrievable like patterns. My sense of self began to collapse despite its apparent unity in my body, multiplying and dividing. The difficult abstractions of philosophy and theory became a world I could see. And vertigo came in the moments when all three times seemed to align. What little I'd read of German philosopher Walter Benjamin would hound my thoughts. His angel of history hovered high.

Of course, material reality, or what we seem to agree is the common rule book of our shared present, was never far away. It was our common language. Political change is not a subjective experience that can be projected outwards. Too often we make the mistake of thinking that knowledge is the major barrier to progress. Important as knowledge might be, if the interests and power relations that structure the world are pitted against its conclusions, the fight for change will be long and bloody. Structures of reform tend to exist within paradigms. Fundamentally challenging the rules of those paradigms, or systems, means a kind of war on the structures that have created, and recreate, what we call our present.

As the pendulum swung ever more clearly towards a counter-revolutionary moment, every institution that looked fragile began to gather itself. My experience of time became much more embodied and entwined in institutions. Alongside the sense of time that I'd esoterically gathered for myself, I began to read how the logic of institutions that was being fought on the streets was present in people. The logic of times past was alive. It was not simply that traditional positions were held strongly, but laws written to suppress dissent during colonial times were being used to imprison revolutionaries in the present day. The way institutions are resourced or indebted became part of the enmeshed fabric of people's daily struggles. And just as I had divided and multiplied my identities, I began to read these institutions in the people around me. The arc of time, and not of history, was far more present than I had imagined, perhaps naively. What I could read in those closest to me was also what I began to read in myself. A violent conception of time had occupied me, and I needed to begin the process of liberating myself from it.

Step one, now I look back on it, was a gradual process of understanding what I still have not yet absorbed: time does not exist as a separable entity. To talk about time without reference to space is like talking about human beings without referring to where and when they lived. My year is not your year unless our institutional rhythms and the capacities of our embodied geographical locations are similar enough to render the differences between our years as negligible. But still, my year is not your year. Inequalities in time are as pervasive and extreme as financial inequality. To be poor is to be more likely to die younger. To be rich in a country with bad healthcare is also to be more likely to die younger. To insist on time as a unit as standard as a litre of liquid, masks how enmeshed it is in other concepts and realities – space, labour, infrastructure, freedoms. Like a moth banging itself against a lightbulb, I would say to myself, 'I need to make time, I need to make time, I need to make time. I need space. I need space. I need space'. Only when the two are alloyed – space and time, space-time – understood as inseparable, would there begin any possibility of actually making a shift: smashing through the lightbulb, reconfiguring the magnetism of its electric charge. The fact that this shift in awareness bears a relationship to the general theory of relativity haunts my mothlike ignorance, or is perhaps foundational. Time on a mountain moves differently to time by the sea. Atomic clocks have measured the difference between time on a moving plane and time on the ground. They are not the same.

In turn, time is a tyrannical agent of guilt and shame. Imagining time as a thing unto itself that exists everywhere in equal quantity internalises the logic of our failures. Rather than say the political and economic system of time and space that exists in this context is insufficient to achieve whatever we are trying to do (organise, rest, read, think, create; care for friends, family or ourselves), we are more likely to internalise the problem and blame ourselves for planning badly or not working hard enough. Often we solve the problem by overworking or over-stretching ourselves (other manifestations of speed), which of course leads to exhaustion. And this exhaustion cleaves to us so closely that we begin to believe that it is just the way things are, and who we are. The status quo becomes normalised, and we no longer have the time or space to escape it. You can only be fast at something you already know how to do, and if you have to be fast and efficient all the time, how and when do you resource an alternative? The warden in our head who insists on measuring our productivity and speed becomes an immensely powerful agent for a corrosive value system that we have collectively naturalised. But there is nothing natural about the ideas of speed that hound our motorways or work routines, the speed at which we cook or reheat meals, even the yield of our crops and the meat on our chickens. The aim is always somehow to achieve more, or as much, for less, without ever really questioning which values are being measured to produce the gradient of the graph, and which are not. Still, speed continues to present itself to us as a blinding miracle. Blinding because of what it makes invisible to us. Caught in a capitalist logic of efficiency and austerity, concepts that first appear as abstract economic descriptions of something distant to us and hard to understand, reveal themselves as guests so intimate that their words tell us how we have done with our day before we go to sleep, and enforce our expectations of tomorrow before it has come to pass.

The shock that is hard to come to terms with, is how much we have to slow down within the terms of one system to create (or even think of) other configurations of space and time – and then how much unravels as we do, how much it can assault what we once thought of as private, and both where and how soon it becomes impossible to alter rhythms as an individual. The labyrinthine structure of the entrapment is hard to isolate and even harder to develop a grammar for. And in the isolation of our inchoate thoughts a kind of political loneliness reigns. The inability to communicate, despite the various manifestations of mounting fury, creates a silence which gradually gathers its energies, eventually exploding in the next rupture, the next revolution or indeed the next counter-revolution. We underestimate the delight of no longer feeling alone, and its political power, particularly when the delight retrieves from the future or the past, space and time for possible worlds that had been foreclosed on, in reality or in our imagination.

In the process of denaturing my relationship with what had seemed simple and inevitable notions of time, I went on a search. Seemingly basic facts stand like totems or signposts, guarding alternative worlds.

The minute hand on the clock is three hundred and thirty years old.

The hour has come to us through the daily division of prayers for monks.

In ancient Egypt the week was ten days long. For millennia, cultures all over the world have been accustomed to a division of days that would shrink or expand according to the time of year. Night was the untouched guardian of sleep and the stars until the advent of street lighting in the eighteenth century.

During the French Revolution *réverbère* lamps were the object of vandalism in a similar way to CCTV cameras today. The Crowley Ironworks was one of the world's first factories. It had a law book that was enforced by the newly created position of a 'warden'. Employees put in six day weeks of eighty hours. Pay was deducted for wasting time. Informing against those who sinned against the clock was encouraged. The ubiquity of the watch begins its journey onto the most privileged of bodies about two hundred years ago; it is issued by colonial powers to the wrists of their soldiers during the 1880s in order to synchronise manoeuvres. In 1884, at the International Meridian Conference held in Washington D.C., twenty-six nations agreed to adopt the Royal Observatory in Greenwich as the location of 0° longitude. Both the telegraph and the need to unify railway timetables were major forces in paving the way.

In 1960, Coordinated Universal Time or UTC was adopted. It is built on the standardisation of the second. Within four years, the process begins in the US Military, which eventually delivers the GPS. The GPS requires four satellites: three to triangulate and one to correct for differences in space-time. Meanwhile, in the realm of physics and quantum cosmology, the very existence of time is in question.

Our experience of the illusion of a global simultaneous present is an acutely modern experience. It is not the intensification of a form of time that has always existed, but an invention that is fundamental to the fabric of our social and political world. It works for some, and not so well for others, or rather it works for some at times in certain places, and not so well for even those very same people at other times and in other places.

Within us all, we might also say exists a child of modernity, and an orphan of modernity. A child who comes from the present and adapts trustingly to the rule book, and an orphan bewildered and alienated by those very same norms – one whose lineage exists elsewhere and elsewhen, on the lookout. I want to guess that at the moment my intersecting clocks gave me a sense of vertigo, my orphan was strong and sensing the possibility of a home. To be clear, I do not mean to romanticise the past or disavow the achievements that underlie the present, but I do mean to recognise that the abyss we face has a genealogy which flows through us, which is also to say that in the tick and the tock of our intimate clocks is a space for disruption and the discovery of other oscillations.

T i m e M a k i n g N e w T i
m e M a k i n g N e w T i m e
M a k i n g N e w T i m e M a
k i n g N e w T i m e M a k i
n g N e w T i m e M a k i n g
N e w T i m e M a k i n g N e
w T i m e M a k i n g N e w T
i m e M a k i n g N e w T i m
e M a k i n g N e w T i m e M
a k i n g N e w T i m e M a k
i n g N e w T i m e M a k i n
g N e w T i m e M a k i n g N
e w T i m e M a k i n g N e w
T i m e M a k i n g N e w T i
m e M a k i n g N e w T i m e

M a k i n g N e w T i m e M a
k i n g N e w T i m e M a k i
n g **T o o** N e w T i m e M a k
i n g N e w T i m e M a k i n
g N e w T i m e **S t u p i d** M
a k i n g N e w T i m e M a k
i n g **T o** N e w T i m e M a k
i n g N e w T i m e M a k i n
g N e w T i m e M a k i n g N
e w T i m e M a k i n g N e w
T i m e M a k i n g N e w T i
m e M a k i n g **F a i l** N e w
T i m e M a k i n g N e w T i
m e M a k i n g N e w T i m e
M a k i n g N e w T i m e M a

'[W]e should no longer think in terms of technology shaping self-perception, but instead of technology simulating the self, and then replacing the self with its simulation'.

—Erkki Kurenniemi

It's amazing, the speed with which our entire species created, perceived, named and then quotidianized the accelerated cultural reality of the contemporary echo chamber. In what feels like a mere ten years, billions of people have morphed from being individual citizens, open to new ideas, into billions of bellicose mobs-of-one, with each new mob-of-one resigned to being an intractable, bitter and compromise-free new normal on almost every issue with every other mob-of-one. Everyone is ready to go fight someone: anyone, anywhere – except face-to-face. The comment sections of YouTube and other similar platforms have become the real world.

Many of us have read enough to understand how we arrived at our hyperfactionalised communal space; it's the reinforcing effect of belief when it encounters a similar belief. Like seeks like – and then, like *amplifies* like – and then, reality goes insane and/or viral and/or global. Facts are downgraded to opinions. Feelings trump facts. Science is ignored. Ours is an era coloured by the absence of nuance and by the collapse of most all of what once existed in the centres between many increasingly obsolete binaries: the left versus the right; male versus female; truth versus falsehood; capitalism versus communism; democracy versus fascism. Right now, no idea is too stupid to fail.

Democracy seems to be the most pronounced institution – hyperobject? – to be dismantled, in order to make way for a post-echo-chamber world. Every new technology unexpectedly allows us to give license to parts of our humanity that were previously considered taboo. Inside the echo chamber, it has never been so easy to attack. Nor has it been so simple to defame, libel and stalk. It's a golden age of psychosis. Even a simple glance at our daily news feeds hurls us into an almost permanent state of cringing. People who were once passionate about everybody voting – *Every vote counts!* – now think, 'Hmm. You *know*, just because 51 percent of the people who voted on this think that something is a good idea is likely a flawed concept. People vote for ridiculous things all the time. What were we thinking?' Majority rule no longer means anything when nobody trusts anybody.

The historical left and right were equally complicit in the cratering of democracy. Both sides of our dissolving dualities now seize upon the smallest slivers of truth or lies in order to define, de-platform and limit the agency of their perceived opposite.

I'm more other than you. No, I'm more other than you.

To paraphrase a recent *e-flux* editorial: the twentieth century was about what belongs to whom, whereas the twenty-first century is about who belongs to what. A vote in the modern electoral universe feels more like a vote against voting itself than like a vote for or against an issue or a person. Down the road, will we be paid to vote? Be conscripted into voting? Pay to vote? Get mileage points for voting? No idea is off the table. For the time being, it would appear that democracy needs morning-after pills, and that political discourse needs a diaper.

When hippies emerged as if from nowhere in the 1960s, people had to explain where these strange new creatures came from. It wasn't hard to figure out that hippies emerged from young brains marinated in TV. The recent arrival of millennials in the world has required the same sort of explanation; and the culprit is, of course, the online universe. God only knows what we're creating next.

Key to the post-echo-chamber universe is the issue of shifting personhood – neopersonhood – how it feels to be an individual in the world. Anyone over thirty knows that the sensations in their heads are now very different from the ones they once felt. The absence of downtime, coupled with too much exposure to too many forms of information devices, has imprisoned us within endless, short-term, dopamine-driven feedback loops. Our brains are vibrating. We want speed. We want acknowledgement. We want granular data *now*. Along the way, our sense of time perception became distorted. Time *is* moving faster. You're not just imagining it, *it's really happening*, and it's not just you – it's everyone. At the same time, everything feels like it happened either ten minutes ago or ten years ago. As with the centres of politics, the entire middle core of our time perception has been hollowed out, and that's just for older people. Young people face the historically unprecedented possibility of never being capable of feeling nostalgia, because their brains have only ever experienced a perpetual present and are unable to process a deep sense of the past. History no longer applies to them – or has society come full circle? Have our brains become prehistorical and, as a species, has our dance with information technology entered its peak state? I think so, and there's no turning back.

M a k i n g N e w T i m e M a
k i n g N e w T i m e M a k i
n g N e w T i m e M a k i n g
N e w T i m e M a k i n g N e
w T i m e M a k i n g N e w T
i m e M a k i n g N e w T i m
e M a k i n g N e w T i m e M
a k i n g N e w T i m e M a k
i n g N e w T i m e M a k i n
g N e w T i m e M a k i n g N
e w T i m e M a k i n g N e w
T i m e M a k i n g N e w T i
m e M a k i n g N e w T i m e
M a k i n g N e w T i m e M a
k i n g N e w T i m e M a k i

i n g N e w T i m e M a k i n

g N e w T i m e M a k i n g N

e w T i m e M a k i n g N e w

E a r l y e T i m e M a k i n

g N e w T i m e M a k i n g N

e w T i m e M a k i n g **i n** N

e w **t h e** T i m e M a k i n g

N e w T i m e M a k i n g N e

w T i m e M a k i n g N e w T

i m e M a k i n g N e w T i m

e M a k i n g N e w T i m e M

a k i n g **M o r n i n g** N e w

T i m e M a k i n g N e w T i

m e M a k i n g N e w T i m e

M a k i n g N e w T i m e M a

From overhead and nowhere, the channel arrived one standard lunch hour, skittering over supermarket tiles and worn carpets and carparks for miles, separating this side from the other side, making both islands, of course. After that regrettable episode, the sun on the other side went out of business and the rain whipped the whole locale until everything in it might sink or be fished out.

But that was over there, where stopping on the road was still stepping on a toad.

Here, you were lucky to avoid a heatwave pothole in the major tax assessment area. Across the window ledges, rubber doggy balls were left to fade to the same tight grey. It got so parching, dry ripples or were they desert whiskers grew up thickly through split tarmac, a mirage. The air out-stank old milk. People started driving out at night to the channel's rim to fill their boots with as much saltwater as the boots could take whilst they were waiting a matter of however-many-years for the ground to once more unboil.

The atmosphere was a hard new drama, come to thrash the living daylights out of you.

This enforced separation into two distinct sections, with the sharpened waves in between, fouled with smears of cloud, was like a double dose of a life-threatening situation. In the sky over the channel, blame sat like a heavy smog, which made for poor visibility. Panoptic vigilance was required with any approaching thingy.

All these wonderful, sore reminders implant in your balloon-like mind that's supposedly the here-and-now.

At least the voluminous sea-spray shower
feels kissy in a cool spot, like your skin's on
a forest floor, soaking up Perrier by the litre.
Continuous bathing risks soft ugly patches
forming on your surfaces, sticking around for
the future or skin-eating fish to chew them off.
But ducks aren't threatened by you in water
because you're only a bobbing head. Grab
your mother and a towel, some mini meat-free
sausages and chilled trunks from the freezer, go
to the edge and get very dripping.

This must be how the toads felt, wet-humping as
the earth crumbled.
Once, in the channel, you rooted for sea-grass
with a herd of at-the-time delighted, later gutted
dugongs. Their nostrils followed you through
the panting waters. When they paused to breach
water, the dugongs danced as if they'd never
seen themselves, or any other marine mammal,
dance in their lives. They laid their aching
bristles in your lap and asked you to be their
girlfriend, though you weren't sure this was an
accurate translation.

Words weigh tonnes with possible meaning.

But there's no use scrutinising memories. At
least not with the naked mind. Their make-up
is as complex as the beach's lip where painfully
unbroken shingled miles and shrieking gullets
and the tide pull back on keen seaweed showing
off its afternoon light crackling against the ends of
the earth so that the warning flags stand flapping
and marginal like thoughts you can really trust.

The view across to the other side.

Using a phone to photograph your genitalia
is the only way to really see into it when the

off-gassing ice-cream van touts its easy jingle against the window, causing you to gyrate on the spot, which makes notable no-filter effects which make your genitalia self-conscious.

Whichever way you slice it – the past and present, here and there, us and them – it's always not-quite-right.

'Darling dollies, my breeze, my consolation', you'd said to the dugongs, 'even though you'll never feel dryness underfoot, we're already part of one climate we can't know. We thought it was a cautionary tale about our insatiable desire for more and it was. It seems the progress of nature, which is us, is to make things the next generation can break ever more easily, dragging each generation deeper through the shit of its ancestors whilst doing little to avoid hysterical screaming from any remaining men. Yet the thirst remains identical, for love to continue and be gradually different'. You'd finished with several rousing rounds of put-him-in-the-scuppers-with-the-hosepipe-on-him and your voice rang out portentously, in a way that made your skin vibrate, bringing the smaller shoalfish out of storage.

You can never see genitalia as it truly is because genitalia's quantum.

The new ice-cream is complete-meal-replacement, frozen, with a slightly gritty texture, available in selected waxy maize flavours. When asked if it's delicious but poisonous, the ice-cream lady makes it very very apparent that it is, definitely. Looking at your intimate pix, she adds, 'I'd be less offended if you'd served me a turd on a platter' and toots her horn approvingly, hitting her boot to the accelerator.

It isn't the weight of the world pressing in on you, just the shower steam bearing against your buttocks.

After the channel poured in, the sun had barely got up before it began to heat everything to helterswelter, slumped down for the night, then heated it all up again. If only it would stay winter for 365 & a quarter days a year and then, every leap year, gain an extra three-quarters of a day of winter. By now, the sky would have stopped melting and a chill would go on forever.

Finger-comb your hair. Smell beneath your fingernails.

No one wants to come back as a cloned dairy cow or a dancing cobra but as a very heavy tuba or as something quieter and blander than your smallest toenail. Licking and sucking at the macronutrients resembles the dog-ends of days, rolled right down to their marrow like loaves of magnolia grease-paint, where this terrible thing thought of as a better life trails the relief that you've never kept track of that racket.

It's not too late for anything to die again, as long as it's kept alive.
Until the day when things go out with a resounding bang and absolve us all of our differences, this side and the other side seem hell-bent on temperature and therefore tolerance imbalances. It isn't a thought you like the feeling of inside your head because it has the texture of IEDs and scratching fingernails. Crusts of unseen detail whang through right and left hemispheres.

The sun has spread like jam a tough bark across all the brains in the vicinity. Maybe the heat over here and all the people inside it are under a collective hypnosis. The idle mind ought to be a jug for casual vexation and dilly-dallying but the fact that everyone's hair smells of old lanolin and the casein clay walls have released their cheesy odours and stink to high heaven yet no longer attract comment makes it seem that, together, we must be suffering from some kind of eternal inattention for which only a sustained Tai Chi practice might be the saviour.

Small particles of macronutrient spatter from your mouth like a layer of edible pargeting.

N e w T i m e M a k i n g N e
w T i m e M a k i n g N e w T
i m e M a k i n g N e w T i m
e M a k i n g N e w T i m e M
a k i n g N e w T i m e M a k
i n g N e w T i m e M a k i n
g N e w T i m e M a k i n g N
e w T i m e M a k i n g N e w
T i m e M a k i n g N e w T i
m e M a k i n g N e w T i m e
M a k i n g N e w T i m e M a
k i n g N e w T i m e M a k i
n g N e w T i m e M a k i n g
N e w T i m e M a k i n g N e
w T i m e M a k i n g N e w T

i m e M a k i n g **T h e** N e w
T i m e M a k i n g N e w T i
m e M a k i n g **O r d e r** N e
w T i m e M a k i n g N e w T
i m e M a k i n g N e w T i m
e M a k i n g N e w T i m e M
a k i n g N e w T i m e M a k
i n g N e w T i m e M a k i n
g N e w T i m e M a k i n g N
e w **o f** T i m e **T i m e** M a k
i n g N e w T i m e M a k i n
g N e w T i m e M a k i n g N
e w T i m e M a k i n g N e w
T i m e M a k i n g N e w T i
m e M a k i n g N e w T i m e

[This was written to be read aloud.]

I spent a part of this summer on a rocky island overlooking the coast of Tunisia. It was a place I'd been before, a place held in my imagination. I had first encountered it in the writings of Khairallah Ali, the Egyptian novelist whose work I stumbled upon whilst doing research at the New York Public Library in 2015. Not that his work was a part of the library's holdings, but archival finds led me to the surrealist painter Ahmed Morsi, who had been living in some sort of exile in Midtown Manhattan, who led me to Avo Boghossian, who led me to Sherif Ibrahim, a childhood neighbor of Ibrahim Aslan, who led me to Khairallah, whose writings were filled with references, both seemingly real and surreal, to a place he described as 'Qawsirah', where he and other Egyptian writers had spent time in the sixties. I looked it up. There was an island historically referred to by that name, but it wasn't evident; I couldn't extract whether this was a place he had borrowed in its entirety, or simply borrowed by name, metaphorically, and adapted.

We landed in the late morning, my girlfriend Julie Mehretu and I, in a bumpy descent over a barren-looking cliff-rimmed coastline in the Strait of Sicily, the water shades of aqua, azure and cobalt blue. The artist Danh Vo was there to pick us up, in his small, white Fiat Panda, parked at an angle at the side of the small airport, windows open, doors unlocked. He had been spending time on the island over the past ten years, and had invited us to visit. It was a place I had held vividly in my mind's eye – the imagination of what it had been conjured to be – so, as we began the drive around the island to its farthest-most point and Danh's *dammuso*, the scenes from one of Khairallah's novels filled my head. The vineyard with Egyptian grapes; the crevasse in the cliffside that spurts water; the hot spring at the foot of the island; the old baker who served as the keeper of history. Did they exist?

We drove through the narrow, winding streets, near the coastline, the cliff's edge, and veered inwards, into the land, before coming out again. Historically known as Cossyra, from the Arabic Qawsirah, the island is better known by its modern-day name, Pantelleria – the largest volcanic satellite island of Sicily, caught in the corridor of Saharan and European winds, and famously located closer to North Africa by way of the tip of Tunisia, than to the Italian mainland. Its history is as seeped in North Africa as in Europe, and goes back 35,000 years, to Ibero-Ligurian origins, before its Carthaginian revival. That history is felt everywhere – in the rock remains of ancient structures and the landscape terraced with primordial-looking stone.

The volcanic sediment makes the island amongst the most fertile places on earth. Fruit, vegetables, herbs, sprout unattended, even out of the sides of raw rock, all born of the volcano itself, thousands of years of life erupted – and eventually, like Aphrodite, out of the sea as it washed ashore. This was the island the Arabs named Bint al-Riyah (Daughter of the Winds), when they conquered it in 700 CE. It was also the land of resilience. Olive trees crawled horizontally across the earth, spanning an acre, rather than growing vertically, to counter the famed winds that were ever present; fig trees reached waist level, and then grew outwards, almost like fields; vines lay sprawled on the dust, grapes nestled in the earth.

Khairallah had written about this resilience: how it provoked him to think differently of his work, the process of making it, the place it occupied in his life, his idea of his day, his writing day, how it should be. He was vague, elliptical, but one got the sense that the island inspired him; its untamed nature, what couldn't be harnessed. In one of his books, he had mentioned a local artist, Elena Buonarotti, a sculptor who created objects out of materials indigenous to the land – its multitude of rocks and shrubs. They were never put in homes, her sculptures, but rather always left in the place where they were made, or sourced, scattered across Pantelleria. I wondered about her and these pieces as we drove, and I looked out at the land. It was unclear if Khairallah had known her, or simply known *of* her. It would be impossible to frame the island's history without her family's background – they were the wealthiest farmers on the island, owing to a claim on 30 percent of the island's land: hundreds of acres, whose crops were harvested and sent to Sicily, and then on to the mainland. What came was always untimed, unpredictable. The same land produced tomatoes, capers, olives, almonds, grapes, figs, oranges, aniseed, rosemary; some crops had a sense of the notion of the seasons, others were more temperamental. In some years, melons, aubergines, squash emerged from the ground. Traders waited in anticipation of forthcoming shipments, despite never knowing when they might arrive, or with what; this was the finest produce in Europe – and they took it all.

We drove for forty-five minutes, and finally pulled up by a small church and a series of old stone buildings. Danh pointed to a narrow staircase across the street. He would go next door and buy bottles of water; we should go down the stairs and choose what we wanted for breakfast. This, it turned out, was the local bakery, exactly as it had been described, as I had read in the novel, standing at the edge of a cliff looking down to the sea. We gestured and tried to make conversation. I mentioned Khairallah by name, his novel *Still Life*, the descriptions of here. *Did he remember him, the Egyptian and his friends?* The baker pointed to a ridge eighty metres down the rock's edge, and to a cone-shaped protrusion two metres tall and one metre wide. A marble cube, the size of a head, seemed to protrude from its front, glimmering in the sun. This was a Buonarotti. Volcanic rock and marble merged like Roman remains.

Over the coming days, Danh took us on long treks through the untamed rock-strewn land, hours of walking, deep into the pit of the island, in the simmering heat, pointing out Buonarotti's sculptures, the decades of them, those that could still be deciphered. The landscape was both timeless and of another time, almost prehistoric, with the sense of the shadow of that history everywhere. The sculptures, some immense and some small, disappeared, and were swallowed into that land; out of the works life had emerged, morphing and obscuring, making new forms. There seemed to be hundreds, more – she had told Danh that she estimated some 2,000 sculptures were etched into that landscape; a lifetime of work, which had continued despite inheriting her father's land at twenty-eight, and then having to oversee the immense harvests that occurred intermittently throughout the year.

We never met her on that trip, but I pieced together stories, ideas about her life, an image of who she might be. Her dedication to her making, to her art, occupied me – these thousands of objects made with no sense of whether they might ever be seen beyond the notion that they were part of this landscape that was otherly, in the way one might imagine another planet to be. This was a land that was unpredictable, yet that always produced, always yielded. A land so harsh that sharp, dark rocks marked its every surface, cliff faces hung like paintings, yet also like daggers; not a single sandy beach at which to arrive. An island so unwelcoming to mankind, and yet, so abundant, so generous. This, you could depend on. This was a place with a different kind of faith in the land, and in time. These were her words, this was what everyone I asked said of her, how she always repeats, 'Here, we have a different kind of faith in time'.

* * *

I told this story as part of a longer lecture at a conference on Perception last week in Rome, 'Suspension of Perception', after Jonathan Crary's tome. I had been invited by some strange fluke of degrees of separation and Italian theoretical physicist Carlo Rovelli, who is a friend of an Italian novelist originally from Alexandria, who had read my novel, in its Italian edition, and wondered about the sense of *time* in it, as much as the place it depicts. The degrees of truth to both of them.

'This life you depict seems to occupy a different sense of time, it disrupts the idea of time as it is believed to be', Rovelli wrote in an email, and then asked if I would consider delivering a short text ahead of the conference, so that he could place my talk. *A rumination on this sense of time, mine, that of the character, that of the novel, this city* – he wasn't sure which.

This is what I wrote:

One's sense of time in the world we inhabit is marked by the absence of it, the diminishing units of measure contained in a day. We experience, each of us, this absence in what appears to be a structured, unified manner, measured by the familiar, universal ticking of the clock. We watch the numbers move forwards, many of us, with the notion that against this diminishing is the measure of what was gained, and what remains to be produced. Time is the value of productivity, gain. This is the organising logic of the world. We think. Most of us. Those of us who inhabit cities of the future. The truth of my character is a different one. One that recognises that time, the essence of time, the sense of time, is entirely tied to place. Cairo is of the past, and to grow up in a place like that is to inherit and be conditioned to an altered notion of time. Time is not in the value of the future, for the past is what is of value, what is revered – what was, not what can be or what is. Your value is not in what you make or have made, your everyday 'making', but in how your life is bound to history. You will never be asked, in Egypt, what you do, but rather, who your father is, what village your family is originally from. In value being attached backwards, rather than forwards, time is slowed down, expanded. There is, in the everyday, a very different sense of time; it almost stands still, feels limitless – at once, as freeing as it can become a burden.

* * *

I will admit, only in writing this, how out of my depth I felt in that auditorium – watched by what seemed like several hundred esteemed scholars and thinkers who had little interest in my short novel, and I'm sure no idea why I might even have been there. Yet my lecture continued, ending with a mandatory Q and A, which to my surprise generated actual questions. Several in the audience knew of Buonarotti's work.

One man, a quantum physicist and art collector with an interest in time-based work and a particular fascination with Julie's paintings – for what he described as their 'timelessness' – asked how one might reconsider the structure of time, push back against its capitalist inclination. Here is the transcript (copyright of the conference) of my response:

I can really only answer this from a very personal place, of being out of step with time, on Cairo time. For this character in my novel, for example, who is nameless, not by coincidence, and for those of you who don't know, she becomes a published writer; there was never the expectation or sense, growing up, that she could be, by way of her work, part of this other structure, these future cities and their economies; her entire conditioning was to the history around her. Not where she was going, but what she came from. The preoccupation being with the latter. We're in Italy, so, of course, Ferrante comes to mind, too. Perhaps that is the only way to make, as we move forwards, and by that I mean art, literature – by resisting time, the notions or ideas of time. By stepping outside of it. [Inaudible.] Ali Smith does this brilliantly in her latest novels, inventing a new form, both out of time and also in it. [Inaudible.] The ancient Egyptian measure of time revolved around agriculture (inundation, growing, harvest). In the sub-Saharan town of Akiraka, time was marked by when the few things planted in that barren desert finally bore fruit. Buonarotti's Pantelleria is perhaps on a similar temperament of time. This is the faith in time she spoke of; knowing, in the end, that time, in its own time, will bear fruit. Maybe the thing to do, individually, is to simply resist the unit of measure, to disrupt the order of time, as we each know it to be.

T i m e M a k i n g N e w T i
m e M a k i n g N e w T i m e
M a k i n g N e w T i m e M a
k i n g N e w T i m e M a k i
n g N e w T i m e M a k i n g
N e w T i m e M a k i n g N e
w T i m e M a k i n g N e w T
i m e M a k i n g N e w T i m
e M a k i n g N e w T i m e M
a k i n g N e w T i m e M a k
i n g N e w T i m e M a k i n
g N e w T i m e M a k i n g N
e w T i m e M a k i n g N e w
T i m e M a k i n g N e w T i
m e M a k i n g N e w T i m e

M a k i n g N e w T i m e M a
k i n g N e w T i m e M a k i
n g N e w T i m e M a k i n g
N e w T i m e M a k i n g N e
w T i m e M a k i n g N e w T
i m e M a k i n g N e w T i m
e M a k i n g N e w T i m e M
a k i n g N e w T i m e M a k
i n g **O u r o b o r o s** N e w
T i m e M a k i n g N e w T i
m e M a k i n g N e w T i m e
M a k i n g N e w T i m e M a
k i n g N e w T i m e M a k i
n g N e w T i m e M a k i n g
N e w T i m e M a k i n g N e

'Motherfucker!'

The rattlesnake stands erect, weaving, dusty coils braced against the stained cardboard I just flipped over, tail throwing out dry, offbeat percussion. We stare each other down.

I'd love to walk away. But unless I get rid of him, this snake is going to be here tomorrow, hiding under something, waiting for me. I've barely started emptying out my ex-girlfriend's dead mother's house, so they can sell it. I feel bad about breaking up with her, after all these years together. She's over at the family business, in an industrial warehouse, which we also have to empty out. We're going to be here for weeks. It's incredibly hot.

'OK. Stay right there. Stay right there...' I run for my snake stick, an electrical cord looped through a hollow metal broomstick, leaning against one of the house's many sheds, next to some rusting golf clubs. The snake is moving away as I run back.

I wave the lasso end of the cord at him, and he dodges, shows his fangs, feints. When I finally scoop the garrotte over his diamond-shaped head and yank my end of the cord tight, the trapped snake thrashes, close to me now, and I realise I haven't breathed for the past minute.

I march off, up towards the ridge, gripping my stupid invention in outstretched arms. The snake plays limp. Considering its next move. 'Motherfucker, don't you know I'm from New York?' I say out loud. I'm so mad at this snake and feel so sorry for him.

From the top of the ridge, it's a fifteen-foot drop to the dry creek bed. I hang the snake over the edge and shake the stick. Stuck. The snake hangs there, burning for payback. I try to loosen the cord, but it's stuck.

The snake lashes its tail at me, and in a spasm, I throw the nunchuck of snake and broomstick into the air; it crashes into the ravine, and the snake instantly wriggles free and vanishes into a crack in the hot, red earth.

The mom's house stands in a clearing below me; other suburban desert homes fall away towards the grid of the streets, lined with small houses and cinder-block workshops, sliced open by the snaking tail lights of the interstate highway.

I light a cigarette, lungs wide open in the hot, dry air, the smells of sulfur and tobacco, ancient and essential. An orange Tucson taxi passes the neighbour's turn-off, bumps towards the house. It's one of the brothers, Liam (chain wallet, heavy metal, heroin) or Trevor (blue hair, techno, meth).

I realise I need to pee, and I do it on the driveway of the departed woman's house, as the smell of dry rot wafts from a nearby shack. A hundred miles away, across the flats of Tucson, the Rincon mountains show dark ravines, bright ridges. I'll trash out this house but I won't belong to her fucking death, it's not mine.

* * *

I sit beside Hussein in the back of the ambulance, staring at Hussein, at the prayer bruise on his smooth forehead. Then I feel I shouldn't stare, so I look at my hands, dirt from this morning still in the deep creases left by years of outdoor work. Ali pulls the ambulance into the hospital car park, stops behind a battered Mercedes, where a man in country clothes is lifting a tall, young woman, unconscious, from the back seat; he puts her over his shoulder and carries her towards the crowd at the hospital door.

Ali is already pulling Hussein on his gurney out of the back and the wheels snap down and lock; then he pulls it fast through holes in the crowds, me pushing the back, past the women staring at space, men leaning on walls, sick people sitting or stretched out on the ground, waiting.

Ali and I wheel Hussein down the narrow corridor to a big, low room, where a couple hundred more family members stand around waiting at doors and office windows. But Ali drives the gurney straight into a small office. Hussein hasn't moved or spoken for five hours now. We worked together, both gardeners, but in separate areas of the garden, and I don't know him that well. But I was near him, this morning, when his eyes turned yellow and he fell like a tree. I tried to wake him, putting metal in his palm, onion under his nose. I drove him in the gardener's service car to town. Naturally, now that we're here, I feel responsible for him.

A man lies shirtless on the floor, propped on one elbow; the beautiful unconscious woman is already there, lying across her brother or husband, who has the one chair; another gurney against the wall holds a man bent over like a fetus. There's a single metal desk, with a young, white-smocked doctor behind it. I tell him, 'We've been to Clinic Jazair, to the Red Crescent, to the Clinique Moderne. They said to come here'. I hold out the letter, stamped and signed, from the rude lady doctor at the previous clinic. 'Profound coma', the young doctor reads, impressed. He rises and walks to look down at Hussein, pulls up a top eyelid with his thumb, shines a little flashlight into the eye. Then he nods to Ali. 'OK, triage'.

Ali is already moving the gurney with Hussein on it through the crowd gathered around the double doors, past the guard, into a slightly less-crowded hallway. In a large room, there are a couple of dozen women, lying on gurneys or standing around the sick ones, waiting. In the hallway, sick men sit on benches and on the floor.

The Doctor moves around fast, wearing blue scrubs, a short, strong man with thick hair. I was in this room once before, and I know that he decides if you wait or go inside to be taken care of. Ali shows the Blue Doctor the letter and shows him Hussein. The Doctor looks at the letter and almost spits.

'The private clinic, did they take care of him? Take his pulse, check his sugar level?' I tell him that they demanded 20,000 – six months' salary – and without that, they said, he wouldn't enter the clinic. 'Did they give him oxygen? Saline? Nothing! That's what they did. So, why do they exist?' He looks at me, demanding a reply. I make a money gesture. He snorts, angrier than I would have imagined.

Because this hospital is famous as a place where people go to die. It's crowded and dirty and noisy, and if the windows are closed, it smells like blood and vomit and shit and bleach. But now, the doctor is leaning over Hussein, slapping his face gently. He blows hard towards Hussein's eyes, frowns. Ali brings him a blood-pressure machine. They have to open the band wide, Hussein's bicep is so big. Most people here are smaller, and look ridiculous in their paper gowns.

Hussein looks just as handsome as when he's awake. His muscles are long under his shirt and jeans. He's tan and his hair and beard are thick, except above his mouth, where he is always clean-shaven, even now. Even the red sports underwear, his pants open for hours now, look like some guy in a magazine photograph. His face, unmoving, looks calm.

The doctor goes away again, and I watch Ali. I've been watching him all day, since he drove Hussein and me from the second clinic to the third one. Ali is a skinny guy, the kind you know stopped smoking cigarettes: his fingers aren't yellow, but he will always have those thin cheeks; and his fingers, when he's sitting in a cafe, will always be busy with a pen or a bottle cap. But his eyes are steady, he knows what to look at without searching.

As he drove the ambulance, he leaned forwards slightly, pushing the cars out of the fast lane with gentle pressure, then accelerating smoothly into the open road ahead, stealing every kilometre, every minute, back from death, to give it to the sick person. He knows just how to deal with the nurses and doctors in those clinics, knows what they will say before they answer. They don't surprise him. But now, he's watching the door where the Blue Doctor went, at the end of the hall, and he's not sure what's going to happen.

Hussein's brothers have come in, quiet and scared. I ask them, 'Was he sick yesterday?' No, they say, he went to the beach. All day? No, he stayed four hours. The brothers look from Ali's face to mine for clues, then at their feet. I point at the ceiling and the brothers nod agreement: inshallah.

The brothers are country guys and don't know how to stand invisibly in this place, so the guard sends them back out, but I grab one brother's hand, pushing him towards the wall next to Hussein on the gurney. He puts his hand on Hussein's foot, and that's all.

Then the door opens and the Blue Doctor gestures, come. Ali is ready, he pushes Hussein down there, quickly but careful of the fucked-up people on the floor, and I look inside the special room. There is air conditioning there, and even before the door closes, a white-shirted Doctor with a mask covering his face has Hussein with a tube of air in his nose, one tube for each nostril, and is fitting a needle into his arm. The White Doctor says to me, 'Get out; go, brother'.

Ali makes a gesture that he is going to move the car. I nod, almost bowing to him. I stand in the hall and I can't believe it. There are hundreds of people out there, waiting, getting nothing, and Hussein is with two doctors in the only room here that has air conditioning.

A small man comes over to me, and I see that he needs to say something to me. I nod at him. He looks at the special room and says it: ‘I have a little one in there’. Behind him on a bench, completely separate, sits a very young woman with a grey headscarf. I say to the man, ‘Is that your wife?’ The door to the special room opens, and I see a girl in a chair who looks up. The White Doctor walks right past us. ‘Go to your wife’, I say. Like a child, he goes and stands silently beside the seated woman, who doesn’t react.

Just then, the door opens and the Blue Doctor walks out, straight past us, without looking. Ali gestures to me, stay back, and then follows him very respectfully. The Doctor snaps back at us, angrily, ‘He’s stable. There’s no “profound coma” – that doctor is an idiot. Go away now and come back in a few hours. Whatever happens, you have to get him out of here tonight’.

A few hours later, I am standing on a hill with my hoe, looking at the ocean, when my phone rings. I don’t recognise the number, but I answer it. ‘Aziz’, the voice says. ‘It’s me’. Hussein.

* * *

The private plane traces a descending arc over the old, white city, the fourteenth-century castle on a cliff, the moon nearly full in the dirty waters of the bay. With great effort, Jonathan, a tall Englishman, lifts his head to look out the window – his godson Lucca instinctively rising to support him – before the pain suddenly closes the old man’s eyes, pushing him down into the reclining seat. Angie, a tall, young woman on his other side, keeps her hand steady on Jonathan’s forearm. Through the open door of the cockpit, the pilot says, ‘Strap in, everyone. We’ll put down shortly’.

The next morning, Jonathan is awake as the light comes down to the Mediterranean, bouncing off the stone-edged swimming pool and through the high glass doors of the former chapel, his bedroom. He notes how discretely the hired nurse has medicalised the room: behind the slightly open door of a Portuguese painted-wood cabinet, the telltale shine of plastic and glass.

His eyes track around the room, professional habit, weighing and judging his own spare composition of objects and artworks, textiles and paint. A baroque tapestry fills one wall, a framed portrait of a native girl hangs on top of it, suspended from a picture rail. Zohra looks out at him – 'gentle and well defended', he had always thought, but today, there's something else in her eyes, a dare to be honest. 'Yes, I suppose I will, soon, Zohra', he says, smiling back at her. He groans softly and Lucca comes in. 'Morning', he says, and takes a pillbox from the pocket of his soft, white jacket, a hand-me-down from his godfather. Jonathan manages to swallow the pill. They both know it will take a while to ease the pain, and Lucca holds his hand until it does.

At midday, Lucca stands looking at music files on a laptop computer. Outside, he hears Angie speaking quietly on the phone, pacing. Telling another friend that Johnny is too weak to see anyone, Lucca can tell. Johnny sleeps, mouth open. Lucca looks at his thick, silver hair on the ochre pillowcase. As Angie comes over to him, Lucca presses a button on the computer, and the opening chords of a slow hymn burst from the speakers. He hits stop; Jonathan opens one eye, then the other in the bed. 'Bit early for that, isn't it?'

Their laughter echoes around Johnny and he looks at them, wry and lucid. Lucca nods at her, and Angie lights a candle and brings over a small home-made cake with the candle in the middle. 'Happy birthday', says Lucca, lifting him to see. Angie brings it to him, blows out the candle and cuts slices for herself and Lucca. With a small smile, he closes his eyes.

Later. More pain. Jonathan is confused. Lucca ever-so-gently lifts up his head, cradling him, and reaches for the glass of water and the pill that Angie has ready. As he swallows the pill, the young man lets him back onto the bed, where Jonathan closes his eyes, chanting inwardly, 'Allah Ameen… Allah Ameen…' He continues the chant, steadily, until sleep stills his lips.

Outside, in the garden, the gardeners finish their day, put their away tools. The houseman, Abdou, comes to speak to them, and they question him. 'It won't be long now', he says. 'Everyone should have their funeral clothes prepared and laid out'. They all look towards the chapel.

A blast of techno explodes over the wall, then stops: a DJ testing a powerful sound system comes to them over the wall. Angie enters the room, taking off a jacket. 'It's no use', she says. 'They're Jordanians, not even Moroccan. It's a big wedding, they've hired some bloody famous DJ'. Normally, they both would have loudly cursed their luck, the rich fools next door, and the Arabs, ungovernable to the end. But today was not for cursing.

The old man sleeps until sunset, then surprises Angie, asking her to locate a book, Keats, in the main house, and read something to him. A phrase he can't recall. She reads:

The moon, like a flower,
In heaven's high bower,
With silent delight

Sits and smiles on the night.

'Sits and smiles', says Jonathan. 'That's right'.

As she finishes, a circular series of notes played on the strings of a lute come from the powerful speakers in the house next door, joined then by a man's strong and delicate voice, singing in Arabic. Johnny recognises the tune, though he can't name the song – the sentimental, funny invocation of a beautiful girl from the country – and smiles. But in the kitchen, the women shake their heads; this is a song for clapping hands and singing along, and now they can't enjoy it, not with him dying in there. Shame on the Jordanians. The new girl in the kitchen moves her lips to the song, whispering to her friend the name of the famous singer, gossip she had learned on the road that day. The singer plays more fine love songs and Jonathan lies awake, listening, as his friends watch light drain out of the evening sky.

Ninety minutes later, the music ends – it is dinner time at the wedding, and music is not customary during the meal – and the old man is still. Lucca closes his eyes, a gesture he will never forget, his godfather's face a death mask now; Angie lowers the blinds, and Lucca goes to telephone for the Moroccan doctor, as they had planned.

On the funeral day, Abdou, the houseman, and Lucca go early to the morgue, where the police kept the body, as they sometimes keep bodies of foreigners, just to be sure. After the usual waiting around, they dress his body: first, in white cotton to keep his mouth closed, and then in fine clothes and raiments that the old man had collected across continents and centuries. Then the Moroccans, the men, the gardeners and the *maalems*, the master artisans, bring Mister Johnny home one last time, carrying him out of the house and down the road to the church.

They arrive to find a hundred Christians in the churchyard – English, French, Americans, Italians, some come from far away. None of them wear black, most are old. They embrace each other and shake hands with the Moroccans. They move aside to let the simple wooden coffin pass into this handsome Anglican church, designed in a Moorish style.

A grave has been dug, by the church doors, amongst the graves of Englishmen going back to the '14–'18 war – the airmen, each with an eagle and a crown, a quotation, a bit of verse. Today, the congregation is different: black African migrants, stopped by the mortal danger of the border crossing, stuck here now, danger ahead of them and behind them, much in need of God. The left nave of the church is full of these parishioners. Jonathan had understood that this was their church for now, and as warden of the church, he had arranged for an African priest to lead it, and that priest now ministers his funeral – a lovely, plain service, with songs and readings.

Jonathan's friends speak as well, and only those Africans who didn't know him well may wonder why this Englishman chose to die and be buried in this foreign land. 'He loved the Moorish people and was their friend'.

The box is carried out to the hole, then. There are five men – Abdou, three gardeners and the gravedigger – working together to lower it down. It takes twenty minutes to fill the hole. The day is sunny and the flowers are in full bloom. The mourners come close and watch the work. For twenty minutes, the African brothers from the church chant call-and-response style: 'Farewell, Jonathan, farewell. We miss you, Jonathan, we miss you'. A Scottish friend takes a harmonica from his pocket and plays, *When the Saints Go Marching In*. The hard lumps of soil rise level with the earth. People place flowers in a mound. Then the east wind kicks up, scattering petals, enjoining us to get on with it.

* * *

The woman reclines in the padded armchair, watching as a muscular, young technician wheels a heavy Lucite-and-lead stand close to her. *Are health techs extra health conscious, because they see sick people every day and don't want to wind up like them?* she wonders.

His own genitals presumably protected by the lead plate and thick glass, the tech unpacks the radioactive fluid and plugs it into her drip. A burst of bright, burning cold, expands around the needle in the back of her hand. She smiles tightly, her usual reaction to pain. 'You might feel, like, a little cold', he says, closing the door. 'Don't get up, don't move at all. See you in an hour'.

An hour, she thinks. *Jesus*. They have forbidden even a book, and her phone is out of the question, of course, not that it would work in this lead-lined room, the size of her walk-in closet at home, tastefully lit with dim halogens in the ceiling. Tasteful, not to offend the dying, she thinks. Once the fluid has worked its way through her system, she knows, she will slide into the donut-shaped scanner; as doctors observe in real time, her body will be rendered in three dimensions, as a series of thousands of lateral slices. Each slice is a lottery scratch ticket. Instant win.

Her mind, pushing off that thought as fast as a swimmer off the pool wall, begins to travel. First, it's visual: recent memories of this summer; the kids at the beach; the light entering the little wooden shack that she and her husband built in the garden; sunlight penetrating a new building for the first time. Why does that feel like a metaphor for something? A dream she had whilst napping in that shack, a book on her chest, a dark creature, soft and malignant, floating in turquoise waters – was her subconscious aware of the sickness before she was? Except for the lump itself, there are no symptoms. She doesn't feel sick at all. *Yes, here I am*, she thinks. She feels the cool touch of her husband's hand on her bicep, then he moves in his sleep, kinder in his sleep. *I'm awake now*. She sees pages describing a project she plans to realise, the paper absorbing the ink until it becomes unseen. Work she will never do. Then she sees her children, adults now; tall, smiling at a joke she can't hear in the kitchen of a country house.

What does it mean, really, if I'm gone? I always supposed we never really think, imagine death, because it's unthinkable. But really, it's perfectly thinkable: I'm gone, that's all. For them, her loves, there will be a tearing sensation, parting pains, but like young, healthy skin, it will hurt at first, then heal quickly.

Forty minutes later, she has entirely made peace with the notion of her own death.

She lifts up her free hand, the left, and slaps herself awkwardly but hard across the cheek. *Stop it. Why are you accepting death? Idiot. You're not dying. It's a scan. You're strong and young. There are doctors for this.*

The door opens and the tech is standing there. 'They are ready for you, madam', he says.

*　　*　　*

I'm still in Tucson. It's been a month. The girl and I are staying at a motel where every room looks at a green, grassy courtyard. They water the grass at night. The pool is empty, broken. We sleep in separate beds. She still has a lot more weeks of paperwork to do, to inherit the house and be able to sell it. I'm almost done with my part.

This afternoon, I'm at the factory, hers now, putting things into a dumpster we rented. Since they stopped paying the bills, the electricity and the air conditioning got shut off, so a lot of the make-up melted in its tubes. The rest of it she is going to sell to a competing company, along with the brand name.

The place is almost emptied out now. It's a high-ceilinged warehouse, with a loading dock at the back and an office in the front, on a street of similar buildings that are empty. At the end of the street is a big road with a family-style Mexican restaurant where I've eaten every day since I've been sorting through the factory; they sell the best Mexican food I've ever had, alive with cilantro and radishes and chillis. Everything around it is dead.

I'm working and waiting for the brother to come out of the bathroom. He's been in there for, like, fifteen minutes, so I know what he's doing. Shooting heroin. I didn't know it took so long, but I guess it's complicated. I keep on hauling boxes of old paperwork out of the dark office and carrying it to the dumpster. It takes a hard shove to get the boxes up over the side, but it's satisfying.

Neither of the brothers has helped with this month of work for more than a few trifling minutes at time. And that was because – separately, and more than once – they came trying to steal stuff from the dead mother's house, to pawn and then buy drugs. Their sister isn't speaking to them, and she got a restraining order, banning them from the house. We check the county prison website sometimes, to see if they're locked up or walking around. When they speak to me, it's usually asking for shit they say is theirs.

Finally, Liam comes out of the bathroom. He's a huge guy – long, black hair in his sweaty face – buckling up a huge pair of jeans and pulling down a long, white T-shirt. Tattoos. He tried to become an outlaw biker, but chasing dope has emptied him out. I remember when he was a sweet, handsome kid, eight years ago. When he speaks, he doesn't look at me, and his voice is thick.

'Man. I don't even know what you're doing out here. But...shit'.

He takes something off his wrist, where there are a lot of leather bracelets, a motorcycle chain. 'This was my dad's'. I've heard stories about his dad, a real piece of work, dead now. 'Want you to have it'.

I look at what he gave me, and my hand jumps on snake instinct: it's a vintage silver bracelet, a diamond-headed snake eating its own tail. Symbol of immortality? 'Gucci 1985 Made in Italy' is stamped inside the buckle. This thing has been around – Rome, Studio 54, Hollywood, all the drug dens out here – catching wind off the front of a Harley until he sold that. Arizona was silver-mine country; the metal might have come from these mountains. Liam could have turned that silver into a week's worth of heroin. I look at him.

'So long, man'. He smiles painfully, avoiding my eyes, and limps out, swallowed by the brightness of the street door.

M a k i n g N e w T i m e M a

k i n g N e w T i m e M a k i

n g N e w T i m e M a k i n g

N e w T i m e M a k i n g N e

w T i m e M a k i n g N e w T

i m e M a k i n g N e w T i m

e M a k i n g N e w T i m e M

a k i n g N e w T i m e M a k

i n g N e w T i m e M a k i n

g N e w T i m e M a k i n g N

e w T i m e M a k i n g N e w

T i m e M a k i n g N e w T i

m e M a k i n g N e w T i m e

M a k i n g N e w T i m e M a

k i n g N e w T i m e M a k i

ng**What**NewTimeMa

kingNewTimeMaki

ng**we**New**talk**Time

MakingNewTimeMa

king**about**NewTim

eMakingNewTimeM

akingNew**when**Tim

eMakingNewTimeM

akingNewTimeMak

ingNewTimeMakin

g**we**New**talk**TimeM

akingNewTimeMak

ingNe**about**wTime

MakingNewTimeMa

king**time**NewTime

Perhaps it is hubristic to take as my own title a very slightly modified one from another author whose story has already once been snatched from him, at least in a way, by an editor anxious to contain – the author would say 'amputate' – the text, whether by word count or word content, it is unclear. I like to think not, and I like to think that we can speak together. In case the reference is not immediately recognisable (and there's no reason it should be), the text in question is Raymond Carver's 1981 *What we talk about when we talk about love*, republished posthumously in 2009 in its original, unamputated form as *Beginners*. One of the things we learn from the first, edited version of the story is that what we talk about when we talk about love is, actually, death. In the second, unedited version, we learn that we talk about death because we haven't yet learnt to love, because we are just beginning. Or something like that. In both, lessons about love are situated temporally, but their temporality is never resolved: in our end is our beginning; but it is equally true that in our beginning is our end. But now, I am seizing and revising the words of another famous and dead and white man. So, I will stop. What matters most is that these ends and these beginnings manifest in the temporality of talking.

When we talk about time, we are all saying different things to each other, and we are saying them all the time. I say the months have stretched forever, and you say it is like yesterday just happened. I say it is too late, and you say it is just at the right time. You say the war is over, and I say we have not yet learnt who won. We all know that time is subjective, but we pretend it is worth the same, literally and figuratively. Of course, it can't be. Time is differentiated and situated, not only individually and experientially, but also historically, geographically and economically. Just now, for example, I googled 'making new time', and arrived at the amazon.com page for the book you are currently reading. My present is already someone else's loss, financially speaking, at the very least, and not just in this instance.

About two weeks ago, and without having been asked, my phone began making new memories for me. I was startled, at first: a quick screen alert was echoed by a ping I did not recognise. In a band of screen space no thicker than my finger, the text told me, 'You have a new memory: Four years of good times with four-legged creatures'. A few days later, I was alerted that I had another new memory, this time about 'Meals with friends'. A few days later, another new memory popped up. It was a bit less precise. Short and to the point, it consisted of the 'Best moments of the last two weeks'. The memories had taken anchor in the photos, photos I took; but these didn't correspond to the photos I had chosen, or the memories I might have made from them. They are not mine, but my phone is giving them to me. They tell stories that were never written, although I suppose it is true that they were written by an algorithm that someone wrote. The point is that unsifted and unpurposed, they take me from a present I think I have made, which I always think I am making, and that is always mine.

I have been asked to write a meditation about time, or rather, to write up what I have come to think after having meditated on time. But, I have had a hard time finding the time in which to do so. I was unable to 'make' the 'new time' that would conjoin my enterprise with that of this book, both in terms of my labour and in regard to the book's thematic content. I kept beginning the task, but stopping before I could finish it. By the time I was able to return to the task, I had forgotten what I started with, or where I had hoped it would take me. I kept reproducing the thing I had wanted to talk about, which was the experience of being simultaneously out of time, yet stuck thick in its weeds. This might be the temporality of the 'echo chamber' through which the curators of this year's Sharjah Biennial want to guide us. The echo chamber they describe is the bubble in which we live. In it sound the calamities of the contemporary, resonant with the incessant reverberations of our self-condemnations, our castigations of the time in which we live and the time we don't have.

Funnily enough, it was my phone – one of the instruments that is responsible for the time-suck that means we have to make 'new time' – that plucked me out of this morass, and not because it is designed to do that or because it has a magical agency I mean to uphold. (This is not my version of *Her*.) No. Instead, it turns out that the two weeks upon which my phone drew to make my new, 'best of' memories correspond precisely with the two weeks in which I was supposed to finish this meditation, which, of course, I didn't do, because I didn't have the time. I am in Beirut, where meditating is not always easy and time is never my own (or anyone else's, really). Causality never seems as predominant here – artistically, intellectually or temporally – as chance, and so, time moves accordingly, not like a flow chart, a timeline or anything that we might recognise as historical time. It moves more like an EKG's clustered scratch marks on a scrolling piece of paper. The paper moves, but the more movement the instrument senses, the more the ink marks knot in static striations. Time here is uncanny in the canniest of ways. In presenting me with my new memory of the 'Best moments of the last two weeks', the phone precisely captured this temporality, both in its own actions and by pointing to one of its most telling examples: an actual echo chamber, albeit an inadvertent one, in which I had sat. But unlike the echo chamber that constitutes the Biennial's view of our contemporaneity, this was an echo chamber I never wanted to leave.

I'm talking about the cement-domed theatre that stands – although just barely – at the centre of the Rashid Karameh International Exhibition Center in Tripoli, Lebanon. Designed by Oscar Niemeyer in 1962, the fairground was commissioned by the administration of then-president Fouad Chehab, who was anxious to unify the fledgling Lebanese nation after it had only barely recovered from the foreshocks of civil war in 1958. Doing so meant, in part, countering Beirut's stronghold on the national economy, reconciling (or at least mediating) sectarian differences, and developing the public institutions of a modern state. The fairground, as Niemeyer conceived it, was part of this vision, and the Brazilian architect imagined that it would unfold onto the doubled urban structure of Tripoli, forming a functional third city, complete with infrastructure for housing and education. It was also meant to consolidate (or at least situate) Lebanon as a power player within a larger, regional unity, linked by transport and transversal trade networks between Baghdad, Tripoli and Damascus. Never completed, and abandoned in 1975 at the start of the Lebanese Civil War, the fairground now stands as the ruins of this unrealised future, already ruined, in fact, before it was left unfinished. A relic from the past, it is nonetheless also a perfect representation of the current state of affairs – and the state – around it: a cryogenically preserved, aborted embryo. This is the time about which we talk, when we talk about time here.

As with the rest of the fairground, the cement-domed theatre-in-the-round (it would have featured a – first of its kind! – floating stage that, elevated by hydraulic pumps, would have imbricated art in the weave of its own public), which my phone had singled out as the focus of my 'best moments' memory, was never finished, and so, sound-insulation panels were never installed. Or, if they were, they were looted, either by a cohort of corrupt contractors and the politicians with whom they conspired, or by any of the several militias and refugees who occupied the theatre after the fairground was left unfinished. Now, because there are no sound panels, words within the dome echo and swell and distort as they travel around, slightly delayed with each reverberation. The events that occurred in the theatre during the war years, when it was occupied by various militia at different moments, remain undocumented and unwritten; but it is nonetheless spoken that acts of torture, or at least their preparations, took place there.

The new memory my phone made for me, as I was trying to meditate on the question of what we talk about when we talk about time, was of sitting in this dome with a group of students, twelve or so, all told. Each of us had played with throwing our voices, singing, calling, whistling, speaking and jumping, as we walked or sat individually around the theatre's perimeter. The more noise we made, the stronger the echo and the more destabilising the experience. It became harder and harder to discern from where each sound came, from which person or in which order. We were all together, bound in sound, but also all temporally untethered. We ceased being the owners of the words we uttered, or the authors of their meaning. Instead, we became something of a collective sound machine moving ever so slightly backwards and forwards in time, joining a history that was collapsing onto itself or, perhaps, already had done so.

I went again to the fairground a week later. This time, to see it repurposed as the site of a temporary art exhibition. In the theatre and under the dome was installed a work of art. The space was dramatically lit, in a rotating sequence of flood beams, first from the pit, then from the top of the dome and then from the sides. Ropes were tethered from dome to ceiling, as if to mimic, in a recognisably contemporary-art idiom, the still-protruding metal rods on which the sound panels might have hung. I think I heard music, but it was almost indiscernible. The art audience came to the threshold of the building, maybe twenty or thirty at a time, despite the fact that the building was in extreme disrepair and should not have been made to withstand such a mass. The art audience did not walk around a building built in the round as a place to unify a public. Those present did not sit and listen. They stood at the doorway, took pictures, bellowed a bit and left, almost before they could catch the reverberations of even their own voices, to say nothing of the voices of the people who joined them, or the pasts that might have been. This was the time of art, and they were its authors.

Their time in the echo chamber, no matter how loud it had been, was a time of not talking, either about the public the building was once hoped to foster – through something that might resemble love, but certainly meant to resemble art – or the death it likely came to contain. I like to think, though, that our time in the chamber (mine with my students, that is) had been something different, even if, or maybe because, it was far from art. According to my phone, it is now a new memory, but it isn't one I chose, at least not at this moment, and so it is also a memory that exceeds the telling of historical time. When it happened, it was in heterogeneous time, but it was shared all the same. For an instant, we were more than singular bodies. We were a community in time, situated neither in the past nor the present, and definitely not in the future. It was neither our end nor our beginning, but it was full of love, although we never spoke directly of it.

N e w T i m e M a k i n g N e

w T i m e M a k i n g N e w T

i m e M a k i n g N e w T i m

e M a k i n g N e w T i m e M

a k i n g N e w T i m e M a k

i n g N e w T i m e M a k i n

g N e w T i m e M a k i n g N

e w T i m e M a k i n g N e w

T i m e M a k i n g N e w T i

m e M a k i n g N e w T i m e

M a k i n g N e w T i m e M a

k i n g N e w T i m e M a k i

n g N e w T i m e M a k i n g

N e w T i m e M a k i n g N e

w T i m e M a k i n g N e w T

i m e M a k i n g N e w T i m
e M a k i n g I ’ m N e w T i
m e M a k i n g N e w T i m e
M a k i n g N e w T i m e M a
k i n g N e w T i m e M a k i
n g N e w T i m e M a k i n g
R e a d y N e w T i m e M a k
i n g N e w T i m e M a k i n
g N e w T i m e M a k i n g N
e w N o w T i m e M a k i n g
N e w T i m e M a k i n g N e
w T i m e M a k i n g N e w T
i m e M a k i n g N e w T i m
e M a k i n g N e w T i m e M
a k i n g N e w T i m e M a k

How boring and dull it would be to make an argument for slowness in these supposedly accelerated times. Slowness has always been constant, unfolding at a pace that might otherwise seem foreign or out of sync with the current rhythms of daily life. It can be imperceptible and, at times, irrelevant, but it's always been plodding along at its own rate. Singer Jonathan Richman of the Modern Lovers has, in another context, announced, 'It seems to be the mood to return to slowness now', and rapper Juvenile has defended the rhythmic contours of slow motion: 'Slow down for me, you moving too fast'. Countless others have made a plea for slowness, arguing, instead, for a kind of conceptual, libidinal or perceptual downshift.

There are many examples of deceleration, many cases of an unhurried approach to time. There are also cases to be made for slowing down in the workplace, a tendency that has more to do with efficiency than with quality of life: 'slow down, but get more done' is the logic.

Art historical, musical and filmic examples abound as well. Is there anything more laborious and beautiful than the forty-five-minute zoom that structures Michael Snow's *Wavelength* (1967)? For the duration of this riveting sequence, eyes lumber along with Snow's camera, playing witness to an experiment as it gives way to a field of vision that diminishes until it is eventually enveloped by a picture of water on an adjacent wall. Sharon Lockhart's *Lunch Break* (2008) is a like-minded testament to slowness: although it arrived more than forty years after *Wavelength*, it was never too late. Slowness is a theme that unifies the two films. In a continuous motion, Lockhart's camera lurches along a corridor, where workers take their midday break. Snippets of conversation flutter in and out of the passing frame. Lockhart designed the soundscape in collaboration with composer Becky Allen and film-maker James Benning; it is a decidedly industrial sound, which can be likened to a kind of grinding of the gears.

Elsewhere, no one doubts the coarse, droning reverberations of the experimental metal band Sunn O))) or the perceptual shift made evident by the late chopped and screwed remixes of maestro DJ Screw. Listening to a typical Screw remix in the company of codeine or promethazine puts slowness into context. The altered musical tempo matches the decline in one's cognitive faculties; slowness becomes the new norm of experience. DJ Screw left an indelible mark on music producers: his influence comes in and out of popular music like the delayed kick of a bass drum. For their part, followers of the druid clan of Sunn O))) divorce themselves from their senses. The guitar duo performs in a sea of smoke and fog, within which only a faint flood of coloured lights and the guttural sounds of the musicians' duelling guitars is made visible. Concertgoers are known to crowd the venue walls as a way of putting their bodies into closer proximity to the detuned sonic waves. Slowness does not begin to describe the rate at which the music of Sunn O))) emanates forth and envelopes its listeners.

Immersed in this muddy drone, all possibility of acceleration is suspended. To this end, writing also comes slowly. It is a painfully slow process, not unlike wading through the mud of a codeine high or a sludgy musical composition. Writing can be such a laborious task, in part, because it is a tactile and rhythmic form. For some, it comes quickly, if it comes at all. For others, it comes slowly, like a set of anaerobic finger exercises. Texts, such as the one you are now reading, tend to arrive late as a result of writerly deceleration.

I am late, because the words came slowly. I'm sorry to be apologetic about this reality. Because writing takes time, and because its clock does not work properly. Writing doesn't give time, it takes time. It consumes it, and it takes time from me. Some might say that writing wastes time. Or, it may be a waste of my time. There are countless daylight hours spent thinking about the words to write, about the unique qualities of language in the form of a sentence. The question remains whether or not it is time well spent. Some writers are able to maintain their deadlines and pride themselves on competency and punctuality. But slowness is an antidote to productivity, to behaving properly, to participating in a meaningful way and in a timely manner.

Perhaps it's worth participating in less-than-meaningful ways. By choosing to eat up time and slow down the momentum of production. For editors, time is as valuable and efficient as language. Editors deal in the efficiency of language, rather than the reckless expenditure of it. Writers, on the other hand, have an innate ability to elongate time. It's not pleasant to have this burden occupy one's self for so long, given that the actual amount of time writing is, in comparison, so brief. There are other sources to consult, other ideas to mine before sitting down to craft the next sentence. Almost every sentence unfolds in this manner. I usually can't be bothered to sit down for so long.

One belaboured string of words begets another, and so on and so forth. If only there were bursts of energy, bursts of speed that could make for a better use of energy. As part of their professional responsibilities, curators also have to write – and the longer that writing takes, the longer any given curator is taken away from his or her curating. It is often argued that writing is a form of curating, of organising one's thoughts or mediating between them. The words of a sentence might even be curatorial fodder. However, this fantasy is just barely enough to transport curators from their social reality to the world they would rather inhabit, to the literary role they might rather play in the drama of art.

To take one's time is to slow down the process and to perform an occupational masquerade. This activity can appear to be as productive as it is gratifying. Writing can be generative, whilst curating is resigned to being forever responsive. Those slow writers, with whom I have worked in my capacity as a curator, tend to cower, to hide from the long arm of an impending deadline. They have masterfully learned to evade the email – subject line: 'Checking In' – or the seemingly more personal SMS. This cat-and-mouse game can weigh heavily on one's conscience. But slowness prevails. Staying true to form, the respected, evasive writer almost always turns in a text only after it's ready and not a moment sooner. Slowness is anti-productive. It is waste, and it won't let the demands for speed get in its way. Where would the worlds of publishing or exhibitions have gone with DJ Screw at its helm, with Sunn O))) as the editorial groundskeeper?

This text was submitted past its due date, but not a moment past its prime. This is because the physical qualities of a body can hardly compete with the pace of rapid ambitions and freewheeling ideas. The interior has a difficult time finding the words to express itself and make itself known to the outside world. If interior thoughts are made available through the writing process, then the speed might as well evade the acceptability of communication. At times, the neurons don't appear to be firing, and all I can do is sit quietly and wait. Therefore, because of slowness, this is overdue. The debilitating difference between acceleration and slowness is manifest in this piece of writing, the first draft of which was submitted six weeks past its initial deadline. I hope it was worth the wait.

T i m e M a k i n g N e w T i

m e M a k i n g N e w T i m e

M a k i n g N e w T i m e M a

k i n g N e w T i m e M a k i

n g N e w T i m e M a k i n g

N e w T i m e M a k i n g N e

w T i m e M a k i n g N e w T

i m e M a k i n g N e w T i m

e M a k i n g N e w T i m e M

a k i n g N e w T i m e M a k

i n g N e w T i m e M a k i n

g N e w T i m e M a k i n g N

e w T i m e M a k i n g N e w

T i m e M a k i n g N e w T i

m e M a k i n g N e w T i m e

M a k i n g N e w T i m e M a
k i n g N e w T i m e M a k i
n g N e w T i m e M a k i n g
N e w T i m e M a k i n g N e
w T i m e M a k i n g N e w T
i m e M a k i n g N e w T i m
e M a k i n g N e w T i m e M
a k i n g N e w T i m e M a k
i n g **P r e t t y** N e w T i m
e M a k i n g **G r e e n** N e w
T i m e **C i t y** M a k i n g N
e w T i m e M a k i n g N e w
T i m e M a k i n g N e w T i
m e M a k i n g N e w T i m e
M a k i n g N e w T i m e M a

'A flower in front of every house and a smile on every face'

—Attributed to Sheikh Sultan bin Muhammad Al-Qasimi, Ruler of Sharjah

Green, like no other colour, bears its own ideologies, its own universe of meanings. These can materialise as images, illusions and mirages. Green is political. Its palette has driven people to move land, sink wells and carve out mountains, all for the possibility that a delicate canopy of green might appear. Green is geopolitical.[1]

For its campaigns, green appropriates other colours: violet, magenta, bright yellow and deep red.

Brown is the only colour imbued with enough consequence to challenge green. Brown performs as green's foil. A green city lives. A brown city dies. Or that is, at least, what some people say.

Shamans 'correlate' green with happiness. Together, the two are all the rage today, just as they were in the past, including in revered religious texts. Their partnership is, at once, clichéd, innate, moral, ethical and, now, scientifically proven.

Legendary despots have planted extravagant green gardens for themselves. Some of these grounds they have given to their people. In the Gulf region, Sheikh Zayed of Abu Dhabi tried to green his capital with millions of trees. Sheikh Rashid of Dubai is said to have built a 'national park' (including swimming pools) in a matter of months for 'millions of dollars'.

In Sharjah, Sheikh Sultan's planned pageantry of green was to have been the most widespread and the most systematic such project ever undertaken there. It was inscribed by master planners, administered by technocrats and, in part, planted by labourers. Its renderings boded happiness, beauty, hygiene and bureaucratic order.

Yet all at once, in the early 1980s, Sharjah had a lot of change to absorb: a second chance at oil wealth, a 'skyrocketing' property market, a ravenous rental market and a scarcity of water and electricity. The water shortage was partially caused by brown sand clogging up pipes that delivered water from deep below the desert. The electricity shortage was blamed on a city growing too fast.

Oil was the cause of and solution to every problem.

In addition to attracting industrial plants, business ventures and apartment towers, Sharjah needed to be beautiful. There were clean-up campaigns. Store owners were entreated to plant trees in front of their shops. Housewives were instructed on how to manage household waste. There was, at least once, a parade of cars and trucks bedecked with cut flowers. Green in these instances was pretty, kind and volunteered.

One might ask if it is possible to *make* Sharjah green, as if it just takes someone to *care*. Up until the 1980s, the city relied on underground sources for its water. Up until it couldn't. To make Sharjah green, it took someone to *pay*.

Green, however, could no longer just adorn. It needed to 'change the face' of Sharjah. Green needed to be designed and, therefore, top-down technical. Green was a concoction of science (biology, botany, psychiatry, meteorology, climatology) at the urban scale. In its own act of narrative-making, science portrayed the city as a nursery of green under attack – not by its own machinations of pollution and consumption, but by something encroaching from the outside.

The Sharjah Green Belt was meant to bind the city together. Sharjah's planners measured out the potential of the Green Belt in kilometres – 150 metres wide and several metres high. It was supposed to wrap around the city's new apartment towers, industrial districts, flyovers and shopping streets. With trees, shrubs, grass and flowers, it was planned to encircle Sharjah in order to treasure and protect it.

'Green belt' is a nifty term that was exported and has been sold the world over, first by British town planners. In the Greater London Plan of 1944, perhaps the most important document in urban-planning history, green belts were drawn as thick membranes around idealised circles of 'New Towns'. Residents nested inside the city, inside the green belt. To leave a New Town meant traversing the green belt, perhaps something like riding through an enchanted forest.

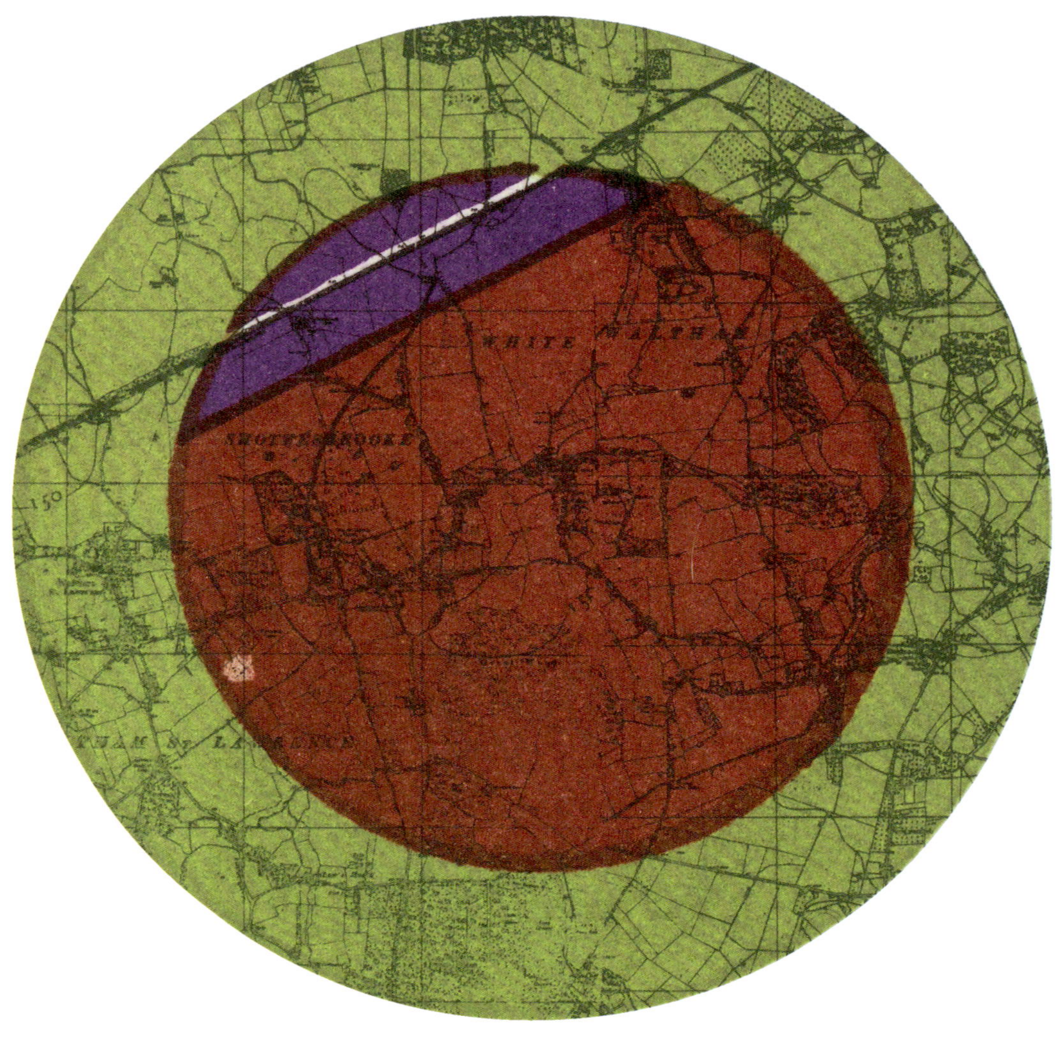

Detail of the Greater London Plan of 1944 that indicates a low-density New Town in red surrounded by a green belt (University of Amsterdam, Bijzondere Collecties)

In the guise of a belt, green took on new powers. It could shape cities and determine regional economies. Its tones and hues performed as a social and financial brigade. Fastened around a British New Town, a green belt was designed to protect against urban sprawl, to keep buildings within it and speculative temptation beyond.

Ramparts protected many ancient cities. Some ramparts were cities in themselves, perforated by rooms and hallways inhabited by soldiers and animals. Damp and dark, these interiors existed for the purpose of preserving the city centre and holding the perimeter against barbarians.

The Sharjah Green Belt's adversary was not the barbarian, but the desert – once an ecosystem integral to Sharjah, it was now considered a menacing force to resist. The green belt was to be armed with lushness and deploy 'huge shade trees as fencing'. A new breed of green grass was made for and named after Sharjah (*sharjah hashish*). Like the ramparts, the Sharjah Green Belt was to host an inhabitable redoubt: 'modern facilities in keeping with the traditional life of the people'. It was to have been 'exclusive', supplying 'amusement facilities', cafeterias and tiled walkways. Green's primary sustenance, water, was supposed to course through fountain pumps and be thrust high into tree-filtered air.

When Sharjah was threatened with a water shortage, moisture no longer seemed like a natural state. It became a high-stakes commodity, a tick on the list of essential infrastructural ingredients. Behold a pretty *and* modern city.

Sharjah got its first desalination plant in 1981. Perhaps it has always imposed a price, but water from then onwards became a product. Like bolts of woven fabric or rolls of smelted aluminium, desalinated water was doled out as it left the plant in standardised units. Units of volume and time. Beauty was no longer just the masking of hard labour with a pretty face. It was an exorbitant luxury. And, as with any luxury, its 'conspicuous spectacle' suspended a pleasing, thickened surface over a deep, pervasive quagmire of environmental controversy. Sharjah got a distillation plant, but it never got its Green Belt.[2] Instead, the city seeped through and sprawled beyond the band's intended path.

1 See Gareth Doherty, *Paradoxes of Green: Landscapes of a City-State* (Oakland: University of California Press, 2017).
2 The 735-metre portion of the Green Belt that was built is today called the Green Belt Ladies Park.

MakingNewTimeMa

kingNewTimeMaki

ngNewTimeMaking

NewTimeMakingNe

wTimeMakingNewT

imeMakingNewTim

eMakingNewTimeM

akingNewTimeMak

ingNewTimeMakin

gNewTimeMakingN

ewTimeMakingNew

TimeMakingNewTi

meMakingNewTime

MakingNewTimeMa

kingNewTimeMaki

n g N e w T i m e M a k i n g

N e w T i m e M a k i n g N e

w T i m e M a k i n g N e w T

i m e M a k i n g N e w T i m

e M a k i n g N e w T i m e M

a k i n g N e w T i m e **T o** M

a k i n g **H o l d** N e w T i m

e M a k i n g N e w T i m e M

a k i n g N e w T i m e M a k

i n g **M y** N e w **B r e a t h** T

i m e M a k i n g N e w T i m

e M a k i n g N e w T i m e M

a k i n g N e w T i m e M a k

i n g N e w T i m e M a k i n

g N e w T i m e M a k i n g N

1

The algorithmic bubble ignores how quickly things move: fleeting interests, transitory relationships, random travels, migratory routes. My email inbox bombards me with messages such as: 'Rabat has some last-minute deals'. 'One deal left'. 'Take me there'. 'Sofia, look no further. The best deals are here'. I trash these emails. I cannot stand the out-of-syncness between my immediate reality and the online world, between the physical and the digital space. I have no intention of travelling to Rabat again anytime soon. Can someone delete this from my search history, please? Damn algorithms. Wait. Rewind? Fast forward? Perhaps I am simply mourning a troubling emotional experience. But how do we stop technology from colonising our brains, choreographing our memories and harassing us with where to 'look', thus determining the direction of our accelerated lives? I begin to think about the best way to put an end to these reverberations, which occupy an endless space within my brain, a space that seems defined by lack, by absence, by a sense of incompleteness or impossibility. Hear me! Hold my breath. If only this voice could stop regretting.[1] I think about silence.

2

The asphyxiating culture of hyperproductivity dictates that one must be *on* at all times. Newsfeeds, Facebook posts, tweets, search engines, emails, screens, surveillance. Shall we accept cookies? Yes or no? The Internet has become a sort of prosthetic extension of our brains. We are digital, online entities with profiles that are defined according to fixed typologies and digitally traceable affiliations. The cloud that stores all of our data epitomises the prevailing network hegemony. The real is abstracted from its material referent. Under digital capitalism, as argued by German artist Anna Zett, 'The more we use the internet, the farther the frontier of privatization moves into our embodied minds....Gmail and Facebook are free because I pay with my attention, my interaction, with the content in the metadata of my life'.[2] Still, I turn to Wikipedia to search the term 'echo chamber' – or, at least, its definition according to whoever wrote or edited that page. The site tells me the following: '[I]t is a metaphorical description of a situation in which beliefs are amplified or reinforced by communication and repetition inside a closed system'. The echo chamber becomes a parable of a world in which polarised views and political extremist positions are hyperbolised and disseminated at high speed, with no critical filter.

3

In a book published nearly two decades ago, *The Great Accelerator*, French author Paul Virilio interrogates time, history, speed and knowledge. In the first paragraph, he states: 'To live every instant as though it were the last – that is the paradox of futurism, of a futurism of the instant that has no future...as if instantaneity suddenly annulled all durability'. He describes that in a 'globalised world constantly traversed by internal exiles in a closed-circuit exodus of just-in-time flows of people...TRACEABILITY is now being imposed on each and every one of us'. *No return beyond this point* – alerts a sign upon my arrival at the security check of a London airport: 'We all know that where there's a wall there has to be a door; but the only real difference between this wall and the old fortified wall that surrounded a city is the virtual nature of the contemporary enclosure of postmodern times, as well as the clinical radiography deployed at the main entrances of our current borders'.[3]

A chapter of Virilio's book titled 'Too Late for Private Life' notes: '*Mode de vie* (lifestyle) and *cardiac rhythms* (heartbeats), *mode de vitesse* (speed mode) and *technical rhythmics* (technical cycles) – that, in a nutshell, is the question posed by the TEMPO of our use of time and space in a vitality that was once run-of-the-mill but is now suffering from everyday life's electrotechnical ARHYTHMIA which never stops rocking people's consciences'.[4] Can we eradicate the vibrations that come from within our own bodies, the echo chamber of our unfulfilled desires? Can we escape who we are?

4

The anechoic chamber is an echo-free enclosure, a space encapsulating the conditions that are the closest we can get to absolute silence. The anechoic chamber has inspired the work of composer John Cage. The story he tells marks a founding moment in his concept of 'silence'.[5] Cage describes the experience: 'In that silent room I heard two sounds: one high, one low. Afterwards, I asked the engineer in charge why if the room was so silent I had heard two sounds. He said: describe them. I did. He said: the high one was your nervous system in operation, the low one was your blood in circulation'.[6] In his autobiographical writings, Cage recalls: 'In the late forties I found out by experiment (I went into the anechoic chamber at Harvard University) that silence is not acoustic. It is a change of mind, a turning around. I devoted my music to it. My work became an exploration of non-intention. To carry it out faithfully I have developed a complicated composing means using *I Ching* chance operations, making my responsibility that of asking questions instead of making choices'.[7] Can silence, as a structural position, defy technology and enable us to imagine other possible worlds beyond the ones prescribed by the 'infosphere'?[8]

5

Silence. How to create spaces of intimacy and empathy in an ever-accelerated present? *Solid Maneuvers* (2018), a performance by Nigerian-born artist Otobong Nkanga, touched me in a visceral way. She dressed in a black outfit and performed machinelike, considered movements. I recall some of her words and actions through the filter of my memory: Skin. Soil. Stones. Sediments. Breathing. Lungs. I can feel the particles going down my lungs. Will they make me cry or will they burn me? The sound of rocks being crushed. Mining and minerals. Iron, calcium, magnesium. Things that we dig and take out of the soil. How do we remember a place of shared histories? Holes. Digs. Becoming landscape. The gestures of the hand. Tools. Machines. Labour. A factory. The redundancy of our gestures. Why not singing? Like coded instructions. Breathing. Exhaustion. Collapse.

6

The physicist Carlo Rovelli talks about the emotional dimension of time as well as human anxiety in relation to the idea of impermanence. He says that 'the time we experience is a multi-layered, complex concept...a mystery that relates to issues ranging from the future of black holes to the enigma of our individual identity and consciousness'.[9] What do we talk about when we talk about time? Is it about making new time? Or, rather, an understanding of time that encompasses different conceptions, perceptions, extraterritorial positions, affections and speeds? And how do we measure it? Against what? The metabolism of our bodies? The bacteria that infect our vulnerable immune systems? The things we possess? The place where we live? The pace of our working lives? The networks that define our daily activities? The challenges of our emotional states? And is it the question of time passing or of time lost that we are measuring? What if we simply refuse time? 'To hold back. To undo. To unsay. To unremember. To Unhappen'.[10]

1 Samuel Beckett, The Unnamable (London: Faber & Faber, 2010), 49 and 87.
2 Anna Zett, 'Sleeping in Public, Working Like Babies', Technosphere Magazine, 15 November 2016, https://technosphere-magazine.hkw.de/p/Sleeping-in-Public-Working-Like-Babies-cC1sQRMqqpdwbMVEfKE2tE.
3 Paul Virilio, The Great Accelerator (Cambridge: Polity Press, 2012), 22.
4 Ibid., 31.
5 For a detailed account, see Julia Robinson, ed., John Cage (Cambridge: MIT Press, 2011), 190.
6 YouTube clip titled 'John Cage, a visit to the anechoic chamber', published 19 March 2013, accessed August 2018, https://www.youtube.com/watch?v=jS9ZOlFB-kI.
7 See John Cage, ROLYWHOLYOVER, A CIRCUS: JOHN CAGE (The Museum of Contemporary Art, Los Angeles, 1993).
8 See artist Cally Spooner's interview with psychiatrist Isabel Vally, which was presented in the exhibition, Cally Spooner: Soundtrack for a troubled time and notes on humiliation at Whitechapel Gallery, 30 August–26 November 2017. Spooner references Franco 'Bifo' Berardi's notion that 'the infosphere appropriates and absorbs our nervous systems, creating an "epidemic of panic and depression" that is "spreading through the circuits of the social brain and the global economy"'.
9 Carlo Rovelli, 'The Physics of Time', FT Weekend Magazine, 21/22 April 2018, 16.
10 William Kentridge, Six Drawing Lessons (Cambridge: Harvard University Press, 2014), 25.

T i m e M a k i n g N e w T i

m e M a k i n g N e w T i m e

M a k i n g N e w T i m e M a

k i n g N e w T i m e M a k i

n g N e w T i m e M a k i n g

N e w T i m e M a k i n g N e

w T i m e M a k i n g N e w T

i m e M a k i n g N e w T i m

e M a k i n g N e w T i m e M

a k i n g N e w T i m e M a k

i n g N e w T i m e M a k i n

g N e w T i m e M a k i n g N

e w T i m e M a k i n g N e w

T i m e M a k i n g N e w T i

m e M a k i n g N e w T i m e

EndingsMakingNe
wTimeMakingNewT
imeMakingNewTim
eMakingNewTimeM
akingNewTimeMak
ingNewTimeMakin
gNewTime**and**Maki
ngNewTimeMaking
NewTimeMakingNe
wTimeMakingNewT
ime**Other**MakingN
ewTimeMakingNew
TimeMakingNewTi
meMakingNewTime
MakingNew**Things**

My six-year-old pointed out a problem to me: a girl was writing a story 'from real life', but couldn't finish it because she kept waiting for the ending. In a way, my daughter was asking about the efficacy of endings when writing in parallel to time, which is effectively what documentary is. So instead, we think of Roald Dahl ('What if someone committed a murder with a frozen leg of lamb?'[1]). My daughter is often preoccupied with notions of the 'real': 'Is this *real*?', for example, when watching E.T. (the extraterrestrial) being rolled off on a stretcher.[2]

In February 2016, an Egyptian high court sentenced novelist Ahmed Naji to two years in prison for public indecency after the publication of one chapter from his book *The Use of Life* (*Istikhdam al-Haya*) in the literary magazine *Akhbar Al-Adab*. In a fascinating conversation with writer and translator Mona Kareem, Naji explains that '[the novelist] Sonallah Ibrahim, Mohamed Salmawy (head of the Arab Writers Union), and Gaber Asfour (former Minister of Culture) will be testifying in court to clarify that [Naji's] novel is a work of imagination and creativity'.[3] It follows, that if the thinking behind Naji's printed matter had been 'real', akin to a child's blur with 'what is real', then the work he made from it could be deemed 'criminal'. Whereas if, literally, the formation of the thoughts behind the making of those phrases came from his imagination, then his book is, in fact, 'lawful'. Clearly, the real is frightening for authoritarian regimes, but it is also fittingly punishable – and so, more controllable. The real is both disturbing and outright alarming. My daughter didn't ask, 'Is this real?' when Elliot and E.T. rode the skies, gliding past the moon on a bicycle in true friendship and love; but rather, when E.T. turned white and sick and deadly. The real is the fantastically wondrous. The ordinary, too. But, the cruel could not possibly be the real.[4]

In Naji's short story *Ambulance* (2016), an erotic moment between two lovers gets interrupted by reality, when one realises that he has given 'grandmother' too strong a dose of her medicine. Through 223 frantic words, we follow the saga of the two characters simply trying to escape reality via lust, but getting pulled back into it. In the middle of this hysterical prose, a wonderful interruption is found in the moment when the protagonist drives behind the ambulance transporting the grandmother to the hospital: instead of focusing on the gravity of the situation, he becomes preoccupied with the radiant lines of red that the truck throws out on itself. In the end, the two return to their erotic moment in a hospital bathroom, 'as granny [keeps] dying'.[5] And so, in the end, an overwhelming event is, in fact, momentary. It inevitably passes, often lending itself to the same kind of ending – that of the mundanity and, also, the cruelty of, quite simply, moving on...

Yet in the search for writing an ending, we often get strangulated by punctuation. We seem to overly rely on the full stop. For a start, because the *dot dot dot* (...) no longer suffices. Eugene Thacker opens his essay *Dark Media* by citing Frederic Brown's 1948 'Knock', the shortest horror story ever written: 'The last man on earth sat alone in a room. There was a knock on the door...'.[6] He then compares it to a variation of the work, published nine years later, titled, 'The Horror Story Shorter by One Letter Than the Shortest Horror Story Ever Written', which reads: 'The last man on earth sat alone in a room. There was a lock on the door...'.[7] The act of comparing the endings of a horror story is intriguing in itself. Thacker contrasts the two-sentence stories by asking, '[W]hich is the greater horror, the something that wants to come in, or the impossibility of ever going out?'[8] Comparisons are, likewise, always being made regarding the cruelty of two different events. If one is finally able to make an utterance about the horror of a show being seen, then the answer often lies in a comparison that kills the details, never allowing it to emerge as a plausible course of action: 'Gaza? But what about Syria?'; 'Syria? But what about Yemen?'

The illustrator and comic-book artist Ayman Al Zorkany once deemed the comic book the most satisfying form of an ending. He described the format of the comic book, specifically, as '*Malikat Al Lahza*' ('the Queen of All Moments'),[9] because, in a full-leaf comic grid, you can actually *see* where and when the end of the event is, if you so wish, and in a single plane of vision. The illustrator can write the whole story, from beginning to end, into one frame. Meanwhile, the reader can control the time and the speed at which s/he is experiencing a story, by pacing the moment a page will be turned. In other words: things are perfectly and ecstatically under control.[10] Plus, the comic-book format shortens the saga.

But how do we flip the page for an ending to an event whose crescendo will just not get fulfilled? How do we force an ending onto a story that will reappear? Thus far in contemporary art, leaving time has been necessarily artful; fictional, science-fictional; spiritual, too. But what do you do when you are the victim or no longer have these artful bounties? How do we narrate events in such a way that allows for poetic transcendence and travel, but still contributes to making cruel events more visible, legible and accountable?

My six-year-old, therefore, asks me: What is to be done if a person is writing a story 'from real life', but can't finish it because she keeps waiting for the ending? I tell her that's a great question. She replies, 'Then wouldn't it be great if we could jump into a hole that doesn't have an end?'

1 From the archives of Roald Dahl, as highlighted by Josh Lacey in https://www.theguardian.com/books/booksblog/2013/sep/13/roald-dahl-great-writers-imagination-lacey, which was the basis of the 1953 novel *In the Lamb to the Slaughter* by Dahl and then the 1958 Hitchcock film *Lamb to the Slaughter*.
2 Steven Spielberg, *E.T. the Extra-Terrestrial* (1982).
3 Mona Kareem, 'The Persecuted Novelist of Dystopian Cairo: Mona Kareem interviews Ahmed Naji', *Los Angeles Review of Books*, 11 January 2016, https://lareviewofbooks.org/article/the-persecuted-novelist-of-dystopian-cairo/#!.
4 Or 'quasi-real', according to Kendall Walton's 1978 essay *Fearing Fiction*.
5 Ahmed Naji, 'Three New Short-short Stories by Imprisoned Writer Ahmed Naji', in Arabic Literature and Translation, 3 December 2016, https://arablit.org/2016/12/03/three-new-short-short-stories-by-imprisoned-writer-ahmed-naji-whose-next-court-date-is-tomorrow/.
6 Alexander R. Galloway, Eugene Thacker and McKenzie Wark, *Excommunication: Three Inquiries in Media and Mediation* (Chicago: University of Chicago Press, 2013), 92.
7 Ibid.
8 Ibid.
9 In the conference 'Imagining the Future', Berlin, Germany, 29–30 May 2018.
10 When that statement begins to sound utopian, we know we are in crisis.

T i m e M a k i n g N e w T i
m e M a k i n g N e w T i m e
M a k i n g N e w T i m e M a
k i n g N e w T i m e M a k i
n g N e w T i m e M a k i n g
N e w T i m e M a k i n g N e
w T i m e M a k i n g N e w T
i m e M a k i n g N e w T i m
e M a k i n g N e w T i m e M
a k i n g N e w T i m e M a k
i n g N e w T i m e M a k i n
g N e w T i m e M a k i n g N
e w T i m e M a k i n g N e w
T i m e M a k i n g N e w T i
m e M a k i n g N e w T i m e

M a k i n g N e w T i m e M a
k i n g **T h e** N e w T i m e M
a k i n g N e w T i m e M a k
i n g N e w T i m e M a k i n
g N e w T i m e M a k i n g N
e w T i m e M a k i n g N e w
T i m e M a k i n g N e w T i
m e **W h i s p e r i n g** M a k
i n g N e w T i m e M a k i n
g N e w T i m e M a k i n g N
e w T i m e **G a l l e r y** M a
k i n g N e w T i m e M a k i
n g N e w T i m e M a k i n g
N e w T i m e M a k i n g N e
w T i m e M a k i n g N e w T

An invitation to leave the echo chamber is certainly an attractive prospect. Let us step out from the dulling effects of big data's intellectual and emotional fortress – from the monochrome shades and into the dazzling light of our dreams of relationality, criticality and, to hell with it, maybe even world peace. Wrench open the door and get down and dirty with complexity, from a safe distance, throwing spanners into the works of Google's ultimate curatorial coup, whose algorithms nod and tut in time with us, as we are confronted with the (fake) news over our morning tea. And whilst we sip our tea, it is too easy to imagine that it is a modern phenomenon, invented to prod the world into increased polarisation and orchestrated by either an army of Russian bots or notebook-touting liberal journalists (depending on which side of the fence your echo chamber lies).

To imagine that the echo chamber is a symptom of the late-capitalist era is, however, a critical error. The ancient Greeks, well versed in barbarianism and tyranny through their own behaviour, warned us of the dangers of capitalism. The word 'echo' comes from the Greek *ēchos*, signifying sound – until a young mythological nymph named Echo gave it new currency. Cursed by Zeus's wife and destined merely to repeat the words of others, Echo also had the bad luck of falling in love with Narcissus. In all variants of the myth, Narcissus is finally destroyed by his enthrallment with his own image and inflated sense of self-importance. He is spurred on and aided by Echo, who perpetuates the hunter's self-aggrandising discourse through her constant repetition of his words.

In the intervening years, somewhere between the moment Narcissus transformed into a daffodil and Donald Trump was elected the 45th President of the United States of America, an individual's capacity to strike out against hegemonic information streams – directed by religious doctrine, monarch or state, or, in many cases, a potent combination of all three – has been largely overestimated. Alternative sources of information to those peddled by figures with authority have, throughout history, been silenced through slaughter or the propagandic bent of literature, images and architecture. As humans, we largely lack the abstraction of thought to imagine our own deaths, and yet in keeping with our total disregard for coherence, every generation thinks it is hers that will see the end of the world. Therefore, why struggle when frightened by what we see? We can be reassured that we are most certainly right: the echo chamber allows our sense of self to remain intact, whilst the world seems to be going up in flames around us.

So, although it may be tantalising to think of leaving the echo chamber, perhaps it is not even a possibility. Perhaps it never has been. For a brief moment, as air travel became financially accessible to large numbers of people and migration across continents was encouraged by former colonial powers, it maybe looked like an increasing diversity of human contact would weave new narratives and complicate people's understanding of the world. Yet, and herein lies the key to, or rather the foundations of, the echo chamber: its fundamental characteristic is not simply the exclusion of alternative points of view, but rather the discrediting thereof. What's more, the structures of the echo chamber's success are today so firmly rooted in how we navigate the world, across national, generational and class lines, that bar a self-imposed exile from consuming the news or using social media, we may be better off attempting to work from within its confines.

Someone interested in visiting physical echo chambers – and there are such people in our rich and esoteric world – may be disappointed to arrive in a city and discover that there are none. However, if accompanied by a savvy tour guide or a local, the echo-chamber enthusiast could very well be redirected to the similarly thrilling *whispering gallery*. Well-known examples include the Gol Gumbaz in Bijapur, India, and the Temple of Heaven in Beijing, China. How many generations have found communion in these spaces? In a whispering gallery, the curved shape of the enclosure allows for the smallest of sound waves to travel, unabated, across its circumference and breadth. Unlike the echo chamber's design, which relies on hard walls for the same sound to be repeated again and again, the whispering gallery's curvature creates the possibility for the gentlest whisper to be heard, despite physical distance.

The whispering gallery is a provocation to think about the forms and structures we can build that do not produce echoes, but rather allow for the softest voices to be amplified and to travel. At RAW Material Company, this is a primary concern of ours, manifested in the importance we place on institutional structure as material for curatorial and critical reflection. This is also at the heart of RAW Académie Session 5: Germination, directed by Nigerian artist Otobong Nkanga and part of her long-term project *Carved to Flow* (2017–ongoing). Germination is an invitation to explore the materiality of social support and nurture, a domain too often assumed to be governed purely by the dialogical. However, shape and texture count, too. From the inside of the echo chamber, is there a way to turn a hard surface into gentle curvature?

If we have now managed to rub down the walls of the echo chamber and create our whispering gallery, to settle into its round enclosure, we must be cognisant of how we occupy the roles that render this structure useful. In the whispering gallery, there are three main components: structure, speaker(s) and listener(s). As speakers, let us not deafen others by speaking too loudly. The form will do the work necessary to support our voices. As listeners, let us be mindful of where we need to stand to hear best. We may need to move closer to the edge of the dome to catch the waves that hug its walls.

If we can't get out of the echo chamber, let us at least listen for whispers.

M a k i n g N e w T i m e M a

k i n g N e w T i m e M a k i

n g N e w T i m e M a k i n g

N e w T i m e M a k i n g N e

w T i m e M a k i n g N e w T

i m e M a k i n g N e w T i m

e M a k i n g N e w T i m e M

a k i n g N e w T i m e M a k

i n g N e w T i m e M a k i n

g N e w T i m e M a k i n g N

e w T i m e M a k i n g N e w

T i m e M a k i n g N e w T i

m e M a k i n g N e w T i m e

M a k i n g N e w T i m e M a

k i n g N e w T i m e M a k i

n g N e w T i m e M a k i n g

N e w T i m e M a k i n g N e

w T i m e M a k i n g N e w T

i m e M a k i n g N e w T i m

e M a k i n g N e w T i m e M

a k i n g N e w T i m e M a k

i n g **C o r d o b a** N e w T i

m e M a k i n g N e w T i m e

H o u s e M a k i n g N e w T

i m e M a k i n g N e w T i m

e M a k i n g N e w T i m e M

a k i n g N e w T i m e M a k

i n g N e w T i m e M a k i n

g N e w T i m e M a k i n g N

An Architecture for Cultural Production of American-Muslim Identity (A Propositional Architecture)

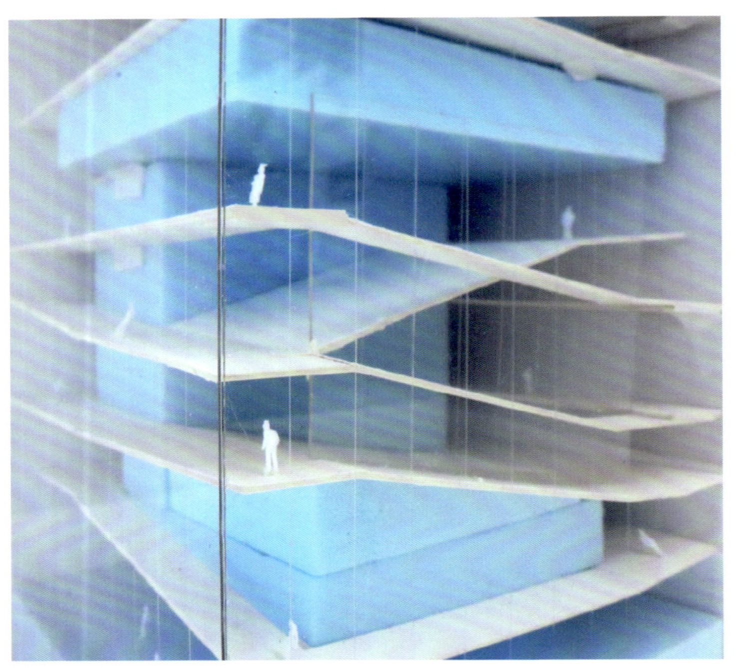

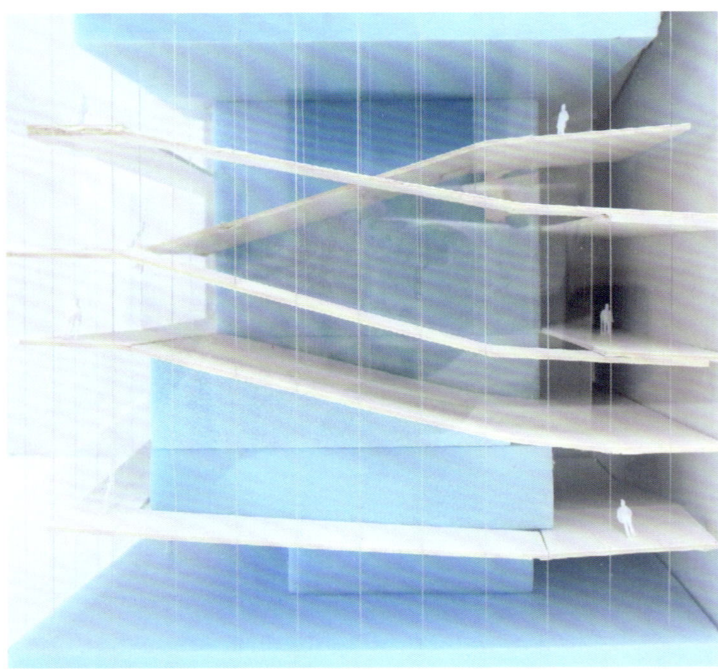

In 2014, the American Society for Muslim Advancement (ASMA) approached Büro Koray Duman (B-KD), my architectural practice, regarding its search for a new Islamic cultural centre. There are between 6 and 8 million Muslims living in the United States, about 700,000 of whom reside in the New York City metro area and are served by 150 mosques. These mosques form the only architectural typology for a Muslim congregation space. There remains no space that anchors the Muslim community and provides education by, and for, Muslims. To create an American-Muslim identity, there is a need to provide a place for cultural production and to differentiate 'religion as practice' and 'religion as culture'. Whereas 'religion as practice' is static, timeless and universal, 'religion as culture' is dynamic and evolutionary. For Islam as a culture to evolve and be relevant, and for American Muslims to nourish a unique identity, one must produce spaces that incubate, cultivate and produce such an identity. Cultivation of the American-Muslim identity in its tremendous diversity is a heterogeneous form that, I believe, should be introduced differently into American society overall. It is, indeed, a crucial task in our time, insomuch as the echo chamber of today's news media has flattened the complexity of this identity.

To tackle this task, B-KD and ASMA researched a variety of historical and contemporary structures, and then discussed what makes an effective space in which to foster and produce culture. One example that resonated with us was the *külliye*, which historically has served as a community centre and cultural space in Islamic cities. Deriving from the Arabic word *küll* (meaning 'the whole', or 'all'), *külliye* is a term that designates a complex of buildings centred around a mosque and managed within a single institution, often based on a *vakif* (foundation) and composed of a *medrese* (school), a *dar-ul-shifa* (hospital), a public kitchen, a hammam and other structures designed for various benevolent services. The *külliye* has been particularly ingrained in the fabric of Ottoman and Seljuk cities, and is regarded as an important community centre.

Inspired by the traditional *külliye*, Cordoba House aims to provide community services, a gathering place, a space for resources and a site for the production of knowledge. It also endeavours to be a portal for communication to Americans, so that they may understand Islam as a culture – its richness as well as its nuances in different parts of the world.

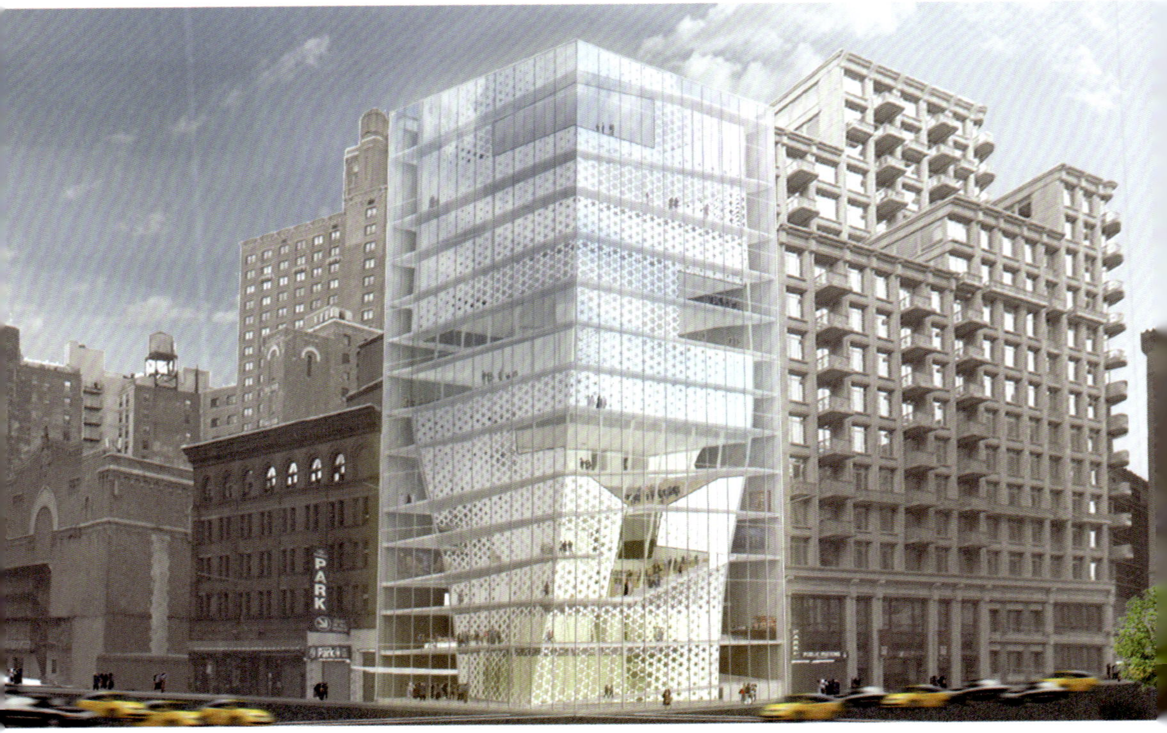

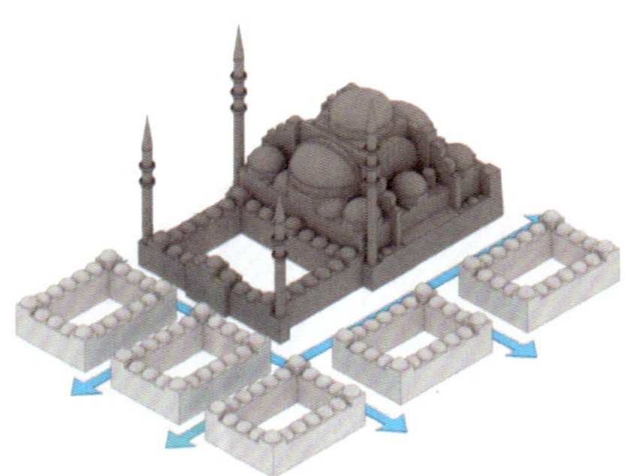

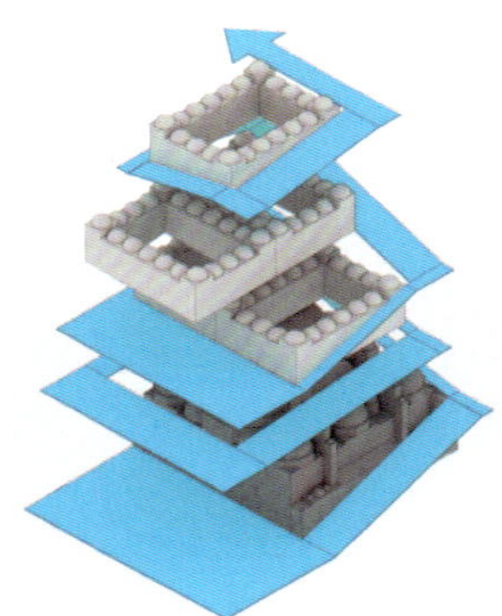

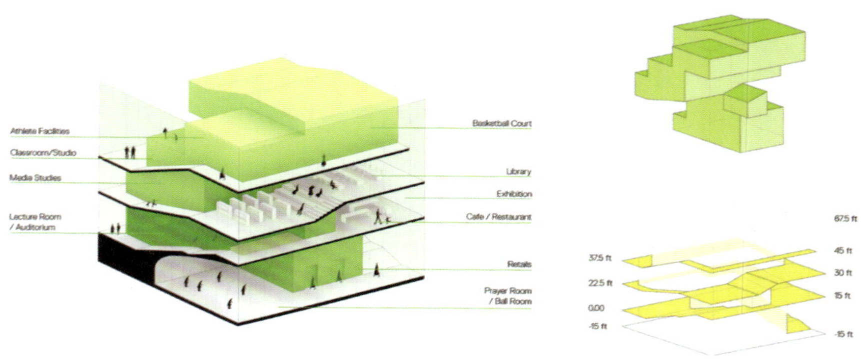
Athlete Facilities
Classroom/Studio
Media Studies
Lecture Room
/ Auditorium
Basketball Court
Library
Exhibition
Cafe / Restaurant
Retails
Prayer Room
/ Ball Room
67.5 ft
37.5 ft
45 ft
30 ft
22.5 ft
15 ft
0.00
-15 ft
-15 ft

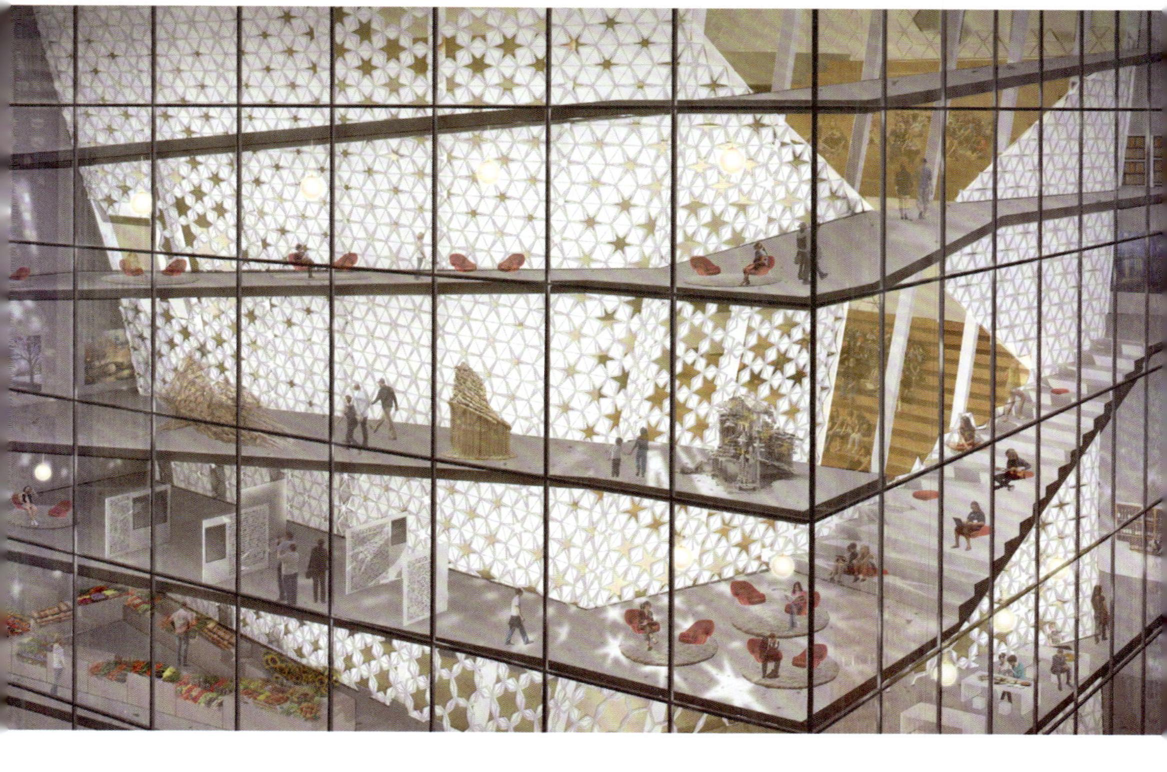

B-KD and ASMA divided the areas for knowledge-building into formal and informal spaces. Formal spaces, such as an auditorium, classrooms, lecture halls and permanent galleries, were planned for education programmes, discussions and performances. Informal spaces were intended to foster discovery and chance encounters: a souk with a restaurant, café and catering hall; temporary exhibition spaces; a library and a bookshop; and a series of rooms for meditating and lounging.

Since ASMA's vision was to build a first-of-its-kind cultural centre in New York City, the 'formal' spaces were architecturally defined as vertically stacked 'volumes' on a regular city block. The informal ones were envisioned to wrap around their perimeter, like a vertical interior street. The aim here was to expose a series of informal and lively spaces ascending upwards, adjacent to the centre's facade. The ultimate goal was to replace the fearful image of Islam, the fear of the unknown, with one that is surprisingly playful and pleasant. The power of open architecture – a physical space that provides the social infrastructure necessary to promote social exchange, conversation and the production of knowledge – can be a welcome antidote to the echo chamber of the digital world.

Architecturally complex but welcoming, strangely familiar but surprisingly distinct, Cordoba House simultaneously reflects history and incubates the future. In the past few years, we have witnessed the limits of the Internet's transparency, its horizontality and its so-called 'non-hierarchical' and 'non-mediated' structure, as well as its threat to elements of democracy. This structure's open, social architectural space seeks to reclaim the importance of an open society that can inspire new ways of thinking.

T i m e M a k i n g N e w T i

m e M a k i n g N e w T i m e

M a k i n g N e w T i m e M a

k i n g N e w T i m e M a k i

n g N e w T i m e M a k i n g

N e w T i m e M a k i n g N e

w T i m e M a k i n g N e w T

i m e M a k i n g N e w T i m

e M a k i n g N e w T i m e M

a k i n g N e w T i m e M a k

i n g N e w T i m e M a k i n

g N e w T i m e M a k i n g N

e w T i m e M a k i n g N e w

T i m e M a k i n g N e w T i

m e M a k i n g N e w T i m e

M a k i n g N e w T i m e M a

k i n g N e w T i m e M a k i

n g **E n c r o a c h m e n t s**

N e w T i m e M a k i n g N e

w T i m e M a k i n g N e w T

i m e M a k i n g N e w T i m

e M a k i n g N e w T i m e M

a k i n g N e w T i m e M a k

i n g N e w T i m e M a k i n

g N e w T i m e M a k i n g N

e w T i m e M a k i n g N e w

T i m e M a k i n g N e w T i

m e M a k i n g N e w T i m e

M a k i n g N e w T i m e M a

k i n g N e w T i m e M a k i

Humanity had been hard-pressed back then. Countries fighting over dwindling resources; riots, revolutions and counter-revolutions, and the constant low-level attrition of netwars; a billion refugees made homeless by famine, flood or extreme weather events. All of this craziness culminating in the Spasm, when more than a dozen capital cities from London to Karachi had been damaged or destroyed by low-yield tactical atomic bombs and a limited nuclear missile exchange.[1]

On the new moon of Ciṭṭī Prime, once we had established an initial climate trajectory, terra-planting and a subterranean hydroponic grid, it fell to each of us to recount our stories. Each story being a city, or at least an amalgam of two or three, where the memory was overlaid and confounded. For you see, some of us were born on the ships, and so our knowledge was hearsay, based on parents who didn't live to see 'earth-fall' in the new colonies. Or, as was so often the case, it derived from half-remembered, addled memories of grandparents, whose Alzheimer's was only accelerated by the FTL drives that allowed extra-systemic escape velocity. There were some who had argued that those over a certain age should be left behind, coming, as they were, from the 'guilty generation', and not just because their shells were so frail. However, it was decided that doing so would make us no better than them; and for better or worse, we wanted to create a set of experiential scenarios in which we could experience first-hand the interlinking political and social narratives particular to place – ones that, when stacked up, caused the whole tapestry to fray and boil over.

I was asked to build a machine interface for Lahore, the great Mughal city, looking at how it had fared after Partition and on into the beginning of the twenty-first century. Partition had brought with it blood and death, causing mass displacement and a scale of mortality so terrifying that it looped forwards as a precursor of world events at the time. So, the cooperative had deemed the period worthy of closer scrutiny. My grandmother Shaheen had maintained that, because of the rivalry between the two cities, you couldn't really speak of Lahore without mentioning Karachi: the ancient capital, where, according to legend, a slave girl had returned the smile of a prince, thus becoming cemented into a wall for her labours. Along with its upstart neighbor, the city of immigrants – along with the dynamism and violence that came with it – and its medieval brutality gave way to modern violence. This was how these two jewels flashed and burnt, and irradiated each other, like digital pomegranate blossoms that lived on in the code-memory of those who cared to remember.

Yet in any history of how these cities came to speak to one another, it must be remembered that outside forces were very much in play. Nani Shaheen would often say: *If only they had just left us alone to find our own destiny, but whose destiny is their own?*

Lines on maps tore rental communities asunder and stirred ethnic and religious tensions that always seemed to be simmering beneath the surface. Even here, in the neutral habitat that space represents, we had our own Mountbattens, Nehrus and Jinnahs, or their equivalents, aplenty – enough to fill a whole series of asylums. With the former colonial administration in tatters, former army buddies found themselves on opposite sides of what gradually would become a very cold war, one that would last well beyond the utopian (for which always read the shadow of dystopian nuance) ideals of the US Embassy Building Program (1954–60):

In 1954 the United States Department of State embarked on a bold embassy-building program that gave American architects a chance to play a new role as representatives of their country. In a major departure from precedent, the State Department appointed an architectural advisory panel of prominent architects to review all building plans for the Foreign Buildings Office (FBO). Under new guidelines, architects were challenged to produce schemes that would harmonize with differing local conditions, respect local customs, and respond to the historical uniqueness of each locale. At the same time, they were asked to create structures with a 'distinguishable American flavor'. To fit the local scene, but to be 'American', to harmonize with the past, yet to be both workable and new – these were the design dilemmas inherent in the FBO building program... The design expressions reveal much about how the United States related to the world and how it viewed itself as well.[2]

American expansionism was challenged by the Soviet invasion of Afghanistan in 1979, which made Pakistan a key theatre of the Cold War and initiated a proxy war that still continued up to Karachi's extensive destruction. A generation before, my grandparents had headed up into the unknown, in a last desperate bid to get up and out and away from the fatigue of the known. It apparently took the obliteration of most of the cities on Earth for humanity to actually, slowly and begrudgingly, begin to call for change. It took equal effort for those in power to shift from advocating intolerance (for what, then, would have been left?) to advocating the best in us – for vision, harmony, community and fellowship – at least enough to get us all working together to get off our now-dying planet.

It was, in fact, the council members and spiritual counsellors who had recommended the creation of archives, such as the one on which I was working: modest records of the cracks and fault lines; those modest but pernicious traces that we used to call 'historiography'. A steady stream of encroachments, disenfranchisement and erosion of social and cultural compacts thus brought about a cyclical knee-jerk response in the form of brute sectarian violence that propelled the social compact back to an earlier, darker age – when romance was all about cementing young women into brick walls...

A cold war has many theatres, and whilst aware that the internal politics of the twin cities were but one spoke of a larger wheel when seen from one point of view, for the tens of millions who lived in them and carried on their daily errands and rivalries, each blossom was a centre, or a central sun unrivalled in the cosmos. The key club was already a myth lost in the sands of time, by the time Nani met her husband, my grandfather, whilst working as part of a voluntary engineer corps helping to create temporary shelters and evacuate children from what was left of the wreckage. The sheer brutality of everyday reality allowed romance and a certain innocence to flourish. I never met my grandfather, but my grandmother often spoke of their courtship and shared optimism for renewal and rebirth: how he was an exception in a city where many of the men still clung to old ethnic rivalries and linguistic divides, as if that mattered 'when the whole roof of the world had fallen in'.

The key club became a metaphor, or perhaps even an allegory, of the bubble in which the wealthy, gilded Karachi elite passed their days – in a decadent haze seemingly straight out of a recontextualised F. Scott Fitzgerald novel, such as *The Beautiful and Damned* or *The Great Gatsby*. Affairs led to children who were not their fathers', and when this, alone, failed to titillate the great and the good, little keys were manufactured and presented for illicit and randomised sexual encounters (from wife to wife, and from husband to husband). Interestingly, although Fitzgerald was writing about the 1920s, this was happening in Karachi in the 1970s, right between the ages of hybrid rock 'n' roll and the video game arcade. Whether it was the British, the Americans, the Saudis or the Soviets in neighbouring Afghanistan, or our former countrymen in India, we were rarely free of influence or response. Whilst this was criticised internally and externally in its day, I would argue that it represents one of the greatest traits of the peculiarly Pakistani genome: adaptability, resilience and a propensity towards the hybrid. You might argue that this was not a choice, but rather imposed from outside. However, compromise – far from being viewed as a mode of defeat (in a Teutonic binary model), as it was viewed from a very particular Earth-bound moral prism – is seen as the base principle for healthy discussion and creativity (both emotional and collaborative).

The rock 'n' roll explosion of the late 1960s was a fascinating case study, as it demonstrated the swift reappropriation of particular Mughal sitar and tabla phrases, along with notations from the 'acid rock' scene that were emerging in California at the time, as in Count Five's 'Psychotic Reaction' (1966) and The Electric Prunes' 'I Had Too Much to Dream (Last Night)' (1966). Likewise, The Byrds adopted classical Indian raga in their seminal acid rock track, 'Eight Miles High', which morphed into an entirely local and reciprocally hybrid form. What this moment also presented was an alternate pathway down which Pakistan might have gone, were it not for American and Saudi bankrolling as well as the exportation of a deeply twisted and perverse pastiche of Islamic credo, which had more in common with the extreme right of today's Republican party in the supposedly United States. It was bitterly ironic how these factions would come to mirror each other and conspire in the days that led up to the end, in a kind of global collusion of the worst in humanity that was hanging on to its violent and patriarchal Old Testament values. It was a good thing that we had left the vengeful God behind on Earth, although 'his' acolytes, like weird genetic aberrations or 'tubers', would emerge from time to time on our would-be utopia: those who refused to be at peace with their neighbours and who had a permanent axe to grind.

Yet going back to the 1960s: what was special about bands such as The Panthers, The Mods, The Aay Jayes, The Abstracts, The Bluebirds and The Fore Thoughts – apart from their use of sitar, harmonium, surf guitar and some extreme organ – was how they mixed different religious persuasions to create a polyvalent social and cultural unity. With their hit tune 'Shahbaz Qalandar', for instance, The Fore Thoughts invoked a paean to the legendary twelfth- to thirteenth-century Sufi philosopher-poet from Sehwan Sharif named Lal Shahbaz Qalandar ('Lal' meaning 'red' for the attire he always wore; 'Qalandar' referencing a type of saint who is so at one with God's creation that he or she is freed from the bonds of time and space). The Panthers rocked out at New Year's pool parties at Midway House (a motel for KLM flight crew near Karachi's airport), with their hybrid Christian-Muslim line-up.

With the end of the 1970s and the outlawing of alcohol, out went the gigs and the clubs; but in their place, and almost as a symptom of cold war politics, came the video arcades. With Ronald 'the Ray Gun' pursuing nuclear proliferation by any means, and his Strategic Defense Initiative (SDI), or Star Wars programme, concocting fantasies of high-tech mass destruction, who were the Space Invaders, anyway? Atari and Intellivision did their best to roll out his vision to the youth of the allied universe, in a bid that was to prove far more successful than the SDI itself, which was cancelled due to its enormous costs and unfeasibility for its day. In other words, and as so often happens, culture and fiction outpaced and outperformed both reality and technology (our utopian or dystopian fictions usually inform the technology of later generations than our own). However, we remaining humans really had to make a concerted effort, after London, to recode our future away from war, and away from nationalism, as dystopian programming is so much more effective than anything with a more positive spin. For the spiritual counsellors, even joy is not an imposition, but a matter of free will. Some of our deepest thinkers are depressives, and we try to make space for that culturally, whilst trying not to neuter it as a form of creative dissent.

Like the antithesis of the key club, the early-twenty-first-century *encroachments* represented the best of human adaptability in the face of insurmountable odds. The disenfranchised simply chose to enfranchise both themselves and their fellows by literally building onto heritage monuments in the Old City of Lahore and creating ad hoc apartment blocks, kebab stands and chai wallahs as appendages to the factories of the great industrialists of Karachi. How dare the great unwashed claim something that was not theirs as their own? One had to laugh, to look at the lengths to which city officials and their wealthy sponsors had to go, to get the encampments 'deconstructed' and their denizens (for which read, 'denigrated citizen', who is legally disenfranchised by the state) moved on, only for them to resettle up the road, with gusto, a mere five minutes away. Lahore even formed its own standing antiencroachment squad, with different designations according to city districts, such as the town of Shalimar (named after the pleasure gardens built by Emperor Shah Jahan in 1640) and the town of Wagha on the Indian border, where the rancour between neighbours was played out nightly as a ritual performance of high melodrama. Meanwhile, in rival Karachi, the employees of the great textile mills would arrive at work with nowhere to park their motorbikes (a whole new lane of shops had popped up overnight; some were robbed at gunpoint by the more unsavoury types that lingered in the no man's land between private and public space). What is a border, after all, but an unsung parallel dimension?

It was always a pleasure to play carrom board game with some of the 'Indian' archivists and dispute who had invented it, even though most of the other colonists couldn't tell us apart – or, for that matter, tell us apart from any of the Persian, Lebanese, Greek or other Indo-Europeans after a few generations of lunar interbreeding. This interbreeding had actually begun many centuries earlier, during the migrations from Kermanshah to the Indus Valley and on into the Proto-Indo-European continent. It started well before the fifteenth- to twentieth-century diversification characteristic of the Portuguese, Dutch, British and French colonies, and latter emigration and colonial alliances after the corporate wars of the mid-twenty-first century, when the Indo-Chinese alliance was able to first blockade and then turn back the Russian-American Federation. It is important to remember that genetic markers were far more diverse and continually mutating from a much earlier time than people's mindsets would ever let on. And thank God – for without those mutations, whole populations would have been wiped out by strains of Ebola, the avian flu, SARS, Zika and adaptive meningitis, which specifically seemed to target more conventional, nationalistic gene pools.

Many more miracles have been wrought through recombinant gene therapy and the introduction of adaptive protein strands into specific functions within lunar society. Who can say what the ultimate outcome of such physiological interventions might be? Possibly crippling side effects later in life? Or susceptibility to new forms of disease based on the hybridisation of classics, such as typhoid or influenza, through fusion with specific bacteria and airborne spores contained within the atmosphere of Ciṭṭī Prime? However, as with progress of any kind, the risks are outweighed by the benefits: we can now largely breathe our moon's atmosphere, and the average human lifespan is worthy of those recounted in the Vedas or the Torah. Yet unlike in those ancient religious books, we seem to have evolved, if only through force of circumstance, not to be continually killing each other...

My name is Tasneem. Remember me with a fond thought, if you care to, and if my entries are pleasing to you.

1 Paul Macauley, *Into Everywhere* (London: Gollancz, 2016), 34.
2 Jane C. Loeffler, 'The Architecture of Diplomacy: Heyday of the United States Embassy-Building Program, 1954–1960' in *Journal of the Society of Architectural Historians*, vol. 49, no. 3 (September 1990), 251.

N e w T i m e M a k i n g N e
w T i m e M a k i n g N e w T
i m e M a k i n g N e w T i m
e M a k i n g N e w T i m e M
a k i n g N e w T i m e M a k
i n g N e w T i m e M a k i n
g N e w T i m e M a k i n g N
e w T i m e M a k i n g N e w
T i m e M a k i n g N e w T i
m e M a k i n g N e w T i m e
M a k i n g N e w T i m e M a
k i n g N e w T i m e M a k i
n g N e w T i m e M a k i n g
N e w T i m e M a k i n g N e
w T i m e M a k i n g N e w T

ime**Making**NewTim
eMakingNewTimeM
akingNewTimeMak
ingNewTimeMakin
gNewTimeMakingT
ime**New**MakingNew
TimeMakingNewTi
meMaking**Time:**Ne
wMakingNewTimeM
aking**An**NewTimeM
akingNewTimeMak
ingNew**Afterword**
TimeMakingNewTi
meMakingNewTime
MakingNewTimeMa

Brexit looms. An algorithm is at play. Humans have programmed it. The netizens all say the same thing. The RSS feeds, without fail, suggest that ‘we’ve won’. ‘REMAIN!’ The graphs on Google that evening reveal an altogether different fate.

Loop I
Insert code
Open the chamber
Close the chamber
Echo...
Is anybody listening?

Loop II
Extrapolate the code
Decode
An ideological block
The Faraday cage
A modern-day version
There’s nothing to listen to anymore, is there?

I take a sip of Diet Coke from a porcelain glass,
the kind made for green tea.
I then take a swig from a glass bottle, then
another sip, this time from a can.
Caffeine overdrive, detritus, bubble tummy,
double trouble, I hope I don't wobble.

Sonic chaos: a non-diegetic sound floods the
atmosphere.
Melancholy (Mellon) and the Infinite Sadness
Softer, Softest
A drumming song

Why I write
Or, rather, why I curate?
I take a leaf from George Orwell
Is it because of sheer egoism, aesthetic
enthusiasm, historical impulse and political
purpose – surely, certainly, maybe?

Money seeps through my hands, it cracks a
tree branch.

M a k i n g N e w T i m e M a
k i n g N e w T i m e M a k i
n g N e w T i m e M a k i n g
N e w T i m e M a k i n g N e
w T i m e M a k i n g N e w T
i m e M a k i n g N e w T i m
e M a k i n g N e w T i m e M
a k i n g N e w T i m e M a k
i n g N e w T i m e M a k i n
g N e w T i m e M a k i n g N
e w T i m e M a k i n g N e w
T i m e M a k i n g N e w T i
m e M a k i n g N e w T i m e
M a k i n g N e w T i m e M a
k i n g N e w T i m e M a k i

n g N e w T i m e M a k i n g

N e w T i m e M a k i n g N e

w T i m e M a k i n g N e w T

i m e M a k i n g N e w T i m

e M a k i n g T i m e M a k i

n g **L i s t** N e w T i m e M a

k i n g N e w T i m e **o f** M a

k i n g **w o r k s** N e w M a k

i n g N e w T i m e M a k i n

g N e w T i m e M a k i n g N

e w T i m e M a k i n g N e w

T i m e M a k i n g N e w T i

m e M a k i n g N e w T i m e

M a k i n g N e w T i m e M a

k i n g N e w T i m e M a k i

Lawrence Abu Hamdan
Once Removed
2019
5 projections, single-channel video, stereo sound
Dimensions variable
Commissioned by Sharjah Art Foundation
Courtesy of the artist

Cory Arcangel
NYARTIST
2019
Pipe organ recording performed by Hampus Lindwall
7 minutes
Commissioned by Sharjah Art Foundation
Courtesy of the artist, Galerie Thaddaeus Ropac, London/Paris/Salzburg and Lisson Gallery, London/New York

Cory Arcangel
Dunk
2019
From 'Dunks'
Laser animation
Dimensions variable
Commissioned by Sharjah Art Foundation
Courtesy of the artist, Galerie Thaddaeus Ropac, London/Paris/Salzburg and Lisson Gallery, London/New York

Cory Arcangel
Destroyed Jeans
2019
From 'Scanner paintings'
8 vinyl banners
250 x 650 cm
Commissioned by Sharjah Art Foundation
Courtesy of the artist, Galerie Thaddaeus Ropac, London/Paris/Salzburg and Lisson Gallery, London/New York

Marwa Arsanios
Who is afraid of ideology? part 2
2019
From 'Who is afraid of ideology?'
Video and installation
27 minutes
Commissioned by Sharjah Art Foundation and co-produced with San Francisco Museum of Modern Art, Onassis Fast Forward Festival 6 and Vooruit Belgium
Courtesy of the artist and Mor-Charpentier Gallery, Paris

Marwa Arsanios
Who is afraid of ideology? part 1
2017
From 'Who is afraid of ideology?'
Video and installation
23 minutes
Courtesy of the artist and Mor-Charpentier Gallery, Paris

Alessandro Balteo-Yazbeck
In collaboration with Attilio Napolitano
Opposable Thumb
2018
From 'All the Lands from Sunrise to Sunset'
Centenary olive wood, rabbit skin collagen-glue, insect-based shellac, cellphone
48.5 x 33 x 26 cm
Commissioned by Sharjah Art Foundation
Courtesy of the artist

Alessandro Balteo-Yazbeck
In collaboration with Attilio Napolitano
Nail Polish, 3000 BC
2018–2019
From 'All the Lands from Sunrise to Sunset'
Acrylic nail polish on centenary olive wood, rabbit skin collagen-glue, insect-based shellac, velvet
56.5 x 34.5 x 17 cm
Commissioned by Sharjah Art Foundation
Courtesy of the artist

Alessandro Balteo-Yazbeck
In collaboration with Attilio Napolitano
Snap
2018–2019
From 'All the Lands from Sunrise to Sunset'
Centenary olive wood, rabbit skin collagen-glue, insect based shellac, IBM Selectric typewriter head
42 x 71 x 42 cm
Commissioned by Sharjah Art Foundation
Courtesy of the artist

Alessandro Balteo-Yazbeck
In collaboration with Attilio Napolitano
Forethought-afterthought (singularity)
2018–2019
From 'All the Lands from Sunrise to Sunset'
Centenary olive wood, rabbit skin collagen-glue, insect based shellac, highlighted printed document: tribute to John von Neumann by Stanislaw Ulam, May 1958
67.5 x 33 x 22.5 cm
Commissioned by Sharjah Art Foundation
Courtesy of the artist

Alessandro Balteo-Yazbeck
In collaboration with Attilio Napolitano
O.K.
2018–2019
From 'All the Lands from Sunrise to Sunset'
Neon spray paint on centenary olive wood, rabbit skin collagen-glue, insect based shellac, felt
48.2 x 30 x 22.5 cm
Commissioned by Sharjah Art Foundation
Courtesy of the artist

Alessandro Balteo-Yazbeck
In collaboration with Attilio Napolitano
Carving (coal) 4000 BC
2018–2019
From 'All the Lands from Sunrise to Sunset'
Acrylic paint on centenary olive wood carving over a coal pile
30 x 41 x 34 cm
Commissioned by Sharjah Art Foundation
Courtesy of the artist

Alessandro Balteo-Yazbeck
In collaboration with Attilio Napolitano
GPS, 1973
2018–2019
From 'All the Lands from Sunrise to Sunset'
Centenary olive wood, oil finishing and telescopic antenna
30 x 24.5 x 13.5 cm
Commissioned by Sharjah Art Foundation
Courtesy of the artist

Alessandro Balteo-Yazbeck
In collaboration with Attilio Napolitano
I've got the infinite
2018–2019
From 'All the Lands from Sunrise to Sunset'
Centenary olive wood, rabbit skin collagen-glue, insect-based shellac, velvet, expanded polystyrene packing peanut

21 x 24 x 22 cm
Commissioned by Sharjah Art Foundation
Courtesy of the artist

Alessandro Balteo-Yazbeck
In collaboration with Attilio Napolitano
Midas
2018–2019
From 'All the Lands from Sunrise to Sunset'
Centenary olive wood, rabbit skin collagen-glue, insect-based shellac, glove finger with touch screen tip
42 x 71 x 42 cm
Commissioned by Sharjah Art Foundation
Courtesy of the artist

Alessandro Balteo-Yazbeck
In collaboration with Attilio Napolitano
VoIP
2018–2019
From 'All the Lands from Sunrise to Sunset'
Centenary olive wood, rabbit skin collagen-glue, insect-based shellac, felt, voice-over Internet protocol hardware
50 x 37.5 x 28 cm
Commissioned by Sharjah Art Foundation
Courtesy of the artist

Alessandro Balteo-Yazbeck
In collaboration with Attilio Napolitano
Cheap
2018–2019
From 'All the Lands from Sunrise to Sunset'
Centenary olive wood, rabbit skin collagen-glue, insect-based shellac, velvet, lead weights, integrated circuit data storage microchip with near field communication technology
22 x 40 x 18 cm
Commissioned by Sharjah Art Foundation
Courtesy of the artist

Alessandro Balteo-Yazbeck
In collaboration with Attilio Napolitano
You!
2018–2019
From 'All the Lands from Sunrise to Sunset'
Centenary olive wood, rabbit skin collagen-glue, insect-based shellac, Fimo clay
20 x 71 x 42 cm
Commissioned by Sharjah Art Foundation
Courtesy of the artist

Alessandro Balteo-Yazbeck
In collaboration with Attilio Napolitano
Man-made
2018–2019
From 'All the Lands from Sunrise to Sunset'
Centenary olive wood, rabbit skin collagen-glue, insect-based shellac, velvet, printed circuit board with various components
12 x 44 x 32.5 cm
Commissioned by Sharjah Art Foundation
Courtesy of the artist

Alessandro Balteo-Yazbeck
In collaboration with Attilio Napolitano
Afterthought-forethought (singularity)
2018–2019
From 'All the Lands from Sunrise to Sunset'
Centenary olive wood, rabbit skin collagen-glue, insect-based shellac, fibre optic lighting components
33.5 x 30 x 18 cm
Commissioned by Sharjah Art Foundation
Courtesy of the artist

Alessandro Balteo-Yazbeck
In collaboration with Attilio Napolitano
In advance of the broken model
2018–2019
From 'All the Lands from Sunrise to Sunset'
Tempered glass on compressed wood, vinyl, glue, solar cell on printed circuit board, coral
5 x 88 x 37 cm
Commissioned by Sharjah Art Foundation
Courtesy of the artist

Semiha Berksoy
My Mother Playing the Oud
1958
Oil on hardboard
99 x 69 cm
Courtesy of the artist and Galerist, Istanbul

Semiha Berksoy
My Mother the Painter Fatma Saime
1972
Oil on hardboard
100 x 70 cm
Courtesy of the artist and Galerist, Istanbul

Semiha Berksoy
Love Story (Self-Portrait)
1968
Oil on hardboard
99 x 69 cm
Courtesy of the artist and Galerist, Istanbul

Semiha Berksoy
Chain Breaker (Self-portrait)
1968
Oil on hardboard
95 x 100 cm
Courtesy of the artist and Galerist, Istanbul

Semiha Berksoy
Climbing (Self-Portrait)
1968
Oil on canvas
100 x 70 cm
Courtesy of the artist and Galerist, Istanbul

Semiha Berksoy
The Girl Protected from Evil by Her Mother
1970
Oil on hardboard
106 x 76 cm
Courtesy of the artist and Galerist, Istanbul

Semiha Berksoy
Zeliha Berksoy
1971
Oil on hardboard
100 x 70 cm
Courtesy of the artist and Galerist, Istanbul

Semiha Berksoy
Mother and I
1974
Oil on hardboard
70 x 100 cm
Courtesy of the artist and Galerist, Istanbul

Candice Breitz
Digest
2019
Multi-channel video installation, wooden shelves, videotape, polypropylene boxes, paper, acrylic paint
300 units: 20.3 x 12 x 2.7 cm each

Commissioned by Sharjah Art Foundation
Courtesy of Goodman Gallery, Johannesburg; Kaufmann Repetto, Milan; and KOW, Berlin

Huguette Caland
Untitled
1978
Oil on linen
72.4 x 59.7 cm
Courtesy of the artist

Huguette Caland
Bribes de corps
1973
Oil on linen
29.8 x 24 cm
Courtesy of the artist

Huguette Caland
Granit I
1985
Oil on linen
49.5 x 148.6 cm
Courtesy of the artist

Huguette Caland
Untitled
1971
Oil on linen
118.1 x 116.8 cm
Courtesy of the artist

Huguette Caland
Untitled
1971
Oil on linen
118.1 x 116.8 cm
Courtesy of the artist

Huguette Caland
Sunrise
ca. 1975
Oil on linen
100.3 x 100.3 cm
Courtesy of the artist

Huguette Caland
Eux
ca. 1975
Oil on linen
100.3 x 100.3 cm
Courtesy of the artist

Huguette Caland
Self Portrait: Bribes de corps
1973
Oil on linen
128.27 x 88.90 cm
Courtesy of the artist

Huguette Caland
Faces
1975
Oil on linen
76.2 x 78.7 cm
Courtesy of the artist

Huguette Caland
Bribes de corps
1973
Oil on linen
149.8 x 149.8 cm
Courtesy of the artist

Huguette Caland
Enlève ton doigt
1971
Oil on canvas
38.1 x 76.2 cm
Courtesy of the artist

Huguette Caland
Tête à tête
1968
Oil on canvas
118.1 x 118.1 cm
Courtesy of the artist

Huguette Caland
Bribes de corps
1973
Oil on linen
129.5 x 130 cm
Courtesy of the artist

Huguette Caland
Caftan designed for Nour Collection, Pierre Cardin
1979
Mixed media on fabric
127.5 cm (center-back length)
Courtesy of the artist

Huguette Caland
Inaash
1975
Embroidery on fabric
137.7 cm (center-back length)
Courtesy of the artist

Huguette Caland
Untitled Caftan
ca. 1990s
Embroidery on fabric
125.7 cm (center-back length)
Courtesy of the artist

Huguette Caland
Untitled Caftan
ca. 1990s
Mixed media on fabric
139 cm (center-back length)
Courtesy of the artist

Huguette Caland
Untitled Caftan
ca. 1990s
Mixed media with embroidery on fabric
110.7 cm (center-back length)
Courtesy of the artist

Huguette Caland
Untitled Painting Smock
1980–2012
Mixed media on fabric
113.7 cm (center-back length)
Courtesy of the artist

Huguette Caland
Untitled Painting Smock
1980–2012
Mixed media on fabric
119.5 cm (center-back length)
Courtesy of the artist

Huguette Caland
Untitled Painting Smock
1980–2012
Mixed media on fabric
109 cm (center-back length)
Courtesy of the artist

Huguette Caland
Untitled Painting Smock
1980–2012
Mixed media on fabric
111.5 cm (center-back length)
Courtesy of the artist

Huguette Caland
Untitled Painting Smock
1980–2012
Mixed media on fabric
105.5 cm (center-back length)
Courtesy of the artist

Ian Cheng
Emissary Sunsets The Self
2017
From 'Emissaries'
2015–2017
Live simulation and story, infinite duration, sound
Dimensions variable
Courtesy of the artist, Pilar Corrias, London; Gladstone Gallery, New York/Brussels and Standard (Oslo)

Ian Cheng
Emissary Forks At Perfection
2015–2016
From 'Emissaries'
2015--2017
Live simulation and story, infinite duration, sound
Dimensions variable
Courtesy of the artist, Pilar Corrias, London; Gladstone

Gallery, New York/Brussels and Standard (Oslo)

Ian Cheng
Emissary in the Squat of Gods
2015
From 'Emissaries'
2015–2017
Live simulation and story, infinite duration, sound
Dimensions variable
Courtesy of the artist, Pilar Corrias, London; Gladstone Gallery, New York/Brussels and Standard (Oslo)

Shezad Dawood
Encroachments
2019
From 'Encroachments'
VR environment
Dimensions variable
Co-commissioned by Sharjah Art Foundation and New Art Exchange, Nottingham.
Generously supported by the Bagri Foundation
Produced by Sharjah Art Foundation and UBIK Productions
Special thanks to the Hashoo Group, Gul Ahmed and EMI Pakistan
Courtesy of the artist; Jhaveri Contemporary, Mumbai and Timothy Taylor, London

Shezad Dawood
Spacewar!
2019
From 'Encroachments'
Tapestry in teak artist's frame
159 x 116 cm
Commissioned by Sharjah Art Foundation
Produced by Sharjah Art Foundation and UBIK Productions
Special thanks to the Hashoo Group, Gul Ahmed and EMI Pakistan
Courtesy of the artist; Jhaveri Contemporary, Mumbai and Timothy Taylor, London

Shezad Dawood
The Directorate
2019
From 'Encroachments'
Tapestry in teak artist's frame
159 x 116 cm
Commissioned by Sharjah Art Foundation
Produced by Sharjah Art Foundation and UBIK Productions
Special thanks to the Hashoo Group, Gul Ahmed and EMI Pakistan
Courtesy of the artist; Jhaveri Contemporary, Mumbai and Timothy Taylor, London

Shezad Dawood
Invasion
2019
From 'Encroachments'
Neon
200 x 200 cm
Commissioned by Sharjah Art Foundation
Produced by Sharjah Art Foundation and UBIK Productions
Special thanks to the Hashoo Group, Gul Ahmed and EMI Pakistan
Courtesy of the artist; Jhaveri Contemporary, Mumbai and Timothy Taylor, London

Shezad Dawood
Folk Tunes of Pakistan on Electric Sitar and Western Instruments
2019
From 'Encroachments'
Screenprint on paper in artist's frame
71.8 x 97 cm
Commissioned by Sharjah Art Foundation
Produced by Sharjah Art Foundation and UBIK Productions
Special thanks to the Hashoo Group, Gul Ahmed and EMI Pakistan
Courtesy of the artist; Jhaveri Contemporary, Mumbai and Timothy Taylor, London

Shezad Dawood
Clifton Beach (Digital terrazzo), [black]
2019
From 'Encroachments'
Fabric wallpaper
Dimensions variable
Co-commissioned by Sharjah Art Foundation and New Art Exchange, Nottingham
Generously supported by the Bagri Foundation
Produced by Sharjah Art Foundation and UBIK Productions
Special thanks to the Hashoo Group, Gul Ahmed and EMI Pakistan
Courtesy of the artist; Jhaveri Contemporary, Mumbai and Timothy Taylor, London

Shezad Dawood
Clifton Beach (Digital terrazzo), [white]
2019
From 'Encroachments'
Fabric wallpaper
Dimensions variable
Co-commissioned by Sharjah Art Foundation and New Art Exchange, Nottingham
Generously supported by the Bagri Foundation
Produced by Sharjah Art Foundation and UBIK Productions
Special thanks to the Hashoo Group, Gul Ahmed and EMI Pakistan
Courtesy of the artist; Jhaveri Contemporary, Mumbai and Timothy Taylor, London

Stan Douglas
RCCR
2017
Discrete cosine transform, lacquered UV ink on gessoed panel
150 x 150 x 5.1 cm
Courtesy of the artist and David Zwirner, New York/London/Hong Kong

Stan Douglas
AMMA
2017
Discrete cosine transform, lacquered UV ink on gessoed panel
150 x 150 x 5.1 cm
Courtesy of the artist and David Zwirner, New York/London/Hong Kong

Stan Douglas
E66E
2017
Discrete cosine transform, lacquered UV ink on gessoed panel
150 x 150 x 5.1 cm
Courtesy of the artist and David Zwirner, New York/London/Hong Kong

Stan Douglas
4400
2017
Discrete cosine transform,

lacquered UV ink on gessoed panel
150 x 150 x 5.1 cm
Courtesy of the artist and David Zwirner, New York/London/Hong Kong

Stan Douglas
6AA6
2017
Discrete cosine transform, lacquered UV ink on gessoed panel
150 x 150 x 5.1 cm
Courtesy of the artist and David Zwirner, New York/London/Hong Kong

Stan Douglas
G44G
2017
Discrete cosine transform, lacquered UV ink on gessoed panel
150 x 150 x 5.1 cm
Courtesy of the artist and David Zwirner, New York/London/Hong Kong

Stan Douglas
4CC4
2017
Discrete cosine transform, lacquered UV ink on gessoed panel
150 x 150 x 5.1 cm
Courtesy of the artist and David Zwirner, New York/London/Hong Kong

Lubaina Himid
Man in a Jumper Drawer
2018
Acrylic on wooden drawer
44 x 37 x 12 cm
Private Collection, London
Courtesy of the artist and Hollybush Gardens, London

Lubaina Himid
Man in Stationary Drawer
2018
Acrylic on wooden drawer
44 x 37 x 12 cm
Private Collection, London
Courtesy of the artist and Hollybush Gardens, London

Lubaina Himid
The Captain and the Mate
2017–2018
Acrylic on canvas
183 x 244 cm
Adam and Mariana Clayton Collection
Courtesy of the artist and the Adam and Mariana Clayton Collection

Lubaina Himid
Act One, No Maps
1992
Acrylic on canvas
150 x 210 x 5.5 cm
Courtesy of the artist and Hollybush Gardens, London

Lubaina Himid
Memorial to Zong
1991
Acrylic on canvas
152.4 x 121.92 x 4.5 cm
Courtesy of the artist and Hollybush Gardens, London

Lubaina Himid
Bone in the China: Success to Africa Trade
1985
Wooden construction, acrylic on plywood with aluminium and acrylic on canvas
244 x 122 x 270 cm
Courtesy of the artist and Hollybush Gardens, London

Alfredo Jaar
33 Women
2014–2019
33 framed pigment prints, 198 light projectors, 198 tripods
Dimensions variable
Commissioned by Sharjah Art Foundation
Courtesy of the artist

Ann Veronica Janssens
Volute
2006–2019
Micro water droplets, air
Dimensions variable
Courtesy of the artist and Bortolami, New York

Barbara Kasten
Collision 6 E
2017
Digital chromogenic print
160 x 122 cm
Courtesy of the artist and Bortolami, New York

Barbara Kasten
Collision 5 T
2016
Digital chromogenic print
160 x 121.9 cm
Courtesy of the artist and Bortolami, New York

Barbara Kasten
Architectural Site 1, June 10, 1986
1986
Cibachrome
94 x 75.6 cm
Courtesy of the artist and Bortolami, New York

Barbara Kasten
Construct 32
1986
Cibachrome
94 x 74.5 cm
Courtesy of the artist and Bortolami, New York

Barbara Kasten
Construct 34
1986
Cibachrome
101.6 x 76.2 cm
Courtesy of the artist and Bortolami, New York

Barbara Kasten
Metaphase 3
1986
Cibachrome
101.6 x 76.2 cm
Courtesy of the artist and Bortolami, New York

Barbara Kasten
Construct NYC 11
1983–84
Cibachrome
101.6 x 76.2 cm
Courtesy of the artist and Bortolami, New York

Barbara Kasten
Triptych II
1983
Cibachrome
Three parts each: 94 x 74.9 cm
Courtesy of the artist and Bortolami, New York

Barbara Kasten
Construct LB 1
1982
Polaroid
20.3 x 25.4 cm
Courtesy of the artist and Bortolami, New York

Barbara Kasten
Construct LB 2
1982
Polaroid
20.3 x 25.5 cm
Courtesy of the artist and Bortolami, New York

Barbara Kasten
Photogram Painting Untitled 77/22
1977
Oil on silver gelatin mural paper on canvas
3 panels: 198 x 56 x 6.5 cm each; 198 x 174 cm overall
Courtesy of the artist and Bortolami, New York

Barbara Kasten
Untitled Torso with Chair
1974
Cyanotype and silver spray paint on paper
64.8 x 50.8 cm
Private collection
Courtesy of the artist and Bortolami, New York

Astrid Klein
Untitled (Better to burn out, than to fade away)
1998
From 'Neon works'
Neon sculpture, rings of neon, ropes imprinted with text
Dimensions variable
Courtesy of the artist and Sprüth Magers, Berlin/London/Los Angeles/Cologne/Hong Kong

Astrid Klein
Untitled, (What are you fighting for)
1988/1993
From 'White paintings'
1988–1993
Acrylic, quartz crystal, alabaster plaster, zinc white on canvas
150 x 204.5 cm
Courtesy of the artist and Sprüth Magers, Berlin/London/Los Angeles/Cologne/Hong Kong

Astrid Klein
Untitled, (Nothing to remember)
1988/1993
From 'White paintings'
1988-1993
Acrylic, gypsum alabaster, tape, paper, zinc white on canvas
230 x 165 cm
Courtesy of the artist and Sprüth Magers, Berlin/London/Los Angeles/Cologne/Hong Kong

Astrid Klein
Fly catcher III
1987–1991
Neon tubes, electric mosquito traps, steel pipe, sound
396.5 (height), 100 (diameter) cm
Courtesy of the artist and Sprüth Magers, Berlin/London/Los Angeles/Cologne/Hong Kong

Marwan
Untitled
2009–2010
Oil on canvas
195 x 260 cm
Sharjah Art Foundation collection
Courtesy of the artist's estate

Marwan
Untitled
2008
Oil on canvas
195 x 162 cm
Collection of the artist's estate
Courtesy of the artist's estate and Sfeir-Semler Gallery Hamburg/Beirut

Marwan
Untitled
2006
Oil on canvas
195 x 146 cm
Collection of the artist's estate
Courtesy of the artist's estate and Sfeir-Semler Gallery, Hamburg/Beirut

Marwan
Untitled
1986
Oil on canvas
195 x 114 cm
Collection of the artist's estate
Courtesy of the artist's estate and Sfeir-Semler Gallery, Hamburg/Beirut

Marwan
Untitled
1969
Oil on canvas
96 x 130 cm
Sharjah Art Foundation collection
Courtesy of the artist's estate

Marwan
Munif al Razzaz
1965
Oil on canvas
130 x 89 cm
Sharjah Art Foundation collection
Courtesy of the artist's estate

Otobong Nkanga & Emeka Ogboh
Aging Ruins Dreaming Only to Recall the Hard Chisel from the Past
2019
Multi-channel sound installation, sculpture and light installation, poetry
Dimensions variable
Commissioned by Sharjah Art Foundation
Courtesy of the artists

Bruno Pacheco
Puff !!!(Sissiphilous)
2018
Oil on canvas
170 x 160 cm
Commissioned by Sharjah Art Foundation
Courtesy of the artist and Hollybush Gardens, London

Bruno Pacheco
Puff !!!(Sissiphilous)
2018
Oil on canvas
180 x 170 cm
Commissioned by Sharjah Art Foundation
Courtesy of the artist and Hollybush Gardens, London

Bruno Pacheco
Puff !!!(Sissiphilous)
2018
Oil on canvas
170 x 160 cm
Commissioned by Sharjah Art Foundation
Courtesy of the artist and Hollybush Gardens, London

Bruno Pacheco
Puff !!!(Sissiphilous)
2017/2018
Oil on canvas
180 x 160 cm
Courtesy of the artist and Hollybush Gardens, London

Bruno Pacheco
Puff !!!(Sissiphilous)
2016/2017
Oil on canvas
170 x 170 cm
Courtesy of the artist and Hollybush Gardens, London

Bruno Pacheco
Puff !!!(Sissiphilous)
2016/2017
Oil on canvas
170 x 170 cm
Courtesy of the artist and Hollybush Gardens, London

Heather Phillipson
Cyclonic Palate Cleanser
2019
Monitors, speakers, burned bread, printed paper, black coir mat, brown coir mat, soil, towels, umbrella, rubber, resin, steel, timber, polythene, enamel spray paint, spotlights
Dimensions variable
Commissioned by Sharjah Art Foundation
Courtesy of the artist

Jon Rafman
Punctured Sky
2019
Mixed media
Dimensions variable
Commissioned by Sharjah Art Foundation with the support of Canada Council for the Arts
Courtesy of the artist

Jon Rafman
Legendary Reality
2017
Single-channel video
15 minutes 43 seconds
Courtesy of the artist

Michael Rakowitz
The Ballad of Special Ops Cody
2017
Video
14 minutes 42 seconds
Commissioned by the Museum of Contemporary Art Chicago
Collection of Al Ma'mal Foundation for Contemporary Art / Contemporary Art Museum Palestine
Courtesy of Jack Persekian

Pamela Rosenkranz
Healer
2019
Robot snake
120 cm
Commissioned by Sharjah Art Foundation. supported by Pro Helvetia and Stiftung Erna und Curt Burgauer

Hrair Sarkissian
Final Flight
2018–2019
Mixed media
Dimensions variable
Partially commissioned by Sharjah Art Foundation
Courtesy of the artist

Hrair Sarkissian
Horizon
2016
Two-channel HD video
6 minutes 58 seconds
Courtesy of the artist

Hrair Sarkissian
Residue
2019
Mixed media
8 x 113 x 192 cm
Commissioned by Sharjah Art Foundation
Courtesy of the artist

Anwar Jalal Shemza
Chessmen
1969
Oil on silkscreen on cotton cloth
60 x 46 cm
Courtesy of the Estate of Anwar Jalal Shemza

Anwar Jalal Shemza
Love Letter 2
1969
Oil on canvas
93.5 x 93 cm
Courtesy of the Estate of Anwar Jalal Shemza

Anwar Jalal Shemza
Blue Blue Jazz
1967
Oil on canvas
91 x 76 cm
Courtesy of the Estate of Anwar Jalal Shemza

Anwar Jalal Shemza
Meem One
1967
Oil on canvas
93 x 93 cm
Courtesy of the Estate of Anwar Jalal Shemza

Anwar Jalal Shemza
Untitled
1966
Wood on chipboard and matt emulsion paint
61.5 x 76 x 11 cm
Courtesy of the Estate of Anwar Jalal Shemza

Anwar Jalal Shemza
Abstract Writing
1965
Pyrography on wood
104 x 77 x 2.5 cm
Courtesy of the Estate of Anwar Jalal Shemza

Anwar Jalal Shemza
Composition in Brown and White
1965
Oil on canvas
78 x 52 cm
Courtesy of the Estate of Anwar Jalal Shemza

Anwar Jalal Shemza
Composition in Green and Black
1965
Oil on canvas
77.5 x 52.2 cm
Courtesy of the Estate of Anwar Jalal Shemza

Anwar Jalal Shemza
Fingerprint
1964
Coloured inks on Japanese hand-made paper on mount board
80.7 x 55.2 cm
Courtesy of the Estate of Anwar Jalal Shemza

Anwar Jalal Shemza
Apple Tree
1962
Oil on hardboard
54 x 43.5 cm
Courtesy of the Estate of Anwar Jalal Shemza

Anwar Jalal Shemza
The Fable
1962
Oil on hand dyed cloth on mount board
68 x 47 cm
Courtesy of the Estate of Anwar Jalal Shemza

Anwar Jalal Shemza
Love Letter
1962
Oil on hand-dyed cloth
76 x 56 cm
Courtesy of the Estate of Anwar Jalal Shemza

Anwar Jalal Shemza
Magic Carpet
1961
Oil on hand-dyed cloth on hardboard
56 x 46 cm
Courtesy of the Estate of Anwar Jalal Shemza

Kemang Wa Lehulere
My Apologies to Time 1
2017
Salvaged school desks, African

grey parrot, wood, steel, string, spray paint
Dimensions variable
Courtesy of the artist and Stevenson, Cape Town/ Johannesburg

Kemang Wa Lehulere
Does This Mirror Have a Memory 1
2015
From 'Does This Mirror Have a Memory', including untitled painting by Gladys Mgudlandlu, 1966; drawing in collaboration with Sophia Lehulere, 2015
Gouache on paper; chalk on blackboard
55 x 75 cm; 70 x 100 cm
Courtesy of the artist and Stevenson, Cape Town/ Johannesburg

Kemang Wa Lehulere
Does This Mirror Have a Memory 4
2015
From 'Does This Mirror Have a Memory', including untitled paintings by Gladys Mgundlandlu, date unknown; drawing in collaboration with Sophia Lehulere, 2015
Gouache on paper, recto and verso; chalk on blackboard
52 x 63 cm; 70 x 100 cm
Courtesy of the artist and Stevenson, Cape Town/ Johannesburg

Kemang Wa Lehulere
Does This Mirror Have a Memory 12
2015
From 'Does This Mirror Have a Memory', including untitled painting by Gladys Mgudlandlu, date unknown; drawing in collaboration with Sophia Lehulere, 2015
Gouache on paper, recto and verso, chalk on blackboard
72 x 22 cm; 70 x 100 cm
Courtesy of the artist and Stevenson, Cape Town/ Johannesburg

Kemang Wa Lehulere
Does This Mirror Have a Memory 11
2015
From 'Does This Mirror Have a Memory', including untitled painting by Gladys Mgudlandlu, date unknown; drawing in collaboration with Sophia Lehulere, 2015
Gouache on paper; chalk on blackboard
28 x 76 cm; 70 x 100 cm
Courtesy of the artist and Stevenson, Cape Town/ Johannesburg

Kemang Wa Lehulere
Does This Mirror Have a Memory 8
2015
From 'Does This Mirror Have a Memory', including untitled painting by Gladys Mgudlandlu, date unknown; drawing in collaboration with Sophia Lehulere, 2015
Gouache on paper, recto and verso; chalk on blackboard
61 x 23 cm; 70 x 100 cm
Courtesy of the artist and Stevenson, Cape Town/ Johannesburg

Kemang Wa Lehulere
Does This Mirror Have a Memory 6
2015
From 'Does This Mirror Have a Memory', including untitled painting by Gladys Mgudlandlu, 1962; drawing in collaboration with Sophia Lehulere, 2015
Gouache on paper, recto and verso; chalk on blackboard
47 x 59 cm; 70 x 100 cm
Courtesy of the artist and Stevenson, Cape Town/ Johannesburg

Kemang Wa Lehulere
Homeless Song #3: The Bird Lady in 9 Layers of Time
2015
Digital video
9 minutes 57 seconds
Courtesy of the artist and Stevenson, Cape Town/ Johannesburg

Munem Wasif
Man Selling Jute
2018
Archival pigment print, wooden frame
76.2 x 50.8 cm
Partially produced by Sharjah Art Foundation
Courtesy of the artist and Project 88, Mumbai

Munem Wasif
Machine Matter
2017-2019
Video; black and white photography; found objects
14 minutes 5 seconds; 76.2 cm x 50.8 cm each; dimensions variable
Partially produced by Sharjah Art Foundation
Courtesy of the artist and Project 88, Mumbai

Akram Zaatari
The Landing
2019
Film, interviews, installation, single photograph
Commissioned by Sharjah Art Foundation with the generous support of Barjeel Art Foundation, Elie Khoury Art Foundation, Ministry of Interior UAE and Fujifilm ME
Courtesy of the artist and Sfeir-Semler Gallery, Hamburg/Beirut

Akram Zaatari
The Landing
2019
Digital cinema, color, surround sound
62 minutes and 55 seconds

Akram Zaatari
The Landing Interviews
2019
Audio interviews with English subtitles and video excerpts of Muhayyar Ali Rashed's wedding in Al-Madam; 1991, color, stereo sound
22 minutes 11 seconds

Akram Zaatari
The Landing. Shaabiyyat Al Ghurayfah
2019
Digital photograph, inkjet print
75.5 x 60 cm

T i m e M a k i n g N e w T i
m e M a k i n g N e w T i m e
M a k i n g N e w T i m e M a
k i n g N e w T i m e M a k i
n g N e w T i m e M a k i n g
N e w T i m e M a k i n g N e
w T i m e M a k i n g N e w T
i m e M a k i n g N e w T i m
e M a k i n g N e w T i m e M
a k i n g N e w T i m e M a k
i n g N e w T i m e M a k i n
g N e w T i m e M a k i n g N
e w T i m e M a k i n g N e w
T i m e M a k i n g N e w T i
m e M a k i n g N e w T i m e

MakingNewTimeMa
kingNewTimeMaki
ngNewTimeMaking
NewTimeMakingNe
wTimeMakingNewT
imeMakingNewTim
eMakingNewTimeM
akingNewTimeMak
ingNewTimeMakin
gNewTimeMakingN
ew **Contributors** T
imeMakingNewTim
eMakingNewTimeM
akingNewTimeMak
ingNewTimeMakin

Omar Kholeif

Dr Omar Kholeif is an Egyptian-British writer, curator and editor. Over the last decade, he has curated more than 100 exhibitions, special projects and commissions globally. He has also authored and/or edited more than twenty books and catalogues on art, including recent publications *Goodbye, World! Looking at Art in the Digital Age* (Sternberg Press, 2018) and *The Artists Who Will Change the World* (Thames and Hudson, 2018). Kholeif is currently serving as co-curator of Sharjah Biennial 14, curator of the V-A-C Pavilion at the 58th Venice Biennale, senior visiting curator at HOME, Manchester, curator for Abu Dhabi Art and guest curator for the Manchester International Festival. Previously, he was Manilow Senior Curator and Director of Global Initiatives at the MCA Chicago, curator at Whitechapel Gallery, London, senior curator at Cornerhouse, Manchester, and curator at FACT, Liverpool. His multiple curatorial projects include *Focus: Middle East, North Africa and the Mediterranean* at the Armory Show, New York, the Abraaj Group Art Prize and the Cyprus Pavilion at the 56th Venice Biennale and the Liverpool Biennial. He is a Churchill Fellow, Fellow of the Royal Society of Arts and member of the International Association of Art Critics. He has served on numerous juries, including those for the Film London Jarman Award and the Thoma Foundation Arts Writing Award in Digital Art, and received awards and grants from major organisations, most recently from the Graham Foundation for Advanced Studies in the Fine Arts and the Andy Warhol Foundation | Creative Capital. Kholeif is currently visiting tutor at the University of Oxford's Ruskin School of Art, and, in 2016, was the Goldberg Visiting Professor at Hunter College, New York. He holds Master of Arts degrees from the University of Glasgow and the Royal College of Art, London, as well as a joint Doctor of Philosophy degree from the Zurich University of the Arts and the University of Reading.

Sophia Al-Maria

Sophia Al-Maria is a writer, artist and film-maker. She studied comparative literature at the American University in Cairo and aural and visual cultures at Goldsmiths, University of London. Her first solo exhibition, *Virgin with a Memory*, was presented at Cornerhouse, Manchester, in 2014. Al-Maria has also shown in the United States at the Whitney Museum of American Art (2016) and the New Museum (2015) in New York; in South Korea at the Gwangju Biennale (2013); in Qatar at the Souq Waqif Art Centre in Doha (2007); and in Egypt at the Townhouse gallery in Cairo (2005). She participated in the

2016 Biennale of Moving Images (BIM), organised by the Centre d'Art Contemporain in Geneva. In 2015, she guest edited issue 8 of *The Happy hypocrite (Fresh Hell)*. Her memoir, *The Girl Who Fell to Earth* (2012), was published by Harper Perennial. She lives and works in London.

Khalid Abdalla
Khalid Abdalla works as an actor, producer and film-maker, but also in cultural production and alternative media. His work balances his creative life and political beliefs, and he is ever aware that infrastructural shifts are as necessary as ideological ones. Currently, Abdalla is focusing on writing, acting and working on what he hopes will be his first feature film as a director. Amongst his acting credits are leading roles in Paul Greengrass's *United 93* (2006) and *Green Zone* (2010), Marc Forster's *The Kite Runner* (2007), Tala Hadid's *The Narrow Frame of Midnight* (2014) and Tamer El Said's *In the Last Days of the City* (2016), which Abdalla also produced. He will be appearing as Jerome Sawyer in David Farr's upcoming Amazon Prime series, *Hanna* (2019). In documentary film, he has producer credits on Hanan Abdalla's *In the Shadow of a Man* (2012) and the upcoming film by Hanan Abdalla and Cressida Trew, *The Vote* (2020). He also appears as himself in Jehane Noujaim's Oscar-nominated *The Square* (2013). Abdalla is a founding member of three collaborative initiatives in Cairo: Cimatheque, Zero Production and Mosireen. Brought up in the United Kingdom by Egyptian parents, he considers Cairo and London his two cities.

Douglas Coupland
Since 1991, Douglas Coupland has written thirteen novels, which have been published in most languages, and has written and performed for England's Royal Shakespeare Company. He is also a columnist for *The Financial Times of London*, as well as a frequent contributor to *The New York Times*, *e-flux*, *DIS* magazine and *Vice*. Coupland recently mounted two separate museum retrospectives: *everywhere is anywhere is anything is everything* at the Vancouver Art Gallery, the Royal Ontario Museum and the Museum of Contemporary Art Toronto Canada (MOCA), and *Bit Rot* at Rotterdam's Witte de With Center for Contemporary Art and Munich's Villa Stuck. In 2015 and 2016, he was artist in residence at the Google Cultural Institute in Paris. His exhibition on ecology, *Vortex*, opened in May 2018 at the Vancouver Aquarium and is travelling globally through 2021. In 2016, Penguin published *The Age of Earthquakes: A Guide to the Extreme Present*, a book co-authored by

Coupland, Shumon Basar and Hans Ulrich Obrist; its sequel, *The Extreme Self*, will be published early 2020.

Heather Phillipson

Heather Phillipson works across video, sculpture, music, drawing and text. Her recent projects include a major commission for Art on the Underground's flagship site at Gloucester Road station in London, an online commission for the Museum of Contemporary Art Chicago and a solo show at BALTIC Centre for Contemporary Art, UK (all 2018). In 2020, she will unveil her giant cherry-and-drone-topped ice cream sundae sculpture on Trafalgar Square's Fourth Plinth. She received the Film London Jarman Award in 2016 and the European Short Film Award Selection from the International Film Festival Rotterdam in 2018. She is also an award-winning poet.

Yasmine El Rashidi

Yasmine El Rashidi is an Egyptian writer. A regular contributor to *The New York Review of Books* and a contributing editor of the Middle East arts journal *Bidoun*, she is the author of *The Battle for Egypt: Dispatches from the Revolution* (2011) and *Chronicle of a Last Summer: A Novel of Egypt* (2017), which was long-listed for the PEN Open Book Award. Her essays have been published in *Artforum*, *Frieze*, *The New York Times*, *Lapham's Quarterly* and *The Guardian*, and her writing has been anthologised widely, including in *Best American Nonrequired Reading* (2014), *The New York Review Abroad: Fifty Years of International Reportage* (2013) and *Diaries of an Unfinished Revolution: Voices from Tunis to Damascus* (2013). A former fellow of the Dorothy and Lewis B. Cullman Center for Scholars and Writers, she is a contributing op-ed writer for *The New York Times*, and is currently working on her second novel.

Sean Gullette

Sean Gullette is a writer, film director, actor and film producer who first gained international recognition playing Max Cohen in *Pi* (1998), the award-winning independent film that he co-wrote with director Darren Aronofsky. He has since acted in many films, and works regularly as a screenwriter, collaborating with directors on scripts. Gullette's debut feature film as writer-director, *TRAITORS* (2013), financed by the Sharjah Art Foundation, received awards at the Venice Film Festival, garnered critical praise and was released internationally. His second film, *UPLAND*, which is currently in development, is based on the eponymous novel by Nobel Prize–winning author Kenzaburo Oe. Also on his slate is the upcoming international thriller *TANGIER*, with Kristen Scott Thomas and Jeremy Irons. Gullette's essays, journalism and fiction have been published in magazines, including *The Face*, *Spy*, *Slate*, *Bidoun*, *Brill's Content*, *Gear*, *Entertainment Weekly*, *Nejma* and *KGB* (the latter of which he founded as editor and publisher in 1991). In addition, his essays appear in *110 Stories: New York Writes After September 11* (NYU Press, 2004) and the Springer-Verlag anthology *Art, Technology, and Cinema*.

Hannah Feldman
Hannah Feldman is an associate professor of modern and contemporary art history at Northwestern University, where she is also core faculty in the programs of Middle East and North African Studies and Comparative Literary Studies. She is the author of *From a Nation Torn: Decolonizing Art and Representation in France, 1945–1962* (Duke University Press, 2014).

Aram Moshayedi
Aram Moshayedi is a writer and curator at the Hammer Museum in Los Angeles, where he recently organised the exhibition and accompanying publication, *Stories of Almost Everyone*, and in 2016, co-curated (with Hamza Walker) *Made in L.A. 2016: a, the, though, only*. Since joining the Hammer in 2013, he has organised projects by artists Lawrence Abu Hamdan, Marwa Arsanios, Andrea Bowers, Andrea Büttner, Simon Denny, Mario García Torres, Shadi Habib Allah, Maria Hassabi, Oliver Payne and Keiichi Tanaami, and Avery Singer, as well as *ALL THE INSTRUMENTS AGREE: an exhibition or a concert*, a two-day program of live music and sound performances by visual artists. He was formerly associate curator at the Roy and Edna Disney/CalArts Theater (REDCAT), where he organised exhibitions and oversaw the production of new works by Tony Cokes, Geoffrey Farmer, Erlea Maneros Zabala, The Otolith Group, Slavs and Tatars, Jordan Wolfson and Ming Wong. He has contributed to numerous exhibition catalogues in addition to *Artforum*, *BOMB Magazine*, *Art in America*, *Frieze*, *Metropolis M*, *Parkett*, *X-TRA Contemporary Art Quarterly* and *Bidoun*, for which he is a contributing editor.

Todd Reisz
Todd Reisz is an architect and writer whose work often examines cities of the Arabian peninsula, from historical and contemporary perspectives. He served for five years as the Daniel Rose Visiting Assistant Professor in Urban Studies at the Yale School of Architecture, where is currently

the Kahn Visiting Assistant Professor of Architectural Design. Reisz has also taught in the Aga Khan Program at the Harvard Graduate School of Design. He edited the *Al Manakh* series (2007, 2010), two essential publications on the urbanisation of the Arabian peninsula, and was the editor and contributing writer for Beirut-based *Portal 9*. For six years, he was a leading designer and researcher at OMA in Rotterdam. In 2020, his decade-long project on Dubai's early modernisation and the architectural career of John Harris will be published by Stanford University Press. He is also co-editing a book with Sultan Al Qassemi about Sharjah's modern architecture and the cultural landscape in which it is rooted. Reisz's work has been featured in several Venice Architecture Biennales, the Sharjah Biennial, *The Guardian*, *Perspecta*, *Log*, *Jadaliyya*, the *Journal of Urban History*, the *International Journal of Middle East Studies*, *Architectural Design*, *Artforum*, *Volume* and *ARCH+*.

Sofia Victorino

Sofia Victorino is the Daskalopoulos Director of Education and Public Programmes at London's Whitechapel Gallery, where she leads a programme of artist residencies and commissions, community projects and public programmes, including performance and film. Previously head of Education and Public Programmes at the Serralves Museum in Porto, Portugal (2002–11), she focuses her research on art, performativity and social practice. Select curatorial projects and commissions include those of artists Mikhail Karikis (2018), Emanuel Almborg (2017), Samson Kambalu (2016), Rivane Neuenschwander (2015), Luke Fowler and Mark Fell (2015), Peter Liversidge (2015), Bart Lodewijks (2014–15), Francis Upritchard (2014), Fraser Muggeridge (2014), Heather and Ivan Morison (2013), Theaster Gates (2013), Claire Pentecost (2013) and the collective Assemble (2017). Victorino serves on the Advisory Committee for the William Townsend Memorial Lecture Series at the Slade School of Fine Art and on the advisory board for the *Documents of Contemporary Art* series, co-published by Whitechapel Gallery and MIT Press. She has lectured on the MA Curating the Contemporary (London Metropolitan University) and the MA in Contemporary Art and Education (Goldsmiths, University of London).

Oraib Toukan

Oraib Toukan is an artist and Clarendon Scholar at the Ruskin School of Art, University of Oxford. Until fall 2015, she was head of the Arts Division and Media Studies program at Bard College at Al-Quds University in

Palestine. Toukan recently exhibited at the Akademie der Künste in Berlin, the Heidelberger Kunstverein, the Qalandiya International, the Centre for Contemporary Arts in Glasgow, the Asia Pacific Triennial, the Mori Art Museum and the 11th Istanbul Biennial. She is the author of *Sundry Modernism: Materials for a Study of Palestinian Modernism*, which was published by Sternberg Press in 2017.

Koray Duman

Koray Duman, AIA, LEED AP, is originally from Turkey, where he earned a B.Arch. from Middle East Technical University. He also received a master's degree in architecture and urban design from UCLA. Duman has worked as the lead architect on several West Coast museum projects in the United States. In 2012, he established Büro Koray Duman (B-KD), an idea- and research-based architectural practice in New York City that creates spaces for cultural production. The studio's recent projects include an extension to the Noguchi Museum and the construction of a foundation for American artist Richard Prince. In 2017, Architizer honoured B-KD as Emerging Firm of the Year for 'its forward-thinking vision for the role of the architect'. Duman is the chair of the AIANY New Practices Committee, on the advisory board of the American Society for Muslim Advancement and the chair of the Leadership Council at the Van Alen Institute. In collaboration with these organisations, he invests in the social, cultural and ecological challenges of our built environment and, in response, explores innovative strategies in architectural practice. He is an adjunct professor in Pratt Institute's Graduate Architecture and Urban Design program, and previously taught at the New School and Rensselaer Polytechnic Institute (RPI). Duman is a registered architect in New York State and in Turkey.

Koyo Kouoh

Koyo Kouoh is the founding artistic director of RAW Material Company, a centre for art, knowledge and society in Dakar, Senegal. She participated in the 57th Carnegie International with *Dig Where You Stand* (2018), an exhibition within the exhibition based on the Carnegie Museum of Art's collection. With Rasha Salti, she co-curated *Saving Bruce Lee: African and Arab Cinema in the Era of Soviet Cultural Diplomacy* (2018) at Haus der Kulturen der Welt in Berlin. Previously, she was the curator of 1:54 FORUM, the educational programme at the Contemporary African Art Fair in London and New York, and served on the curatorial teams for documenta 12 (2007) and documenta 13 (2012). Kouoh was the curator of *Still (the) Barbarians* (2016) at the 37th EVA International, Ireland's Biennial of Contemporary Art in Limerick, and has curated multiple exhibitions internationally. She has also published widely, including *WORD! WORD? WORD! Issa Samb and the Undecipherable Form* (2013), RAW Material Company/OCA/Sternberg Press, the first monograph dedicated to the work of seminal Senegalese artist Issa Samb (aka Joe Ouakam); *Condition Report: Symosium on Building Art Institutions in Africa* (2012), a collection of essays resulting from the eponymous symposium held in Dakar; and *Chronicle of a Revolt: Photographs of a Season of Protest* (2012), RAW Material Company and Haus der Kulturen der Welt. In addition to a sustained theoretical, exhibition and residency program at RAW Material Company, she continues critical curatorial and advisory activities, and regularly takes part in artist juries and selection committees. She lives and works between Dakar and Basel.

Shezad Dawood

Shezad Dawood works across disciplines – film, painting, neon, sculpture and, more recently, virtual reality – to deconstruct systems of image, language, site and narrative. Using the editing process as a method to explore both meanings and forms, his practice often involves collaboration and knowledge exchange, as well as mapping across geographic borders and communities. Through a fascination with the esoteric, otherness and science fiction, Dawood interweaves histories, realities and symbolism to create richly layered artworks. He has exhibited widely internationally, including his recent solo exhibition, *Leviathan* (2018), at MOSTYN in Wales. His film works have also been screened internationally, including at Art Rotterdam (2018); New Adelphi Exhibition Gallery, Manchester (2018); and Screen City Biennial, Stavanger (2017). His works are held in major public and private collections, including the Tate, London; LACMA, Los Angeles; and the British Museum, London, amongst other prominent institutions. Dawood is a Jarman Award nominee (2012) and one of the winners of the Abraaj Capital Art Prize (2011). He was born in London in 1974, and trained at Central Saint Martin's and the Royal College of Art before undertaking a PhD at Leeds Metropolitan University. Dawood is a research fellow in experimental media at the University of Westminster. He lives and works in London.